T0329077

FRENCH CONNECTIONS

Networks of Influence

FRENCH CONNECTIONS

Networks of Influence

Sophie Coignard
and
Marie-Thérèse Guichard

Translated by Keith Torjoc

ALGORA

Algora Publishing, New York
© 2000 by Algora Publishing
All rights reserved. Published 2000.
Printed in the United States of America
ISBN: 1-892941-02-3
Editors@algora.com

Originally published as *Les Bonnes fréquentations,* © Éditions
Grasset & Fasquelle, 1997.

Library of Congress Cataloging-in-Publication Data

Coignard, Sophie.
    [Bonnes fréquentations. English]
    French connections : networks of influence / Sophie Coignard and
    Marie-Thérèse Guichard.
    p. cm.
Includes bibliographical references.
    ISBN 1-892941-02-3 (alk. paper)
    1. Secret societies—France—History. I. Guichard, Marie-Thérèse.
    II. Title.
HS254 .C6413 1999
366.0944—dc21
                                                                99-050700

*This work was published with
the support of the
French Ministry of Culture
through the
Centre National du Livre*

New York
www.algora.com

Table of Contents

Introduction

"Thirteen men gathered, under the Empire; . . . thirteen men who were savvy enough to dissimulate the sacred ties that united them, strong enough to place themselves above the law, bold enough to do anything. . ." They were thirteen "anonymous heroes to whom the entire society was secretly subjugated." This is how, in 1831, Honoré de Balzac introduced his intriguing novel *The Thirteen* in *Revue de Paris*. The book was published in serial form and became an overnight success. The reading public went crazy for these thirteen "masters of the universe" and their adventures.

Balzac excels in describing the settings where fraternity, secrecy, plots, and thirst for power mix with the will to fight for a better world. His works frequently make reference to exclusive groups: the Knights of Idleness in *The Rabouilleuse*; the Cenacle, a group of friends of the sciences and arts in *Lost Illusions*; the Brothers of Consolation in *The Inverse of Contemporary History*. The son of a freemason, Balzac himself founded a mutual support network: the Red Horse Society.

These more or less secret societies that flourished in the nineteenth century are the direct ancestors of the influential networks that rule contemporary France. The group called the Thirteen, that Balzac describes so well, is strangely reminiscent of the groups involved in the affairs of state, business, and knowledge at the end of the twentieth century. Or, simply put, the majority of French citizens who, without always knowing it, are to some extent part of a network. Everyone, through his regional roots, through the schools he attends, the sports he plays, the organization he serves, and by what he believes in, cultivates a network of sorts. But like the air that we breathe, networks in France are such a part of life that one doesn't always notice them.

The country moves into the new millennium in a depressed state. Over the past few decades, France has experienced the failure of ideologies, the weakening of political parties and unions, and popular loss of confidence in institutions and elected officials. The public is desperately looking for some new affiliation, something to bring people together. "Evidence suggests that small groups of existential networks are multiplying," testifies sociologist Michel Maffesoli. According to Mike Burke, another sociologist, the Eighties were the apogee of individualism in everyday life and in the world of work — in business, it was the era of revolving doors. These days, individuals no longer want to follow that destiny; they join "networks" or "clubs." In business, two types of groups are emerging: the old-fashioned type (closed, exclusive, pulling strings for each other), and a more supple kind of group that horizontally joins people working in different companies but sharing a common interest.

This delicious rediscovery of a warm and reassuring sense of belonging to a group creates a slightly idealized image of networks. To imagine these groups as innocent assemblies preoccupied only with the betterment of humanity would be as great an exaggeration as the fantasies about their plotting and conniving that the term "old boy's club" often suggests. "The network of secret societies," Victor Hugo wrote, "is beginning to be felt across the country." A shiver runs up the reader's spine. Balzac had to stand up to his Thirteen, even though he had invented them. While the Thirteen didn't impose their order on society, they did weave plots and little personal intrigues, even joining forces with their enemies in order to achieve their ends. The group turns into a gang, into a den of unprincipled adventurers.

They are not lobbies, since they go well beyond the strict alliance of economic interests, nor actual clubs, since they carefully avoid any sign of institutionalization. Networks deserve neither excessive fascination nor excessive scorn. Simply, they play an essential part in the operation of society. While some are amusingly arcane, others — the connections that give the French nomenklatura its structure — are not insignificant when it comes to major decisions and nominations. From tax inspectors to the Corréziens of Paris, former "collaborationists" to freemason wheeler-dealers, homosexuals to aristocrats, from the circle of people who sit on multiple corporate boards to those former cabinet ministers, hunters and golfers who recognize each other, the "inner circles" dominate the comedy of power and the drama of money.

These networks, all together, whether acting in concert or in competition, make up the true organizational chart of France, the one that is never made public but which explains better than any official speech or press release how policy decisions are made.

From his observation post in the Elysée (France's White House), where he was an advisor to François Mitterrand but a stranger to those coteries most visible at the highest echelons of the State, Régis Debray was stunned to realize "the astounding amateurism of the professionals." "Everyone imagines that these people's decisions are the fruit of experienced and knowledgeable consideration, pondered at length, and well-documented. But they generally result from a nod of the head, a fit of temper, old grudges, whims or passions. A contact from someone's hometown, a recommendation from a cousin or a sister-in-law given behind half-closed doors, a quick word in the elevator, an easy-going gentlemen's agreement can decide who is nominated as head of a public establishment, a ministry or an administrative office — more surely than a solid resume, track record or character. And it goes without saying that, as the major decisions are made, so are the minor ones."[1]

This disillusioned vision of the games of influence combines string-pulling, nepotism and "the network effect." The mechanics of networks, like fluid mechanics, obeys laws that are far more codified than simple favoritism. And the rules are all the more immutable since they originate at a distance.

"Since I am neither a practicing Jew, a freemason, a provincial, a proletarian, nor a grand-bourgeois, and I belong neither to the Tax Inspectorate nor to any great corpus, I have every possible handicap. . . ." Thus joked Alain Boublil, François Mitterrand's former advisor for industrial affairs at the Elysée and ex-director of Pierre Bérégovoy's cabinet at the Finance Ministry, when his name was linked with the Pechiney-Triangle insider-trading scandal. Sentenced to jail although his guilt was never clearly proven, he also suggests that his penalty would have been less severe if he had belonged to one of the important networks.

Influence peddling, among the French, follows criteria of strict utility: help each other, socialize together, boost each other's career, but also make money, conspire together, protect each other in the event of serious failure. And, the supreme distinction, become President. . .

Corsicans, Corréziens, Savoyards, Bretons and people from the Auvergne have always worked together to "make it," in the unfamiliar and hostile capital, and in life at large. In the City Hall of Paris, the Corsicans have always competed with the Corréziens. The latter were visible long before the Chirac reign; and the former have extended their pseudopods as far as Africa.

Help each other: that is a premier mission for any self-respecting network. Various brotherhoods are distinguished in this art. They band together around their shared marginality — of mores, for the homosexuals, of religion for the Jews and the Protestants (in Catholic France) — or around a common passion. A group of hunters established the club "Take It Easy," led by the count de Beaumont (long-time head of Rivaud Bank); they know that hunting can open many doors. And the golf-playing corporate chairmen who belong to "The Presidents' Trophy" take the same approach.

But nothing really serious, in France, can be finalized far away from the pleasures of the table, the altar of shared bonds. Today, as yesterday, 200 to 300 people gather in Paris at "dinners in town." High-ranking civil servants, real estate magnates, heirs to famous dynasties, these convicts of worldliness are condemned to get along with each other — they so often meet. Clubs and associations still rely on the meal (not always a gastronomical delight) as a central event, dissimulating behind their facades an interesting solidarity. "Feet in the Water," for example, brings together politicians, high-ranking civil servants, advertising executives and business owners, some of whom hold opposite partisan sympathies.

But fun isn't all there is to life. Careers are important, too. And networks are good for careers. Invincible mascots of the French government, the finance inspectors are supposed to have lost of their power and their prestige when the State disengaged from the financial sphere, and especially because of the role they played in two major failures for the French economy, those of Crédit Lyonnais and Crédit Foncier de France. But quite to the contrary, they are amazingly resilient. They still reign today at a surprising number of high positions, in spite of the manifest incompetence displayed by many of them. By comparison, the engineers of the Mining Corps have had to become a little more discrete, and take refuge in certain large bastions that are still well-defended. And — a sign of a new liberal wind? — new loyalties are taking shape in the private sector, where a few virtuosos of marketing, formerly with the multinational Procter and Gamble, are serving as commandos; and they are imitated by others.

Making money, is that an individualistic and solitary activity? Not according to the philosophy of certain freemason cliques who strayed into the murky area between business and politics. Under cover of metaphysical debate, they engage in speculation that is much more material than the search for the Great Architect of the Universe. From the Victor-Schoelcher lodge (the base of a fraud scheme) to the scandal over funds raised for cancer research, not to mention the Buildings and Public Works (BTP) and the racket that operates under the warm Mediterranean sun, these "terrible brothers" have become so renowned that their behavior frightens their peers.

But some connections are entirely legal and function for the greatest material benefit of their associates. In the business world, where the Lazard banking firm, for example, is a virtuoso construct in the shape of rake, which enables it to have a hand in (almost) every re-structuring of the large French companies. The heads of those companies, some forty men, have finagled positions on various boards of directors centered around two "gurus," Ambroise Roux, former chairman of the Compagnie générale d'électricité, and Claude Bébéar, the much-publicized owner of Axa.

Monopolizing the levers of the economy in this way bears a certain similarity to the persistent dominance of some heavily mediatized intellectuals who reign over the empire of the word, thanks to the clans they have bred.

On the other end of the spectrum from these peaceful arrangements, some have found that networks can be the ideal structure for forging conspiracies. But, fortunately for the French Republic, such plotting was not very fruitful in the twentieth century. However, there have been plenty who were willing to give it a try, from the *Cagoule* of the pre-war period to today's "red-brown" alliance of Communists and fascists.

The most imprudent of them betrayed their country during the War. Did they all pay the price of their collaboration? Some, like the militiaman Paul Touvier, benefited for many decades from the complicity of those who knew them, and were able to escape justice. Others, more daring still, took advantage of discrete connections and image retooling; they started over with honorable careers in banking, industry, journalism, even high government posts.

Are such networks fiendish in their pragmatism? Not always. From the reforms spurred by the leftist Catholics during the Fifties to today's crusades for or against abortion, special-interest groups are motivated more by personal conviction than by personal interest.

Furthermore, politicians sometimes rely on them to test or transmit their messages. For, to become President, the ultimate ambition, requires having antennas in every demographic and social circle, in every community, in every clique. Controlling the networks is like conducting a symphony.

These criteria of utility, ranging from the most natural (having a common birthplace) to the most contrived (seeking favors in order to attain the supreme office), reveal the networks' *raison d'être* but not their origin. One seldom belongs to a network by chance or because the light was on and you just walked in.

Shared hardships and trials can forge indestructible loyalties. The war-time Resistance, which took the concept of the network to new heights, was one such. It shaped the power structure in France for nearly forty years. When Pierre Mendès France became President of the Council in 1954, he called in all his old buddies from the "Alsace-Lorraine" squadron. In 1958, de Gaulle, back in power and surrounded by former members of the Resistance, found himself facing opposition from another group of resistance fighters, banded together in the Jean-Moulin Club, who saw the General's return to power as a potentially authoritarian regime.

Pierre Guillain de Bénouville, a dignitary of the Resistance (and not an insignificant one), remembered that Raoul Salan was a companion from day one. For Bénouville, having resisted in 1940 is more important than having plotted in 1961. So, after the putsch in Algiers, he paid a visit to General Salan during his detention in the Tulle prison. He arrived in a chauffeur-driven limousine, with a bottle of fine champagne — to the astonishment of the prefect, who couldn't do anything about it: Bénouville had a written authorization signed by the Head of State. One day, Roger Frey, Minister for the Interior, proposed in the Council of Ministers that the policy of safe conduct should not be extended. De Gaulle refused, and retorted: "And if the same thing happened to me that happened to the people in Tulle, how many Bénouvilles would there be?"

One day in 1969, the Reverend Father Michel Riquet created a sensation in the head office of the DST (the equivalent of the CIA). Prefect Rachet, the security agency chief, was not cooperating quickly enough for the priest, who was vice-president of the National Veterans' Office and the National Union of Deportees. "You should understand, my good Sir, that in France, it is we, the Resistance, who are in charge," flashed the priest.[2]

The Resistance was the "network to end all networks," for many decades, even though certain sectors such as the business world remained largely outside its influence. It was so powerful that in banking, and even in industry, it was in fact networks purged of collaborationists that held power after the war.[3]

It is the same memory of the trial endured together that bonded the network of repatriates (pretty much inactive since the assassination of Jacques Roseau, in 1993) and that of the former Communists who were rejected by the Party and left on their own after years of ideological and professional cocooning.

Not everyone has experienced heroic action, a traumatic exodus or agonizing revisionism, but everyone had a youth. It is there, during the age of nonchalance, friendship and informal intimacy that the first lines of complicity are drawn. With adulthood, nostalgia awakens old memories. Sometimes it is simply a question of regional origin,[4] and a question of school and university courses. But there again, the inequality persists: the good will that exists among alumni of a small local college is nothing compared to the "Mafia" of the Polytechnical Institute or ENA alumni, even less that of the large trades. For some, the first job makes the difference. And so we see the "Procterians" (Procter and Gamble) and the "lessiviers" who, after finishing trade school, start their career by marketing a fabric softener, household cleansers or disposable diapers.[5]

Such ties from the early days — and dynamic early days they were — are shared among the journalists who began their career on France 5, the last radio and television network of French Algeria. There was Jean-Pierre Elkabbach, his successor with France-Television Xavier Gouyou Beauchamps, the former owner of Antenne 2, Jean-Claude Héberlé, the announcer Jean-Claude Narcy, known as Narcissus who, they say, excelled as the Emcee of variety shows, the wise man of CSA Pierre Wiehn, the former chairman of the AFP (French Press Agency) Jean-Louis Guillaud. The "Apollo" of this band was no older than the others. But at barely the age of 25, his legend already preceded him. Philippe Labro, the novelist, screen writer, owner of RTL, recounted this outstanding epic of

Algiers in his book, *The Fire's Not Out.*[6]

"Sins" of youth, ideological convictions also produce miracles of allegiance, even after the goal or the sense of combat has faded away. Extremism unquestionably forges the strongest ties. The Trotskyites of yore continue to render services to each other long after being integrated, often happily, into the influential circles of French society. Old "fachos" do not all suffer for their past mistakes, quite to the contrary, even if they try to avoid having them mentioned. For effective liaisons have contributed to "white-washing" their history in order to integrate them into more respectable and more "republican" circles.[7]

More recent, and perhaps even more solid, the homosexual networks seek to derive an advantage from the marginality that has often confined them to the shadows or to duplicity. More or less overt in the worlds of fashion, art and culture, homosexuality largely remains silent in the world of politics, where the former socialist minister André Labarrère was exceptional for his relaxed attitude on the subject. It remains strictly taboo in business and national government.

Long excluded from French the networks, women have woken up and are organizing, too. Along with those initiatives that were primarily of feminist inspiration, yesterday for "equality," today for "parity," some are getting past the male ostracism that still prohibits their entry into certain cliques; they are creating their own structures. In *L'Express* of June 6, 1996, ten women politicians made headlines by signing a proclamation for parity. Less militant, the "Women's Forum Club L" decided in 1994 to make itself known to the general public on its tenth birthday, presenting itself as a "genuine network of influence, based on the 'excellence' of the participants." Among them are one of François Pinault's "lieutenants," Patricia Barbizet; the businesswoman Gilberte Beaux; the writer-editor Thérèse de Saint-Phalle, the visionary Yaguel Didier, Judge Myriam Ezratty, former minister Elisabeth Guigou, producer and ENA alumna Simone Harari, the chairman of Pathé-Television Janine Langlois-Glandier, and Françoise Monod, who is a lawyer, the wife of the chairman of Lyonnaise des Eaux, and a very active godmother to the Correzien clan.

Similarly, since most of the Masonic organizations refuse to mix the genders, women's lodges are showing up as they take advantage of the vacuum left by their brothers in terms of ideas and social innovation. They played a part, for example, in the debate on male-female parity that cropped up in spring 1996.

A sign of the times, the induction of a woman seems to be imminent for the tightly closed club of representatives of "big capital." Ambroise Roux, president of the AFEP (Association of French Private Companies), which brings together the presidents of the 69 largest private companies in France, promised he would soon add a woman to this coterie, which is considered to be one of the most powerful networks of France. The common bond here is shared financial interest, pure and simple. "Concentrated wealth that is organized in a network is infinitely more powerful, even if it is less conspicuous, than the diffuse poverty that the trade unions represent," says Jean-François Kahn in an article on networks of influence published in the *L'Evénement du Jeudi*.[8] It took some 500,000 demonstrators in the street to block the revision of the Falloux law. But the export of a few thousands of patrimonial capital were enough to make Alain Juppé reconsider the increase in the wealth tax."[9]

However, this observation neglects the distinction between a network and a lobby. Contrary to the Working Force for Civil Servants or the FNSEA for Agriculture, the AFEP does not simply defend its members' interests with regard to institutions. It runs the French economic system, monopolizes the boards of directors, and selects the future leaders.[10]

All the charm of this underground geography of French society lies in its discrete, sometimes almost unconscious operation. The network man (or woman) that sleeps inside each one of us devotes time, energy, and intelligence to exploit the semi-emotional, semi-utilitarian web of his relationships and contacts.

But who, finally, are these men (or women) of the ideal network? They are ambitious, often, but know the virtues of patience. They know that the system functions on an egalitarian basis, that the network, generally, is not hierarchical but on the contrary horizontal, transverse, that it must extend a broad enough reach to encompass varied pillars of support, yet remain sufficiently closed to ensure the group's cohesion.

Its members, however, are equal only in appearance. "The network benefits most the one who created it and who leads it," explains a specialist. "He holds all the cards, and it is principally he who can accumulate connections and belong to several networks at the same time." This is a comprehensive insurance policy that helps one to climb through the ranks, to avoid career risks and, why not, make it to the top of the national government.

Chapter 1

MAKING IT

They form the largest of the networks, that of "the internal exiles." Swarming around the capital, regional associations and networks, whether they are Breton (the most numerous), Corréziens (the most media-conscious), or Lorraine (the most discrete), all display the same vocation from the start: to give a hand to forlorn neophytes arriving in the City of Light.

The Basque Andre-Jean Lafaurie, exiled without a penny in the Seventies, now a golfer emeritus and a talented journalist, has a story to tell about that. "I was hopelessly trying to find my way, and I was practically starving," he says. "One day, I came across a compatriot, Jean-Paul Aphecetche, who then owned the restaurant 'La Gaulloise,' in the XVth arrondissement. I was too proud to ask for anything, but he spontaneously offered to cover me. He fed me for weeks, . . . and gave me a chance to hold out until I found work."

But Aphecetche, today owner of the restaurant "Le Pichet," on rue Pierre-Charron, where he continues to welcome his band of buddies, rugby players and golfers, is obviously only maintaining a solid tradition. Three other Basque restaurateurs in Paris have straightforwardly created an "ethnic" labor exchange, "Eskualduna," that directs young people from the countryside toward "friendly" restaurants when they are looking for work. Better yet, those who fail to adapt to the Parisian climate can always use this micro-network to go and settle in Mexico, in Argentina, or the USA, where compatriots will take them in hand.

The "café-owners' connection" also works for the Alsatians. Jean-Paul Bucher, prolific owner of Parisian brasseries, including "Flo" and "La Coupole," keeps an eye out for his fellow countrymen. He hasn't forgotten his own beginnings. At the age of 16, in 1958, he found his way to the kitchen at "Hansi," a restaurant in Montparnasse, where a few dozen locals had already preceded him as apprentices. But the Basque and Alsatian networks pale beside the Auvergne "bistrocracy." Just think — that "community" holds 80% of the bar-tobaccoists and 6,000 bar-restaurants in Paris. Perfectly organized, it even has its own newspaper, the *Auvergnat de Paris*, the bible of bistro managers.

But the interested parties are less likely to brag about it when the sense of regional solidarity goes beyond a "helping hand for the poor." The "zinc Mafia" learned how to run its business using ancestral methods founded on mutual confidence and communal self-financing. Let a young person from the Auvergne take a job behind the counter and presently he is taken in hand by one of the representatives of the beer distributors, a fellow "countryman." If he performs satisfactorily, the distributor will guarantee a bank loan for him. With plenty in return: once he's set up, and moving up through the ranks, the coffee boy will sell exclusively the products of so friendly a lender.

This is a system from which some families profit very nicely. Many of them are former coal merchants, who consolidated their power through matrimonial alliances that rival those of the royal families. In this way, they have created a subtle geopolitics of café-owners. The most powerful of these families is the Richards, whose patriarch, Henri, began modestly in 1920 under a compatriot in Clichy; now the family reigns over the distribution of wine and coffee. Among the brands of coffee distributed are the Ladoux coffees. Now they are part of the family, since Pierre Richard, one of the clan's two heirs, married the Ladoux girl. Andre Ladoux, head of a powerful business consultancy, is impossible to circumvent in any buying and selling of a business, or a liquor license. And then, isn't he the husband of one of the Tafanel girls, a family that holds the exclusive distribution rights for the BSN Group's beers and mineral waters (Kronenbourg, Evian, etc.) in Paris? Of course, Guy Tafanel manages the distributorship, but his sister still has an interest there.

This Auvergne clan that rules the roost in Parisian coffee shops does not, however, own many establishments outright. They are the godfathers of the network. If they give the nod, the Paris subsidiary of the Auvergne Agricultural Credit Agency or Monod French Bank will not hesitate to grant a loan.

The "Red Collars" from the Mountains

The "Savoyards" of the Hotel Drouot, which has been self-managed for more than a century, scrupulously respect these principles. The 110 commission agents from the Drouot auction salesrooms constitute an astonishing self-encapsulated community right in the heart of Paris. These "curious Swiss guards," as the academician Maurice Rheims puts it so nicely, are all Savoyard, without exception. They can be recognized by their black jackets, the collars bordered in red braid, with their number embroidered in gold on the collar. Among themselves, they no longer go by their real names but by nicknames like Narcissus, the Pipe, Baron, etc.. This is a way of distinguishing themselves, since whole families (Pasquier, Emprin, Arnaud and Bottolier, to cite only the most prolific "dynasties") are intermingled on the sales floor.

For over a century, they have held a *de facto* monopoly on everything related to the prestigious Parisian auction rooms. The origin of this "corps," which is at least as solid as the tax inspectorate, is rather obscure. Was it a gift from Napoleon in exchange for the annexation of Savoy, as some claim, or gradual seizure through regional co-optation? The "red collars" don't care, provided that they can continue to recruit from one valley to the other as they did in the past. One town, moreover, is clearly dominant: Sallanches, which provides great battalions of commission agents. But Bourg-Saint-Maurice is not badly represented either.

The system of recruiting has not varied in a century and a half. Each pensioner chooses his successor, who will be put to the test for six months before being adopted collectively. And if it happens that an accident deprives one of them of his employment as a commission agent, a physically demanding trade, he is not dropped.

Contrary to what the casual purchasers might think, the "Savoyards" do not merely convey the furniture and paintings for the 3,500 annual sales to the rooms where the appraisers officiate. These apparently impassive men are always on the look-out for a good bargain, which the regulars call "wild ones." They can also collect buying orders from customers and assemble auctions in their place — a lucrative trade and very tightly organized. The 110 "red collars" have a collectively owned company (one share apiece), the Union of Salesroom Commission Agents, which very modestly defines its purpose as "the carrying of goods."

Three "managing sergeants" represent them but, in fact, direct democracy prevails. Thus, these curious associates play dice to assign the day's tasks. Whoever rolls the lowest number has to look over the exhibition of the objects to be sold, the day before the sale. The next day, he and two of his compatriots follow the course of the sale, occasionally prodding too timid purchasers. And, every five years, one of them quits his job in one of the sixteen sales halls, to become a chauffeur for twelve months.

Associates when it comes to good bargains, they are also interdependent in times of trouble. In the event of a loss, they engage to reimburse themselves for the goods, without involving any bank or insurance company.

Other communities have found ways to develop this "informal mutual support" with formidable effectiveness, which enables them to escape adversity.

The Chouchen Connection

It makes no difference that Edouard Leclerc and his son, Michel-Edouard, have their social address at Issy-les-Moulineaux, in the Paris region; they are still the "grocers from Landernau." And they are proud of it. While they are less visible than the Auvergnat community that has practically made a trust company of the bistro business in the last century, the Bretons are the most numerous of the "exiles." A million and half of them, distributed throughout the central district of Paris, have spread out through all the professions without forming any particular monopoly.

Nowadays, these are not the legendary naïve little small-town visitors, easy prey on the sidewalks of Paris, but owners who are very savvy and who have organized themselves to force the "central power" to take an interest in their area. "Catholic influences? A resurgence of a classless ancient Celtic society?" questions Yannick Bourdonnec, author of *The Breton Miracle*.[12] Their solidarity, he maintains, is stronger now than ever before, even to the point of becoming a "real network culture." In the center of the Celtic region, clubs abound: Synergy 5 in Pontivy and Club 35 in Rennes, to name only the two most visible institutions.

Proud of their success, some "external" Breton industrialists are even associated within a very discrete "Club of Thirty." "Thirty" is a reference to the legendary battle of March 27, 1351, in which thirty knights of the French party of Charles de Blois clashed with thirty other knights defending the cause of Montfort, between Josselin and Ploërmel. Today, the economic knights are named Vincent Bolloré, Michel-Edouard Leclerc, Alexis Gourvennec and Jean Calvez. Bolloré, one of the founders of the league, spends all his summers in Saint-Tropez, but he does not want anyone to think that he has forgotten his family home on the banks of the Odet, close to Quimper. He cultivates his Breton relations assiduously. A few years ago he created a joint venture in tourism, Leclerc Evasions, with Michel-Edouard Leclerc, whom he met during a regatta at the Glénans. But (business is business) he withdrew some time later rather abruptly, and, since then, relations have been a little strained.

Celts in bandoliers: the same Bolloré, owner of the Delmas-Vieljeux shipping company, cosied up to Alexis Gourvennec (the impetuous ex-trade unionist and chairman of Brittany Ferries), who helped him via his relations with other French ship-owners. And he named Philippe Giffard to be administrator of the group — the former owner of Crédit Industriel de l'ouest (Western Industrial Credit), who had had the good taste to lend money to him in his early days.

The members of the "Club of Thirty" are extremely discrete. Their paths cross and re-cross around the current president, Jean Calvez, owner of a trucking business, Louis Duff, chairman of the fast food chain La Brioche Doré (the Gilded Brioche), George Coudray, president of Mutual Credit of Brittany, and Auguste Génovèse, general manager of Citroën Rennes (he is Niçois by origin, Breton by adoption), etc.. Every one of them hates to have people talk about their get-togethers. "Some act like members of a secret society," comments one Breton observer; "for some, it's a lobby that does not dare to say its name, for others, it is mostly an emotional network."

Emotional? Ambroise Roux, the former chairman of Compagnie

générale d'électricité (which became Alcatel-Alsthom), feels moved whenever anyone speaks to him about Brittany. This Auvergnat, with the character of hardened steel, has a passion for granite. His salon-boudoir, where he takes tea with his visitors, is enlivened with splendid black and white photographs of Breton landscapes. Every summer, the corporate *éminence grise* enjoys long weeks in his house in Trégastel. In Paris, he displays a particular weakness for certain select Breton business owners. He not only "hung out" with the Saint Malo resident François Pinault (he intervened on Pinault's behalf with an establishment that was too suspicious, and got them to digest Pinault's tender offer on the Printemps group in 1991). Pinault, in thanks, initially named him head of the board of directors of Pinault-Printemps, then made him a consultant to each of his companies.

Brittany, note the Celtic fundamentalists, doesn't seem to matter much to Pinault, who prefers to spend his summers on the Riviera and his weekends at his château, Mormaire, in Yvelines. But when fire devastated several dozen acres of the mythical forest of Brocéliande, he paid some of the re-forestation costs. Even in Saint-Tropez, his summer visitors are pleased to taste lobsters flown in from his native Brittany. And this corsair who is envied for his success has, as if by chance, more than one point in common with another Breton, another adventurer in his own way, Loïk Le Floch-Prigent.

It is Roux who introduced Pinault to the former chairman of Elf Aquitaine at the time of the tender offer on the Pinault-Printemps group. The socialist boss is indeed "an old friend" of Ambroise: they mey each other in 1982, right before CGE was nationalized. Le Floch was the young private secretary of Pierre Dreyfus, Minister of Industry, and he had shown such courtesy that the old business veteran had been charmed. Pinault and Le Floch, two "fellow countrymen," each of a decided and direct temperament, got along well together. Le Floch made Elf invest in Printemps and he soon found himself on the heavily Breton board of trustees composed by Pinault. In 1993, always so accommodating, Le Floch intervened and even gave a bit of financial help when the Pinault-Printemps group was transferring the Armand Thiéry chain to his friend Maurice Biderman.

As a friend, Pinault made it up to him immediately: later in 1993, Le Floch had to give up his position at Elf to Philippe Jaffré, and it was on a private jet belonging to the Pinault group that Le Floch made his round of good-byes to the African heads of state that were partners of the oil firm. More useful still, as a friend of Chirac, Pinault successfully pleaded Le Floch's cause in January 1996, when the Elysée was casting about for a president for the SNCF. But while Pinault is faithful in friendship, he apparently knows how to be discrete. Too discrete? Quite a few scandalmongers noticed that his name was missing, like that of Ambroise Roux, from the list of the dozen chairmen who had given public support to Le Floch in July 1996, during his inquest and detention.

Their discretion won't raise any eyebrows among the members of the "Group of Bretons in the Ministerial Cabinets." That club, founded in 1986 by a Breton by adoption, Paul Anselin, once a very busy "ministerial" (he was a member of ten cabinets in 26 years) acts exclusively in the background. A friend of Jacques Chirac since the Algerian war (Chirac saved his life during combat), this *éminence grise* of the Celts dashes back and forth between Brittany (he is mayor of Ploërmel in Morbihan) and Paris, where he is Hervé de Charette's head of the mission to the Quai d'Orsay (site of the French Foreign Ministry). Every month, he invites the thirty members of this informal but powerful network to meet. Together, they endeavor to mitigate the lack of a Breton minister in the Juppé government and to keep certain matters moving in the right direction, such as the University of South Brittany and the state and regional plan in general.

To give themselves a stronger voice, this group has reminded several heavy-hitters of their regional origins. In addition to Christian Noyer, the former director of the Treasury and Jean Arthuis's chief of staff, Marie-Christine Lepetit is Juppé's advisor on taxation, Bernadette Malgorn (ex-staff manager of Philippe Séguin and the first woman to be a regional prefect), Pierre-Eric Pommellet, chief of staff of the Minister for PMI-PME (small and mid-sized businesses and industry), and Pierre-Henri Paillet, chief of staff for the Minister of Industry. "What makes them strong," says Hubert Coudurier, head of the Parisian office of the *Télégramme de Brest*, "is that they have someone in a position of power in almost every field."

The Corsicans' Floor

"One day I was going to see someone from back home in the Paris City Hall, and I got lost. 'You are on the wrong floor,' I was told. 'This is the Corsicans, here.'" The Corrézien writer Denis Tillinac always likes to tell that anecdote, which to him illustrates the "preference" that City Hall shows towards its buddies. He is not entirely wrong. It may have been proven that the capital was for a long time a haven for unemployed Corréziens (every native of Ussel, Jacques Chirac's district, was cordially welcomed there), but the Corsicans, too, have carved out quite a stronghold since 1977. "Getting a Corsican in position to replace Chirac at City Hall was an error," regrets someone from the island. "Now we are too exposed."

Visibility is not always good for networks; quite to the contrary. The Corsicans have long understood that. Their island is the only area of France that has neither a Province House nor an official tourist bureau in Paris. "What matters," jokes a senior civil servant from Corsica, "is having a cousin in the right place."

Blood ties play an important part in the geography of insular influence in Paris. In the Tiberi family, son Dominique has been made private secretary to Roger Romani, Minister for Parliamentary Relations. In the Dominati family, Laurent has been destined since the cradle to succeed his father Jacques as deputy in Paris. Pierre Pasqua, son of Charles, a real estate agent in Grasse, does not work officially with his father, but he too has an affinity for Africa. Like a right-wing equivalent to Jean-Christophe Mitterrand on the left, Pasqua has ties with the Mimran group from Senegal. And due to his African interests, he turns up at the fringes of "Cooperation 92," a government-controlled corporation that his father created in the Hauts-de-Seine, officially to serve as a catalyst for development assistance.

But the Corsicans also have a sense of the "extended" family. Henri Antona is the influential chairman of Techni, a subsidiary of the Générale des Eaux (which controls a myriad of companies in the cleaning, heating, security and public works sectors), all of them well-established in the Hauts-de-Seine. He has no direct family tie with Charles Ceccaldi-Reynaud, the mayor of Puteaux and a pillar of the Corsican networks in the Paris area; but he knows he can count on his unfailing support. When the impetuous young Jean-Marie Messier, who succeeded Guy Dejouany as head of Générale des Eaux, wanted to clean house in his subsidiary companies (including Techni), the mayor of Puteaux sent him an unambiguous message: "Don't touch Antona."

The "Corsican connection," is a taboo subject in the Hauts-de-Seine, and they are also touchy about media coverage of their relations with Africa. The black continent, however, is one of the islanders' favorite areas for conquest. Lacking natural resources and industrial activities, they have made a career in the colonies or left to try their chances overseas. After the end of the colonial period, the tradition persists. "African affairs" seldom get far without a Corsican showing up in the leading role.

Born in Centuri, on the Corsican cape, André Tarallo is the son of a tax collector. He is also considering a career in the administration, and has been accepted into ENA* on the promotion of Jacques Chirac. But his friendships from the ENA will be less valuable to him in his career than the fraternity between "home-boys."

For nearly thirty years, André Tarallo managed Elf's interests in Africa — a position very much in the public eye, requiring a diplomat's talents and a secret agent's sixth sense, the authority of clan chieftain and the financial acumen of a Swiss banker. In the oil company's sphere of influence, Tarallo gathered Corsicans as his right-hand men: Pierre Graziani, from the Elf Foundation, Louis Dominici, former French ambassador to Gabon (Tarallo's principal area of activity), and more recently Charles-Henri Filippi, formerly of the socialist ministerial cabinets and director of Crédit Commercial de France, manager of the group's financial companies, who was set aside by the new chairman Philippe Jaffré.

Tarallo is at the heart of all of Elf's African activities. In Gabon as in all the other oil-bearing zones, they are pumping oil. . . and money — two delicate activities that cannot be accomplished without "Uncle André's" know-how. Loïk Le Floch-Prigent learned his lesson when he arrived as head of the group in May 1989. He wanted to get rid of Tarallo and retired him at the age of 64, in September 1991. But Le Floch was obliged to leave him with the titles of Chairman of Elf-Congo, Elf-Gabon and Elf-Trading, a financial subsidiary in Geneva. During his legal troubles, Le Floch tried in vain to shift some of the charges onto Tarallo. But the "Corsican Uncle" still has influential friends, at home and abroad — far more than the now-deposed chairman.

There is no better example than Charles Pasqua as a symbol of the solidarity of the "Corsican clan." His successful rise in politics was due to the support of various quite select godfathers. Without Achilles

---

* The École national d'administration is a prestigious college that trains future government officials.

Peretti, a native of Ajaccio, former president of the National Assembly and mayor of Neuilly since 1947, without René Tomasini, one of the pillars of the old UDR, and without Alexandre Sanguinetti, a hothead who for many years sailed from one ministerial cabinet to another, the young scion of the Ricard house would never have had such a brilliant run.

Charles Pasqua became godfather in his turn. In the Hauts-de-Seine, a Département over which he reigns single-handedly, all his close confidants are Corsican. He even engaged Bernard Tomasini, son of his old friend René, for a while as assistant to the Ministry for the Interior before making him prefect in the Orne. As for Michèle Merli, daughter of Pierre (the UDF deputy-mayor of the Antibes), she was hired by the Paris police prefect Philippe Massoni, a compatriot who wove his own networks within the police force.

Edouard Balladur, before he took advantage of the Pasqua networks during the May 1995 presidential campaign, had been openly wary about them. "They are going to put Corsicans all around you," he whispered to Jacques Chirac in March 1986, when Chirac was about to appoint the essential "Charlie" Minister for the Interior. Perfidiously, Balladur even added, "You can't leave the hostages' fate to a bunch of casino dealers!"

It is no casino dealer that Pasqua then appointed as anti-terrorism specialist but a former officer parachutist and honorable correspondent of the SDECE (the French Intelligence Service, until 1982), whom he had known for more than twenty years — Jean-Charles Marchiani. Hated by George Pompidou's widow since the Markovic affair (a sordid event organized to destabilize the President, which isolated him from the SDECE), Marchiani conducted a discrete career as director of personnel at Servair, the food-service subsidiary of Air France, then at Thomson, in the armaments sector, until 1986. A shadowy figure, he works only with his own pals, all Corsicans, with whom he communicates exclusively in his mother tongue to discourage indiscretion. That enabled him to prevent anyone from "listening in" during his negotiations in Lebanon, then in Bosnia, freeing French hostages — from simple tourists like the Valente couple, to journalists like Jean-Paul Kauffmann and military men like Lt. Souvignet and Capt. Chiffot.

His independence seriously irritates the other anointed intermediaries of the RPR (Rassemblement pour la République, a right-wing party), *inter alia* the Lebanese Shiite lawyer Robert Bourgi. Twin brother of the owner of *Young African*, he is an effective link between Chirac and the African heads of state. This former professor of law in Abidjan hates Marchiani and he has good reasons for it: Marchiani, gun in hand, blew away Mr. and Mrs. Valente, whom Hezbollah had just released onto the sidewalk in front of the Ambassador Hotel in Beirut! These are hateful squabbles that spoil the climate within an RPR that is very sensitive on African matters through its "Club 89," where Bourgi is Deputy for Development.

But it all ended up being worked out, thanks to the "clan." Bourgi was friendly with Charles d'Ornano, deputy-mayor of Ajaccio and, incidentally, "godfather" of Charles Pasqua. Ornano thus called in Pasqua to explain to him that Bourgi must be considered part of the clan "through friendship" and that he did not want to hear of any trouble. Adapting, "Charlie" convened the two plaintiffs and divided the territory: Marchiani would deal with the Middle East (and the Var, since 1996 when he was promoted prefect), and Bourgi would take Black Africa.

In Africa, the Lebanese lawyer also had to compromise with a former sergeant-chief from Sartène, assigned for a while to a police station in Clichy-la-Garenne. Charles Pasqua chose this minor police officer, Daniel Léandri, to manage his "personal business" with the Ministry for the Interior. This balding man served him as bodyguard for a long time. The guards at the Bourbon Palace still haven't forgotten the day when he tried to keep his gun, when he entered the hemicycle behind his boss! Léandri was promoted. From the time when Pasqua occupied Beauvau place, Léandri (whom Pasqua's entourage called "the monk") worked in an office contiguous to his. This faithful and effective Corsican seems at ease in Africa, where the families in power function more or less like the clans of his home area. "When he travels on the continent," writes François Sudan in *Jeune Africa*,[2] "no one (or practically no one) knows. He does not stay at hotels, does not visit the French ambassador at his residence, and almost never visits expatriates." The Quai d'Orsay itself usually only hears about it afterwards!

In July 1994, Léandri was even promoted officer of the national order of the Ivory Coast in the presence of President Henri Konan Bédié, who honored another compatriot that day as well, the prefect Philippe Massoni.

"But since the last presidential election," notes a specialist,

"Léandri goes much less often to Africa, all the exchanges are conducted now via 'Cooperation 92.'" But "Léandri the African" still keeps his eyes open. For, parallel to the political networks, business alliances are formed. It's useless for Pasqua to swear that there is an impermeable wall between them and him (although he is clearly more attracted by power than by money); there are, at the very least, connections between all these islanders. Thus, the former Minister for the Interior maintains friendly relations with Michel Tomi, enterprising promoter of horse betting in Africa. The PMU (*note:* Pari mutuel urbain, like the OTB) is a gold mine: in the bush, large bets are placed on the races at Vincennes and Maisons-Laffitte; the races can be watched on TV. The same Michel Tomi, whose brother Jean-Baptiste (former owner of the casino Bandol) is the extremely influential mayor of Tasso, in Southern Corsican. He is also associated in another field, just as lucrative — slot machines — with Robert Feliciaggi, Mayor of Pila-Canale. Another friend of Pasqua and Tarallo, he runs some fifty casinos in Africa.

In addition to their lucrative African activities, these Corsicans play another, more political role, by occasionally passing "messages" to the local militant nationalists. Until the fall of 1996, the continuity from Pasqua's cabinet to Jean-Louis Debré's was ensured by Léandri. Upon his arrival, the new Interior Minister had tried to throw him out. But he came back, and Debré gave in. It took the resumption of the terrorist attacks, the breakdown of negotiations, and terrorist blackmail to discredit Pasqua's network; the trouble reached as far as the President of the Republic. Sanctions hit hard. Léandri, who had been one of Chirac's bodyguards early on (in November 1978, he was at the door of Chirac's room at the Cochin hospital after his accident in Corrèze), was fired by Debré on orders from the Elysée. Pasqua, on chilly terms with Matignon, could only sulk and openly criticize the ousting of his protégé. And he continued to protect Léandri in his inner circle.

A Corsican at every strategic post. Pasqua continued to apply this rule. Even though his contacts are varied, from old companions from the Resistance to his colleagues at Ricard, with whom he had marketed the famous *pastis*, only a Corsican can claim to enjoy his total confidence. "It is impossible to make a career in the Hauts-de-Seine if one is not Corsican," claims one of his rivals. The assertion may be exaggerated, but "sensitive" posts are, indeed, reserved to them. Thus, since 1981 he entrusted to one of his close friends, Dominique Vescovali (a long-time executive at Bull), the job of managing the finances of the companies that were opportunely created along the course of his career. As colorless as Daniel Léandri, this computer specialist who was dispatched to the Var to counter both the PR (parti républicain, on the right) and the FN (Front national), was often suspected of playing a decisive part in financing the RPR (although he vigorously denied it).

Corsicans and dirty tricks often go together. It was through 100% Corsican connections that Pasqua arranged Yves Chalier's escape to Brazil in May 1986. Chalier was one of the protagonists in the "Crossroads of Development" affair, an explosive series of embezzlements at the Ministry for Cooperation.

Across the Atlantic, two compatriots of the Minister for the Interior, Julien Fillipedu and Jean-Paul Rocca-Serra (manufacturers of electronic poker games), welcomed Chalier with open arms. And a young doctor, a native of Corsica, traveling to Brazil, brought back to Pasqua's trusted aides the detailed account of the adventures of the "Crossroads" file that Chalier had calmly written.

From Africa to Brazil, the Corsican "Mafia" doesn't stop at any border. But its preferred universe remains the political, where it expands without any partisan inclination. For years, Corsican freemasons of every political stripe attended the same Masonic lodge attached to the Grand Orient, created in 1985 and dubbed the "Pasquale-Paoli Lodge," to reflect the nationalist tensions. Thus, José Rossi from the UDF discussed the Joxe plan there with industrialist Henri Antona, who was for many years with the SFIO before leaning in favor of the RPR.

Even if the parliamentary joint committee that had brought together (in the Sixties) close to 65 Corsican deputies and senators is history, another association took its place, the "Members of Parliament and Members of the Economic and Social Council of Corsican Origin." It pulls in Corsicans by birth, like Jean Tiberi and Dominati (father and son) for Paris City Hall, the ministers Xavier Emmanuelli and Pierre Pasquini, elected officials from the Hauts-de-Seine like Charles Ceccaldi-Reynaud, André Santini and Charles Pasqua, the president of the Economic and Social Council Jean Mattéoli, and also François Léotard and Michel Charasse (Corsican through their mother). It even adopted a man from the continent, the advisor who is very influential with the Elysée, Maurice Ulrich, who divides his time between Paris and his residence at Propriano.

According to the rule this club, chaired by Paul d'Ornano (one of the two senators representing Frenchmen from abroad), meets every two months for dinner at one of the Corsican ministers'. A group of guitarists sometimes joined the guests, to sing old local tunes. Today, no one's heart is in the music any more, it seems. Perhaps the group is worried by the "hot issues" going on in Corsica and fears being supplanted by a regional network that is in full expansion since Jacques Chirac was elected.

Corrèze*, the Capital City of the Presidential Palace

To each his turn: the Auvergnats had their hour of glory with Valéry Giscard d'Estaing, those from Nevers with François Mitterrand. Sometimes horizontally (between expatriates) and sometimes vertically (from Paris toward the Département), the Corrézien networks have been fully functional since May 1995. "I am the caretaker of Corrèze," jokes Bernard Murat (the deputy-mayor of Brive), who has discovered the power of the Corréziens in Paris. "At Parisian dinners, my seat keeps getting closer to that of the hostess, since Chirac was elected."

A pilgrimage to Brive has become essential for all the ministers under Chirac; in fact, they have been promoted to honorary members of the Corrézien brotherhood. Corinne Lepage, Guy Drut, Jean-Louis Debré, Eric Raoult, Jacques Toubon, Philippe Douste-Blazy, Anne-Marie Couderc, they have all paid a visit. A boon for Bernard Murat. A former executive in the pharmaceutical industry, rather new to politics, he uses the Corréziens' influential in Paris to expand his influence locally. The head of Havas, Pierre Dauzier (who is also president of the Athletic Club of Brive, or "CAB"), for example, gave him access to his own networks. "As if by miracle," Murat says, "the doors opened: Jean-Claude Decaux came to see me, Martin Bouygues invited me over."

Far more prestigious still, a certain Patrick Boudot, a one-time high school student of Argentat, better known to TV audiences under the name of Patrick Sebastien, made his return to the media stage in autumn 1996 on France 2 (a television station) directly (or almost) from the Brive town hall. In the first row, Mister Mayor and his wife

---

*Corrèze is Jacques Chirac's home *département*, in the Limousin region, south central France; Tulle is the capital and Brive-la-Gaillarde is the principal town.

applauded as hard as they could for this showman who had set up his cameras for a show in homage to George Brassens. President of the rugby section of the CAB, Sebastien ensured that Brive would get excellent publicity, and Brive returned the favor: the municipality spent 500,000 francs to welcome this native son.

Irresistible Corrèze! The Corsican Jean Tiberi, Mayor of Paris (and employer at the City Hall of almost 2,000 exiles from the plateau of Millevaches and the surrounding area), and his wife Xavière welcomed with open arms, starting in early 1996, the annual meeting of the Association of People from the Arrondissement of Ussel. That is an association of almost 1,000 members, presided over by the lawyer Françoise Gallot-Monod, the granddaughter of Henri Queuille (the former president of the State Council) and wife of the Chirac supporter Jerome Monod, owner of Lyonnaise des Eaux.

Jerome Cordelier (a Parisian journalist with Corrézien ties) notes that, "even in the capital, one is from either upper or lower Corrèze;" but the label Corrézien — whatever the village of origin — never sounded so good.

"Corrèze Développement," one of many "Corrèzish" associations, doesn't look too hard at the nature of "roots." "We write to membership candidates," explains one of its representatives, that "we regard as originating from Corrèze all those who are associated with our Département, even if they were not born there. Family ties, especially if you have anything to do with rugby, are generally sufficient to be allowed to join Corrèze Développement, which is a very convivial group."

A very new group, also recruiting, the "Corréziens of Paris" was born precisely one year after the providential election. Initiated by a lawyer who is a native of Brivezac, Olivier Chazoule, Esq., it claims to serve very down-to-earth needs: to find housing for new arrivals, to establish contact between "regional" restaurant managers and meat suppliers, to locate training opportunities among Corréziens in business, etc. Corrézien businesses are, admittedly, numerous: Dumez, City-Bank, Rhône-Poulenc, and Havas are among the companies that welcome exiles. In order to help the new folks find their ways in the Parisian jungle, an accountant, Pierre Godet, has even come up with a "Who's Who" ("Quo Quë" in patois) that includes nearly 2,000 compatriots out of a community of 20,000 to 50,000. The first edition (1997) of this Corrézien Who's Who is a gold mine for anyone who wants to make the best use of the regional web. Barely a month after this guide was published, a private banking advisor at one of the large Parisian banks was already prospecting among his countrymen.

"Corréziens are more malignant than the others, but they do not want that to be known," jokes the writer Denis Tillinac in a book in homage to his compatriots. The book is a census of local celebrities, co-written with Pierre Dauzier.[3] "They manage remarkably well," vouch-safes the northerner Jacques Duquesne, citizen-by-adoption of Eygurande thanks to his wife, "Corrèze exports men who get important roles."

The older ones help the most struggling. "As for myself," says Tillinac, "I remember a bar on boulevard Beaumarchais where, as a poor young student, I used to go to borrow a few bucks with my Corrézien identity card!" The "system" of mutual aid is perfectly oiled. "Every canton, every village, has a 'big guy' who receives young people looking for jobs or housing. No one deviates from this tradition of mutual aid." Clearly!

Chirac, while hiring Corréziens into City Hall by the truckload, was only keeping up a "custom" initiated by "the good Doctor Queuille." Any Corrézien coming into the Austerlitz station in the Fifties would, indeed, make straight for the rue du Cherche-Midi to ask for a hand from the former president of the State Council.

This tradition is so well-established that a faithful Corrézien like the Socialist René Teulade acknowledges without any qualms that he did a good job in placing the alumni of his college in Argentat in jobs with the Federation nationale de la mutualité française when he was the president. The same Teulade had a network of friendly mayors in the suburbs whom he solicited regularly to lodge a "countryman."

For his part Pierre Dauzier, the chairman of Havas, reckons that he has placed at least two hundred Corréziens. Daniel Broussouloux, promoter of the association "Corrèze Développement," presents himself as a "typical example of a Corrézien that other Corréziens helped to get started." After earning his doctorate in law, he got into COFACE (an export insurance company) where, by lucky coincidence, the personnel manager is Corrézien.

"If I was able to buy my restaurant 'The Carpenters,'" says Pierre Bardèche (who also owns a fish restaurant in the VIth arrondissement, "it is because a Corrézien legal adviser helped me out. The owners were Corrézien, too. I did not have the cash to buy the restaurant, but they trusted me." Since then, Bardèche has become one of the pillars of the clan. Chirac celebrated his sixtieth birthday at his place and organized several dinners there during the presidential campaign. Similarly, the owner of the Thoumieux brewery which, out of a staff of forty, employs many natives of the Départemente.

In the law courts, the Interprofessional Club of Corrézien Lawyers of the Paris Bar trusts its customers from the area. Jean-Louis Aujol, Esq., born at the beginning of the 20th century, who pleaded cases during the lawsuit of the Cagoule and the Observatory affair, had (among others) customers in Rungis among the local shippers. In 1946, he joined Jean-Louis Lachaud, Esq., a man from Brive who was atavistically impassioned with rugby, and a defender of the French Rugby Federation. In his turn, Lachaud recruited in 1988 another Brivist, Grégory Martin, Esq.. The solidarity of lawyers from Corrèze (about sixty are indexed in "Quo Quë") is such that they are flattered to have had two presidents of the bar among them, Jean Couturon Esq. and more recently Philippe Lafarge, Esq., who counted seven members of his family in the Palais de Justice! "And of course the lawyer of Round Table Publishing is Corrézien," its chairman, Denis Tillinac, notes with amusement.

In high public office also, the Corrézien connection reinforce ties from the ENA: two old ENA alumni from the neighborhood created a "Corrézien section" within the old association!

But the most original of the professional and regional alliances is "The School of Brive," which is half a gang of merry epicureans, half a literary salon. The founder of this friendly fraternity, Jacques Peuchmaurd, son of a butcher's assistant who went up to Paris, has been a literary director at Robert Laffont for more than forty years. During a stay in Corrèze, in the early Fifties, he met the Limousin George-Emmanuel Clancier, author of the series *Le Pain noir* (Black Bread), who introduced the writer Michel Peyramaure to him. This name was familiar: their wives attended the same college. . .

A few years later, Peyramaure warmly recommended a country friend and writer to him, Claude Michelet. That was in 1974 at a reception given during the first Book Fair to be held in the great hall of Brive, which has by now become a highly regarded book exposition. An irony of history: Claude Michelet is the son of the Gaullist Edmond Michelet, who had, in the Thirties, initiated a "School of Brive," a sort of Christian-Democrat intellectual circle.

Christian Signol is the son of a tradesman from the old country, with whom the editor does his marketing. One day, his mother confides that "the boy" writes. . . Under Peuchemaurd's wing, he starts producing best-sellers. As for Tillinac, a journalist in Tulle before emigrating to Paris, his book with the nostalgic title *Spleen in Corrèze* that moved "Peuch" to adopt him.

Thus "the band of five" was formed. According to Tillinac, they share "the awareness of being affiliated with poor but maligned peasants, obstinate yet capable of diplomacy, a little bit secretive yet open to others as our mountaintops open on the lands of the South." They put out large volumes of popular literature in the great tradition of the authors of the 19th century, and they share an acute sense of solidarity. When one author is interviewed, he mentions the others. They have made the School of Brive an effective brand name and a means of asserting themselves vis-à-vis the Parisian intelligentsia, which resists them in spite of their best-selling books — between 50,000 and 500,000 copies.

The band of five, further enriched by the eventual addition of a sixth member, Gilbert Bordes, is no longer quite what it was in the time of Robert Laffont. The arrival of the editor Bernard Fixot, who took the place of the founder, precipitated Christian Signol (author of very successfully televised *Rivière Espérance* ["The River Hope"], into the arms of the editor Albin Michel. *Spleen in Corrèze?* As Tillinac would say, "It doesn't matter; we had fun."

Corréziens in Paris do not acknowledge it publicly, but they miss the days when "Jacques" reigned at City Hall. It is unthinkable of going to the "Château" now to make a request on such familiar terms as before. Admittedly, an informal "Corrèze" group, that is not shown on the official organizational chart, was set up at the Elysée under the eye of the Treignacois Jean-Louis Fargeas (the ex-Secretary General of the prefecture). It handles "local" demands but answers to Annie Lhéritier, executive assistant to the President. She serves as an umbilical cord to the départemente; for a long time she was head of an identical group at the Paris City Hall, then she was promoted to prefect in the summer of 1996, all the while keeping her position with the Elysée. This native of Aix in Corrèze continues to watch over the favorable progress of Corrézien matters. It also happens, from time to time, that the President intervenes directly to give a lift to his "homeboys." Thus, the general manager of Printemps received a phone call from Chirac, recommending that he treat well a certain department head in the store. The reason for such solicitude? He was quite open about it: the lady is. . . Corrézienne. Bernadette Chirac, elected by the canton of Sarran, also mobilized herself for the cause. Petitions pile up on her desk, asking for help in establishing a company in lower Corrèze, to find a job or housing for a young person who has just arrived.

This discrete diaspora, in stubborn competition with the Corsicans at City Hall, must also find a *modus vivendi* with the "businesses." They scarcely thought that the politician-businessmen of the RPR at City Hall could cast suspicion on practices that until then had been considered as well-understood solidarity. Nearly a thousand Corréziens squeezed into the rooms of the House of Chemistry, in Paris, on June 10, 1996, at the invitation of five local councillors and of the very active president of the Corrèze Chamber of Commerce, Michèle Chezabiel, to open an exposition of "industrial expertise" from the region; nobody brought up any contentious issues at the time. However, the network deplores that specific events set up one of its members as a superstar, thus illustrating the perversities of a system of mutual aid pushed to the extremes of caricature. This system is denounced by dertain militant ecologists, members of the activist group "Taxpayers' Forum," whose goal is nothing less than "to control the management of public finances and to obtain greater transparency in the use of tax revenues."

The militants decided to target an obscure activist from the RPR federation of Corrèze, Philippe Ceaux. A former coffee boy, he was happy to be given a "job" at City Hall. The "Taxpayers' Forum" referred his case to the administrative court but the court rejected their demand, according to the plaintiff's testimony. "My job," he naïvely confided to the authors of *La Razzia* (*The Raid*), two journalists from *Le Canard enchâiné*,[4] "consisted in accepting requests for work and housing from Corréziens settling in Paris." You can't beat that for honesty. Since then, he was rehabilitated by his protector, the former minister and mayor of Tulle Raymond-Max Aubert. The RPR activist was not the only one to benefit from such assistance. André Vidal, the mayor of Soursac, was also "employed" at city hall in Paris until 1992. As for Annie Lhéritier, she had four city employees working just for the benefit of people from Ussel and its surroundings.

Another Corrézien, quite as concerned as his fellow-citizens, had to answer to the court for deeds that were a little more serious. George Pérol, former mayor of Meymac and head of the HLM, the Paris subsidized housing office, was questioned for "influence peddling" by judge Eric Halphen. If his former assistant François Ciolina is to be believed, the Corrézien identity would open every door. According to him, architects with Corrézien ties would often find themselves at the head of some lucrative design studio, the required intermediaries between the housing agency and house-building industry. More comically, when OTIS wanted to beat out its competitors for a contract on 3,000 elevator cars with the Paris agency, some of its workers made sure to mention their Corrézien origins! The argument was surely not the most decisive, but OTIS (and its Corréziens) did win the deal.

"Regional affiliation won out over political considerations in obtaining HLM housing," too, says an elected official from the left. He helped several fellow-citizens take advantage of this "Corrézien preference." This attention to the electorate was not enough to allow George Pérol a peaceful end of career. He was, however, persuaded that Corrézien immunity would play in his favor. "Now that Jacques is in the Elysée, I will be talking with those journalists that report anything you tell them," he would say to anyone who would listen, after the presidential election. Ay! Support from "Jacques" was not much political help to him, for the Meymacois themselves, tired of this mayor who seemed not to be very sensitive to their everyday problems, threw him out in June 1995 after three municipal mandates.

"Business" or no business, the Corrézien network is the subject of so many fantasies that some people assert an improbable Corrézien origin, even if they do not have any legitimacy. The restaurateur Pierre Bardèche, who for a long time signed his letters to Jacques Chirac "Very corréziennally yours," notes with humor that the formula became a hit. This usurpation of identity amuses the autochtones as much as it reassures them: "The Corsicans' floor" may be in jeopardy!

Chapter 2

A HELPING HAND

The Interior Minister thought he knew his way around when it came to networks. Wasn't he always leaning on old friends he'd picked up in the course of all his activities? The Corsicans, the resistance fighters, veterans of Ricard, reconverted soldiers from French Algeria, hard-core right-wingers — so many perfectly identified pools that he knew he could count on. But, for the first time in his career, in March 1987, Charles Pasqua felt himself powerless. He was facing a "fraternal order" that all his experience, however eclectic, was insufficient to handle.

One of his collaborators, Dominique Latournerie, director of public freedom and judicial affairs, had just committed a blunder. He had threatened to ban a dozen periodicals for "representing a danger to youth, because of their licentious or pornographic character, or simply the amount of space given to crime and violence." Among them was *Gai-Pied*, a weekly review with a circulation of 20,000, to which all the fashionable sympathizers of the community (from Dalida to Jean-Paul Sartre) had contributed. Yves Mourousi posed in it, to publicize a gay bar in Les Halles. Jack Lang gave a long interview, saying: "This is a well-crafted review; I read it regularly. It is intelligent, fine and courageous. I find original studies and facts there. In that sense, it is cultural, in the fullest sense of the term." In short, the former Minister of Culture was full of enthusiasm.

In truth, Dominique Latournerie was only carrying out orders. Pasqua, who did not intend to leave the defense of the moral order to the extreme right, had decided to launch a campaign to "clean up" the press. *L'Echo des savanes* and *Newlook* were also affected. But it was the banning of *Gai-Pied* that caused a fuss.

Hugo Marsan, editor of *Gai-Pied*, and Gerard Vappereau, the director of the publication, called for help. The "network," which is informal yet organized, was immediately mobilized. According to the law, the publication had fifteen days to respond. In fact, twenty minutes after receiving the "liberticide" letter, a war council was established. "Dash off a public statement to every editorial house, unleash the dispatch riders to the four corners of the earth, spill out your databases with the public personalities to be contacted, crack open your personal address books;" this is the picture later given by those who were there.[1]

Homosexuals in the "Movement of Liberal Gays" (a movement close to the majority), alerted the deputies of their camp. François Léotard joined the club that *Gai-Pied* improvised to organize its defense. Alerted by homosexual advisers in his cabinet, the Minister of Culture praised the publication on "Press Club," a television show, saying, "I discovered this newspaper for the first time during this mess. I read it attentively and found it quite interesting."

Reinforced by other left-leaning figures, Jack Lang gave the magazine his support. At the National Assembly, he ostentatiously offered the Interior Minister the complete works of Rabelais. And he visited the "Museum of the Horrible," an exhibition of turpitudes of a certain type, organized by Dominique Latournerie, including a reproduction of a pornographic drawing by Picasso.

Chirac understood that the gays would not quit. Pasqua was trying to justify this moralizing bent, but the Prime Minister answered curtly: "Drop the threat against *Gai-Pied*, and calm the homos that are stirring everybody up." The Minister gave in. A few days later, Dominique Latournerie wrote to the magazine, "I have decided that the trial currently underway will not be pursued . . ."

"Is Charles Pasqua soft-pedaling now?" a journalist delicately asked in the just-rehabilitated magazine, as he announced that the man whom *Libération* had dubbed "the chief censor" had run out of steam.

The *Gai-Pied* had plenty to celebrate — the "homos" had made the "heteros" fold.

Neither Rightists Nor Leftists: The Gays

Homosexuals, of course, do not form a homogeneous population. "Without question, there are bars, bookshops, and disco's serving this identity group. But in this case there is no one 'community,'" explains Frederic Martel, a young sociologist who has authored a book on the history of the gay movements since 1968.[2] "On the other hand, there probably exists a 'community of destiny,' ill-defined and fluid, that is conscious of certain forms of discrimination, and that combats AIDS. And in the United States, there is a more political homosexual militancy."

In France, dissension has persisted since the Seventies between a very loud minority, avid for "visibility," and a silent majority that prefers discrete complicity — not to mention the bisexuals, who shelter behind a conjugal façade but know to play on their "special friendships," when necessary.

Often, sexual affiliation erases political allegiance. In May 1979, observers were astonished to see, at the 2nd Congress of Arcadie (an association of "homophiles," as they were called themselves, classified on the right and headed up by a former seminarist André Baudry), writers whose sympathies were on the left, such as Jean-Paul Aron and Dominique Fernandez, and the philosopher Michel Foucault. In fact, since its creation in 1954, Arcadie serves as a network of friends of every persuasion. New members are subjected to a rite of admission. Accompanied by a "godfather," they are presented to André Baudry under their true identity. But with respect to the outside world, they take refuge behind a pseudonym, for example when they sign articles in their magazine. This includes the director of the publication, a high-ranking functionary at the Archives of France, and occasional freelance journalists, a former officer of the French army, a well-known magistrate, and certain university professors.

The popes of this very closed club are, in addition to the young philosophy professor Baudry, the writer André du Dognon, the socialite Jacques de Ricaumont, and the diplomat Roger Peyrefitte. All these who love the stronger sex want to be as clandestine as possible — with the notable exception of Roger Peyrefitte. Grandfather of "outing," the militant practice that consists of denouncing gays for hiding in shame, he "goes both ways" without any preference. Twenty years on, Arcadie accepted a second generation of homosexuals, often more militant; some of them created other movements that were more vociferously leftist, thus precipitating the disappearance of this distinguished club.

There remains, in spite of the risks and the vicissitudes of all these more or less transitory, more or less provocative "liberation" movements, a society of mutual support. It is founded in a shared marginality, as a reaction against what is perceived, wrongly or rightly, as ambient homophobia.

"I came to understand this," explains a "hetero" former Minister, "one evening in June, 1981, when one of my buddies, a gay, took me along to have dinner 'with the guys' at one on his friends'. There, on Avenue Foch, in the huge apartment of the chairman of a big metallurgical company, I witnessed cohabitation before its time. God knows whether, at that very hour, the right was making noise against Mitterrand. However, before my very eyes, I saw a miracle: former ministers under Giscard conversing more than pleasantly with members of the Mauroy cabinet. Around the table, two State advisers, a prefect and some writers whose intimacy I did not doubt, were exchanging information and seeking ways to render each other service. That evening, I witnessed the power of the homosexual network."

The network is all the more solid since it is confident, given the prevailing policy (in France) of respect for private life, of anonymity. Writing in 1986 a work on *The Intellocrats*, Hervé Hamon and Patrick Rotman decided not to evoke the complicity among homosexuals. However, more than one art critic, following the example of Gilles Barbedette, René de Ceccaty and Hugo Marsan, journalists in the "major media," had already signed their names openly in *Gai-Pied*. Not because they confine themselves to the criticism of works by friendly authors, but because the choice of an editor, the launching of a book or a show, the assurance of television coverage also depend, sometimes, on these loyalties that are no less effective than the cliquishness supported by the big schools.

As in every milieu, this network seems to be most effective in what a British journalist, Tim Heald (author of *Networks*[3]) called "the high homosexual community." "A homosexual from London who has good connections," he writes, "was always received by the correspond-ing level of society in New York and in Paris."

Some overt militants for the cause are irritated by these secret complicities when they influence political life clandestinely. "I am a little bit annoyed by these ministerial get-togethers where everything is done in the shadows," fulminated Jean-Paul Pouliquen in the gay maga-zine *Illico*, May, 1995. As head of the Collective for the Civil Union Con-tract, a sort of legal entity of the cohabitation, he presents himself as a lobbyist acting in full view.

In the same magazine, Henri Maurel (the former executive assis-tant to Yvette Roudy, today owner of the radio station "The Gay Fre-quency,") was quick to underline, on the contrary, the role of the net-work in securing the vote on certain laws. "When Yvette Roudy man-aged to have her anti-sexist law extended to apply to homosexual cases, no editorials in the newspapers were required. Similarly, it was by working on the inside that it was possible to get assurance that Bérégovoy's law on social welfare coverage of partners would not be discriminatory with respect to homosexuals."

The politicians themselves grant sufficient importance to this community to surround themselves with representatives — semi-official, perhaps, but whose role is clearly perceived by the interested parties. "Gaston Defferre's success is due to the fact that he had always had his Armenians, his Greeks. . . When it had to do with fags, he had fags," is the crude explanation of Jacques Fortin (president of the Ho-mosexual Liberation Group in Marseilles in the Eighties, and author of the book *The Pink and the Black*. Even the very traditionalist Hervé Gay-mard, Alain Juppé's Health Minister, secured a link with the homosex-ual world by recruiting to City Hall a former leader in the fight against AIDS.

A leading expert on networks, the socialist Laurent Fabius was convinced by his wife Françoise (his "homing device" in many milieux), of the importance of this kind of contact. In 1981, there was indeed an association "Homosexuality and Socialism," but it was close to Lionel Jospin. Fabius thus encouraged the creation of another association, "Gays for Liberation" (LPG), in 1984. The ways of populism are many. Chaired by Henri Maurel, who admits he loves networking, LPG organ-izes event after event: the "cross-country race for liberation," dinner-debates, official receptions at the Opera. Françoise Fabius came up with the idea of that famous gala reception, so well-suited to the "caviar leftists" and very liberally subsidized. "My little darlings," she announced at the end of 1985 to Jean Javanni (vice-president of the movement) and some friends, at a meeting in Toulouse, "I have a terrific idea! We'll sell art objects at the Paris Opera. And you, Jean, since you're HIV positive, I will kiss you on stage!"[4] The gala was a great success (some seats were sold at $500) but when it was time to close the books, there was some gnashing of teeth: too many dubious invoices, too much money that had mysteriously disappeared, not enough funds actually sent to their intended destination, the fight against AIDS.

That did not discourage these activists, who mobilized their networks to support François Mitterrand in 1988. At the same time, they participate according to their means in the legislative campaigns. Thus, Maurice Bennassayag, a candidate in the 4th district of Paris, the Marais, made the rounds of the gay bars accompanied by Maurel and his friends.

However, the idyll between Fabius and the LPG ended abruptly. Maurel, who took up residence in the offices of the Hotel de Lassay, after 1988, thanks to the new president of the national Assembly, dropped his protector as soon as the latter hit hard times. Attacked in the contaminated blood scandal, Fabius found himself alone, with the anti-AIDS associations portraying him as having acted out of industrial cynicism by not hastening the installation of an American blood-test tracking system.

The Vacillating Gays

If it is in the nature of a network is to cross party lines, then "the homo network" is very powerful. During the 1990's, France experienced two governmental cohabitations that only reinforced the allegiances that are independent of traditional loyalties. During the May 1995 presidential campaign, two pillars of the left, Pierre Bergé and Frederic Mitterrand, brought around the opposing camp by getting many friends to come along. The craftsman of these spectacular rallies (and other, more discrete events), is a man little known to the general public but much appreciated in the back corridors by people of all parties. During the presidential campaign he was working in the cultural affairs administration at City Hall; he understands perfectly the ways of the capital.

Originally, he was a professor of history and geography at Egle-tons and at Tulle, in Corrèze. Then he took classes in Paris under the wand of Michel Guy, Culture Minister for Valéry Giscard-d'Estaing, whom he met at the Festival of Avignon — a cultivated minister, very open, who often invited his dancer and choreographer friends to dinner at "Sept." This hot spot of Parisian gay life was owned by the Minister's friend, Fabrice Emaer, who also owned a night club that was in vogue, the acclaimed "Palace." The same Emaer, very much in tune with the cohabitation, also mobilized himself for François Mitterrand in May, 1981, with famous homosexuals like Yves Navarre, Dominique Fernan-dez, and Jean-Paul Aron.

Michel Guy encouraged him not to spend too long teaching in the provinces, where he was hiding his lantern under a bushel basket. He directed his young protégé into the General Delegation of Education, where the general manager is the Gaullist Jean Musy.

Musy becomes the young professor's protector. In 1985, the faith-ful Musy called him to join the administration of the Cultural Affairs of Paris. Once there, this interesting recruit caught Chirac's eye by open-ing doors to a community that the future president had had little suc-cess in cultivating heretofore. The President, far from being a homo-phobe, affects an amused distance with respect to gays. When he was a deputy-mayor of Paris, he used to ask one of his aides, while entering the Chamber of the National Assembly, "So remind me, who are the fags in the RPR?" — an adolescent curiosity that his predecessor Fran-çois Mitterrand, more or less fascinated by female homosexuality, also felt from time to time, so that he encouraged his friend Pierre Bergé to update the "Gay Who's Who."

The Good Works of Pierre Bergé

How can we describe the secret influence of the homosexual *no-menklatura* without mentioning Pierre Bergé, a Giscard supporter in the Seventies, then a Mitterrandian and, finally, a Chiraquian? This man with a constant eye out for opportunities dreamed in his youth of con-quering Paris. A Charentais like Mitterrand, he came to Paris after the war and, like him, dreamed of frequenting the literary circles. Far more liberated than the boarding school boy with the good family back-ground, the young Bergé, without a diploma but already very strong in people skills, knocked on the doors of André Gide and Jean Giono. A friend of pacifist Gary Davis, he proclaimed himself a "citizen of the world" and became impassioned in 1949 for the ephemeral newspaper *La Patrie mondiale* (*The Global Fatherland*). Impresario of the painter Bernard Buffet, then pygmalion to the dressmaker Yves St. Laurent, this tough businessman now sees himself as the patron and the protector of the gay community.

His network of personal friendships, woven for forty years in the milieux of haute couture, business and theater, has indeed long since earned him a reputation as a generous intermediary. When Copi, the Argentinian cartoonist, disembarked in Paris, who did people advise him to go and see? Bergé, of course, who directed him toward Françoise Giroud at *L'Express*. In fact, it was *Le Nouvel observateur* (another major newpaper in Paris) that hired him, but in any event the artist soon turned to other matters. As a service to Communist gay friends, who were rather unpopular in their Party, he organized a very smart fashion show with Yves St. Laurent in 1978 at a party for *L'Humanité* (the Communist paper)!

More serious, and more costly were Bergé's engagements in the fight against AIDS. In early 1986, he and Christophe Girard, number-two man at Yves St. Laurent, became respectively president and General Secretary of Arcat-SIDA. They were called to the rescue by the two bankrupt doctors who had founded association a few months before. In the same way, when a Gay and Lesbian Center was created in Paris in March, 1994 as a meeting place, subsidized by the Health Ministry, Bergé served as guarantor for the lease. He also helps Act-Up, and finances *Têtu*, a glossy gay magazine, where he buys ads for Yves St. Laurent and his Opium perfume.

But what he is most proud of is that he won the presidency of the "Ensemble Against AIDS," the organization run by Sidaction, whose use of donations is, however, somewhat controversial.

In fact, rare are the "notables" who are pleased, like him, to openly display their homosexuality and sponsor so visibly any action to help their peers. "Of course, there are individuals who admit to being homosexual. But how many company owners, national deputies or actors in France are willing to sign an appeal that makes it clear that they are homosexual? We still have a long way to go!"[5] Indeed, the gay networks are still operating largely in secrecy. In the same interview,

Bergé says he doesn't intend to practice any "outing," except perhaps against those who publicly take positions unfavorable to homosexuals. This scarcely veiled threat is addressed, among others, toward a prominent deputy of the majority party who is very influential on family questions and who had decided against the "Contract of Civil Union" that would enable gay couples to enjoy the same advantages as a heterosexual couple.

"Maoist Cells" versus "Gay Cells"

The "official" story of the début of *Libération* ("*Libé*," a popular and unconventional paper) recalls only the sense of a chaotic launching of a leftist daily newspaper developed by the old stalwarts of the proletarian Left. They were astonishing beginnings, indeed, sponsored by an enthusiastic but overextended Jean-Paul Sartre. One of the nerve centers of the newspaper was the rather shocking "Maoist cell," in which a handful of doctrinaire firebrands intended to lay down the new rules of the revolutionary press. Yikes! The young hot-bloods tore into each other with such ferocity that Serge July, a self-proclaimed Citizen Kane, resolved in July 1973 to disband the overly disruptive group. Exit the Great Helmsman's merry band, enter the other friends of Serge July, this time from the network of journalism students, firmly committed to transforming what they called "the rag" into a real newspaper.

This change of direction also benefited a rival network that was trying to get a foothold in the editorial staff. For this newspaper that was striving, in the mid-Seventies, to be attuned to every sensibility, also harbored another "cell," far more over the top than that of the Maoists. The pillar of this mini-network was Jean-Luc Hennig. A highly qualified professor of language, he arrived at *Libération* in 1974 after having been removed from the national education hierarchy for reading to his students from "Three billion perverts," a special edition of the review *Recherches,* on homosexuality. Hennig, who did a column on homosexual topics day by day, and created a section of "specialized" personal advertisements, brought in his friend Guy Hocquenghem, who himself enlisted the journalist Michel Cressole, to deal with television. Along with them, Christian Hennion, a veteran of the Revolutionary Homosexual Front (a post-Sixties movement), wrote a column called "Flagrante Delicto." "If you include Alain Pacadis for music, Serge

45

Daney and Louella Intérim on cinema, and Hélène Hazéra, a transsexual, for entertainment, the 'gay' team was complete," wrote Frederic Martel in *The Pink and the Black*.

To this team was added Copi, the Argentinian, a cartoonist by now famous and who was the darling of an editorial team that ignored the censor. But *Libé* began to age and sober up: when the daily decided in 1981 to close down for a few weeks, to reappear in the form of a newspaper that would be more "pro", with a "real" editorial staff and a hierarchy, the "homo" cell was requested to be less conspicuous and to handle the news in a less "militant" way.

If All the Gays in the World . . .

As an almost overt network, the "gay" group at *Libération* was by no means exceptional. Particularly close when confronting disease (with the AIDS epidemic, friendly support networks were spontaneously generated, in addition to associations of mutual aid) homosexuals also clearly know how to advance each other's careers. That's a private subject, as taboo as the promotion of women who sleep their way to the top. It works differently, however, since in the one case it is an "exchange" between two people, in the other, it is a whole community that mobilizes to support one of its own.

Examples abound, even if they can be reported only anonymously. There is a Minister of Transport, assisted by his chief adviser, who manages his sphere of influence with particular attention to his friends among the boys. One of them, who had begun a promising career under the tender tutelage of a president of public television, would thus win an elevated position in a newly created TV channel. In his domain, the same minister warmly recommended a good dozen of his protégés to the (heterosexual and utterly stunned) Director of the regional station, *France 3*. Among the candidates thus recommended was a manual laborer who had recently discovered a vocation for international journalism, and a young Asian producer whose only reference was a documentary on the gay community in the minister's home city — an audio-visual piece poetically entitled "The Pink End of It" (sic), and some other pretty young men who were out of work.

Another example of professional solidarity: the director of a radio station with international scope made a point since his arrival of promoting around him some carefully selected male friendships. On the other hand, a Minister for the Balladur government ended up finding his assistant's preference for the homosexual race a little too exclusive. The heteros started to be so under-represented in his office that the fellow had to be removed and asked to exert his friendly talents in a different ministry. Funnier yet, an activist of one of the very masculine agencies of the Paris Chamber of Commerce and Industry was exiled to Lebanon for having harassed one of his colleagues, himself a homosexual!

Conversely, it is rather well received if one recruits homosexuals at the Ministry of Culture. Philippe Douste-Blazy, who knew this community when he went into the Health Ministry, surrounded himself with homosexuals in his office. "For convenience, I suppose," remarks a high-level (heterosexual) official, "because that gives him access to the cultural milieux, particularly dance and music. The majority of the men who have succeeded each other as head of the Paris Opera are homosexual. Without necessarily intending any favoritism, they turn to their friends who have the same inclinations."

The same phenomenon is at work in the field of baroque music, where few heteros can be found. At one time, all the musical periodicals were directed by women. They have all been replaced by homosexuals. Like all networks, this one strives to hold onto any territory it acquires. Thus, there may be a sense that certain areas, in the culture and communication sectors, not to mention the sphere of diplomacy (immortalized by Roger Peyrefitte), are more or less reserved for gays.

This type of mutual aid, particularly common in politics, the press, and literature, plays out very discreetly in the business world where the financial stakes outweigh sentimental considerations. In this universe, Pierre Bergé appears to be an exception. But it happens all the same that gays are making incursions there surreptitiously. Thus one could find the talented but provocative Copi in the act of concocting, for the chairman of Perrier, Gustave Leven, the famous slogan "Perrier, c'est fou!" (something like, "Perrier, it's a rave!"). A bit of a sly pun, his friends would say, given that so much of his work was dominated by "raving queens." Perhaps the none too conformist Leven was secretly pleased that his board of directors did not catch this erotic allusion. . . Similarly, an advertising executive who preferred the stronger sex sold Mercedes an unambiguous slogan that apparently delights the listeners on the Gay Frequency: "The queen of cars! The car of queens!"

These few examples should not, however, obscure a persistent reality. In the business world homosexuality, which for the most part remains very much taboo, is only very seldom a "plus" for one's career. "Except in *haute couture*, there is no field of business that is a gay fiefdom," comments a designer. "Most of my friends who work in less frivolous sectors don't dare to raise an eyebrow. They are afraid of becoming 'the fag' of the place. Secret friendships and sleeping one's way up happen more in the executive levels, where things are more insulated, less competitive."

The upper managers, apparently rather prudish, hardly appreciate these "special relationships," as Jacques Calvet, the chairman of Peugeot, called them. He was talking about the mishaps of the "Little Prince of Real Estate," Pascal Jeandet, under whose charm the head of SOFIB, a banking subsidiary of Peugeot, had fallen. The "Little Prince," without fortune or diploma, had succeeded in the Eighties, the boom years, in building a real fortune in no time at all. "Special relationships" had encouraged him until the crisis toppled the prices, and him too. This flamboyant man, who loved nothing more than to have fun every summer with his friends in Ibiza, died brutally at 32 — disowned by all those who had helped him to build his fortune.

"Privileged relationships," which must be hidden in the financial world, on the contrary are completely open in the commercial "gay ghetto." So much so that mutual aid has become very organized. Every month, the specialized magazine *Illico* publishes classified advertisements of bar owners, moving firms and construction companies, all homosexual. According to the sociologist Frederic Martel, who notes in his book the attraction of having an identity group, a symbolic fringe of gays is pushing the meaning of solidarity to the point of patronizing only "gay" establishments. Restaurants, discos, clothing stores, bookshops, movies — they form a closed loop.

Moreover, a gay trade union that claims to include nearly 600 companies in France was created five years ago. SNEG (the National Trade Union of Gay Companies) engages "to give hiring preference to gays: architects, lawyers, personnel, etc.," like the fraternal Masonic professionals who publish annual directories of the "brothers" in every trade so that they can give each other work. SNEG even says it has obtained preferential rates with certain insurance companies.

Other homosexuals, meeting at Gay and Lesbian centers, have

come across as a sufficiently structured association to be able to negotiate specific conditions with a mutual insurance company and for bank loans.

From this point of view, homosexuals have nothing to learn from anybody when it comes to effectiveness. Not even from the denominational networks, Jewish or Protestant, that for so long fed all the fantasies of exclusive mutual aid and solidarity.

The President's Jews

On Thursday, January 11, 1996, press releases were pouring into the Agence France-Presse (AFP). Three days before, François Mitterrand had died, at his Parisian residence on avenue Frederic-Le-Play. There wasn't an organization or an institution that could resist marking its reaction to the disappearance of the former President. Most of the statements, conventional and expected, were quickly lost in piles of paper. But there was one that could hold people's attention, its contents were so surprising.

The statement from the Consistory of Paris (the authority charged with looking after the religious life of the Jewish community in the capital and the surrounding areas), picked up the theme of a speech given the same day by Moïse Cohen, president of the institution, to his board of directors. First of all, he evoked the memory of Mitterrand; then he commented, somewhat bitterly, on certain traits of the recently deceased. For example, his friendship with René Bousquet and his stubborn refusal to present, in the name of the Republic, an apology for the French attitude with regard to the Jews during the Occupation. But Cohen then made a point of stressing that Mitterrand was surrounded at every level by networks controlled by Jews. And he enumerated: the Parents' Club, with Roger Hanin; his advisors, with Jacques Attali; the senior civil servants, with George Dayan; his circle of confidants, with George-Marc Benamou. . . "And so many others," exclaimed the president of the Consistory, in conclusion.

Not everyone in the Jewish community who had access to this text appreciated it. Some feared that the right-wing press might exploit it for detrimental purposes. The statement could lend support to the coarsest anti-Semitic fantasies, which portray the Jews as clandestine leaders manipulating the power behind the scenes.

This was a painful subject, for the principal interested parties felt, in the overwhelming majority, alien to the very notion of a network. When the magazine *Passages*, a publication whose identity is clear, devoted its February 1989 front page to "100 Jews Who Count," it began with a lengthy justification of the survey. Part of the community, whose members think of themselves as "French, of Jewish origin," rather than "Jewish, from France," like ethnologist Claude Lévi-Strauss, did not think much of the initiative.

"Why the Jews, and only they?" questions Emile Malet, editor of the monthly magazine, in his editorial, "Since all year long we see comparable surveys about the Protestants, the Catholics, the hit-parade of the richest men, the rankings and 'top 10's of every classification — why should only the Jews not be the object of a survey? Like the others (and it's better to make this statement calmly), the Jews constitute an active minority. A minority that expresses its sympathy for Israel, . . . a minority often engaged in the struggle for progress and solidarity."

But, since September 1791, when the Constituent Assembly granted French citizenship to the Jews, membership in the nation has voided (in the eyes of most) the very concept of a network, which would be associated with the idea of an oppressed minority. The most elementary statistics support this majority thesis. Barely 10% of the Jews of France belong to a communal association, and of the 350,000 people of Jewish origin who live in the Paris area, only 40,000 only are recorded by the Consistory. In a 1990 study controlled by the Unified Jewish Social Funds (FSJU), sociologist Erik Cohen was interested in mixed marriages: 30% of married Jews, from 18 to 29 years old, had married a non-Jew. This is a phenomenon of exogamy that worried the chief rabbi of France, Joseph Sitruk, so much that he compares the phenomenon of the mixed marriage with genocide. Is he an extremist? Certainly. But lawyer Henri Hajdenberg, creator of Jewish Revival (in 1995 he became the president of CRIF, the Representative Council of the Jewish Institutions of France) declared in 1992, during the big Judéoscope event that he had organized, "Each of us senses, more or less confusedly, that the Jewish community of France is moving toward an assimilation that may be slower or faster, but will be total."[6]

A paradox: whereas it is taboo to mention the "Jewish networks," the most eminent representatives of the community deplore that several of theirs are no longer living first and foremost as Jews.

Many ascribe this de-Judaïzation to rising on the social ladder: the financial, fashionable and international face erases the Jewish identity. We only have to examine the family trees of some great Israelite families to be convinced. The Pereires, Foulds, David-Weills, Halphens, Rothschilds, and Sterns have woven the strands of the generations through matrimonial alliances, among themselves but also with the catholic aristocracy, which looks more like a well-advised management of their "social capital" than the strict observance of identity rules.

Very Catholic Alliances

In the Stern family, the ancestor, Antoine, founded the bank of the same name in Frankfurt in the middle of the 19th century. His son and successor Jacques awaited his death before marrying the actress Sophie Croizette, unfortunate rival of Sarah Bernhardt on the Parisian stage. Jacques Stern died without descent. But three of his four nephews and nieces made "good matches" (the last remained unmarried). The elder one married a Lambert de Rothschild (from the Brussels branch), while his two sisters became, respectively, marquise de Chasseloup-Laubat and baroness de Langlade.

The marchioness married off her two daughters very honorably: the elder to Baron Fernand de Séroux, the junior to Prince Achille Murat. The marquise's children, and great-grandchildren of Antoine Stern, confirmed the family's ties in the social register. Salome married the politician Albin Chalandon; Thamar united herself with Count Antoine de Boissieu; Francois, known as Prince Murat-Chasseloup-Laubat, pled his troth to Huguette, daughter of the banker Henri Arminjon. The descendants of the baroness contracted similarly advantageous matrimonial alliances.

The Worms family also moved away, in the space of a few generations, from any communal activity, and even from any Jewish identity. The banker Olry-Hayem Worms, born in the mid-18th century, exerted all his life an activity supported within the Jewish institutions, in particular as chair of the central Consistory. His daughter, married to a German banker converted to Catholicism, gave birth to three heiresses, all of whom married worthy representatives of the French aristocracy: the marquis de Grouchy, the count de Villers and the count de Kerjégu.

Among Olry-Hayem's nephews, Hypolite was the originator of the current Worms Bank. Married to the daughter of a Lorraine banking family, Sephora Goudchaux, he showed an intuitive and profitable flair for business. His grandson and namesake Hypolite took over the business in 1916. Baptized, the son of a Christian woman, he married the Anglican Gladys Mary Lewis-Morgan. Their daughter tied the knot with the very Anglican son of the English ambassador to Japan. From this union was born Nicolas Cleaves-Worms, who would become managing associate of the company MM Worms and Co., which remained private after the nationalization of the Worms Bank, in 1982.

The Rothschilds were just as comfortable with these extra-community marriages. So much so that, in 1985, there was an event that the press called "the Rothschild incident." For the first time, a chief rabbi of France refused a religious marriage for a Rothschild (for Eric, son of Alain, a distant cousin of David) and a non-Jew.

But in spite of these lapses of tradition, the acclaimed dynasty long occupied, and still occupies to a lesser extent, a special place within the community. It represents the quintessence of what is commonly called the notables: rich people, well established in society, who give parties for charity while keeping their distance from hardship. Since the 18th century, the Rothschilds built their fortune and their reputation on undeniable financial creativity, of course, but also on the careful management of a vast network of relations, inside as well as outside the community.

Their weight was exerted almost monopolistically on the Jewish institutions until the beginning of the Eighties. "In 1979, the Roths-childs reigned unchallenged over the Jewish community of France," explains Yves Azeroual and Yves Derai in *Mitterrand, Israel and the Jews*.[7] "The baron Guy was president of the United Jewish Social Fund. He was the uncontested chief of the clan. His cousins, the brothers Elie and Alain, also held important responsibilities. The first was president of the Consistory and of CRIF since 1976; the second was head of the United Appeal (AUJF), the fundraising organization. In June 1967, Alain de Rothschild was elected president of the Consistory, a post that he occupied until 1982. He was also president of many Jewish enterprises including the Israelite Committee of Social Action of Paris, and the Rothschild Foundation. The youngest Rothschild, David, was treasurer of the AUJF and president of the Orientation Commission. A few years later, he would become its president. At that time, no one was disputing their authority."

But the Eighties were less friendly for the dynasty. Alain de Rothschild passed away after a heart attack, in New York, in 1982. His cousin Guy, depressed by the victory of the left, exiled himself to the United States — an exaggeratedly pessimistic gesture. The Rothschilds, indeed, had a faithful supporter in the entourage close to Mitterrand, in the person of the hyperactive special advisor, Jacques Attali. He and his twin brother, Bernard, were long-time members of the National Council of United Jewish Social Fund, of which he was a vice-president.

During the Mitterrand years this support partly compensated for the rebellious climate that had developed within the community. The Rothschilds were still seen favorably in their role as leaders of the charity circuit, but their political legitimacy was disputed. Fundamentally, the Sephardics (including many repatriates from North Africa) rose against the monopolization of communal responsibilities by the Ashkenazi upper classes. Did they form a network, or a special interest group? Both. As special interest groups, the various clans of the Jewish community clashed, internally, in a traditional fight for position. As a network, the "family" presented a unified front in the face of adversity.

The Universal Law of Pulling Strings

"The economic crisis," noted a journalist who, as a very public figure, refuses to be reduced to his Jewish origins, "allowed us to renew the bonds of solidarity that had been gradually eroded. I was often asked to help out financially for difficult cases." "We were always ready to lend each other a hand in adversity," agrees Paul Benmussa, owner of the restaurant "Chez Edgar," a popular spot for politicians and the media. He had emigrated from Tunisia in 1967 after the Six-Day War. He himself found some support among his Parisian friends, exiled like him) who had attended the same classes at Carnot College in Tunis.

These practices go back to the pre-war period, a time when the Jews of Eastern Europe were flooding into Paris, fleeing the pogroms or feeling the looming pressure of the Nazi threat. Social groups sprang up for people from specific locales or villages, as the Aveyronnais and the Auvergnats had been doing for decades. People chipped in to help each other buy lots in the cemetery, or to get a young man his first suit, and people got together to dance. The new arrivals also received help from the Jewish bourgeoisie that was already established, already assimilated; however, the latter behaved with a distant and irritating paternalism in the eyes of these immigrants, who were often militant leftists.

The Rothschilds didn't think much of these *"parvenu"* compatriots — they even baptized them, with a cruel irony, the "Piaf's," that is,
"patriotic Israelites, French anti-Semites"! Still, they redoubled their
charitable support, without distinction or prejudice. And they openly
made it a point of honor to help a maximum number of immigrants and
to provide them with housing. "These charitable donations ended up
becoming the trademark of the 'barons,' note the journalists Claude
Askolovitch and Sylvain Attal.[8]

After the war, they explained, mutual aid societies were mobilized
more than ever to take care of the camp survivors. The Federation of
Jewish Societies of France created a "Start-Up Fund." It lent money to
buy sewing machines or to create new workshops in the clothes industry. The children of deportees were taken into homes and vacation re-
sorts, efforts were made to reconstitute around them the family fabric
that they had lost. The Communist Party did not want to be seen sitting on its hands, so they too formed a support group, the Union of
Jews for Resistance and Mutual Aid, which brought together many
Jewish militants from Eastern Europe. But the most structured organization and the most active remained the charitable entity that became,
in the Fifties, the Unified Jewish Social Fund. All the successive waves
of refugees of the post-war period flocked to its offices: Hungarian and
Egyptian Jews, after Budapest and the Suez War, plus Tunisians, Mo-
roccans, and Algerians. These exiles helped out in their turn. For in-
stance, the Egyptian Jewish women who fled Nasser's regime in 1956;
they created a chain of mutual support within the Galleries Lafayette,
where some of them had been hired as saleswomen on the recommendation of Adam Loss (then president of the FSJU). They were equally
at ease in French and English, and gifted for trade; they did the same as
the Savoyards who co-opted for themselves the salerooms of Drouot,
the same as the Tunisians of Djerba who buy up the groceries, and the
West-Indians who pull each other into the police force.

"This mutual help is both very solid and very relaxed," offers a Parisian lawyer. "It is true that there is a temptation to stay within the
group. It is true that certain Jewish customers prefer to have a Jewish
lawyer because they have the vague sense that they will be better understood, therefore better defended. It is true that those customers often have Jewish accountants and doctors. But the opposite instinct
exists too. I know many Jews in the business world who make sure

they have non-Jews among their partners, their bankers, their suppliers, precisely to avoid being suspected of being part of a network of interests based on religious affiliation."

The solidarity is all the more subtle and difficult to analyze in that it is closely related to historical and cultural tendencies. While "the network effect" has, objectively, always functioned fairly well in finance, textiles, and publicity, that has not been the case in diplomacy, the army or the police force. An old anti-Dreyfus residue in the army? A monopoly in the traditionally pro-Arabic corps of the Quai d'Orsay? The review *Passages*, already mentioned, raised the question, without deciding either way. And there are cases where mutual support can be a response to anti-Semitism. If the Jewish lawyers had not closed ranks in the Fifties, they would never have been able to break the implicit *numerus clausus* that forbade to them to have more than one Israelite on the Conseil de l'Ordre. One year, the door was opened. A second fellow-member was elected, thanks to his peers who had tacitly decided to play the identity card. In the same way, the "mandarins" of the hospitals, of old French and Catholic stock, were co-opted, thus dividing the hospital landscape between Jewish and non-Jewish services. This distinction has been seriously attenuated with the fast-changing medical demography of today, and can no longer be seen except in some very rare establishments.

The "Calf's Brains Right-wing" Against the "Caviar Left"

Deeply divided between reformed orthodox, traditionalists, Zionist shock troops, and liberal intellectuals, the Jewish community has no real influence, as some believe, on French politics. On its own, it does not have a sufficiently unified opinion, even with respect to Israel, to make or break an election. In truth, the "Jewish lobby" so dear to Abbot Pierre does not exist in the sense of a methodically organized clan. On the other hand, there does exist, more than in any other community, political networks that have shown themselves capable of mobilizing support for their champion.

Thus, in 1981, part of the community, joined together under the banner of Henri Hajdenberg's "Jewish Revival," clearly wanted to bring down Valéry Giscard d'Estaing. The indifference that he had shown after the attack on rue Copernic, in 1980, was deeply shocking. Was there a "Jewish vote" against him, even so? That is difficult to determine, even if the lawyer Théo Klein had called Mitterrand the "best President for the Jews." Fourteen years later, in May 1995, the "Jewish street" shifted, at the same time as most Frenchmen, in favor of Jacques Chirac. Meanwhile, relations between Mitterrand and his Jewish networks had cooled markedly. The President's continued good relations with his old friend René Bousquet, compliant executant of German dirty work, and his apparent desire to dust over the incriminating details of the Vichy years, disturbed some of his strongest supporters, even the most faithful like Robert Badinter and George Kiejman. The Mitterrandian network of Jews from the Resistance — with, at their head, Henri Bulawko — shifted their loyalties to Lionel Jospin in vain; that was not enough for the new candidate. Nor was the support of the president of the LICRA, Pierre Aidenbaum; of the repatriates' spokesman, the cordial Maurice Bennassayag; of the deputy George the Saar, however closely tied he may have been to part of the Jewish community thanks to Jean-Yves Camus (the particularly enterprising former director of communications of the Consistory of Paris). Or, for that matter, the support of Jean-Michel Rosenfeld, Pierre Mauroy's faithful fellow-traveler, weary of being regarded as "Mauroy's Jew"! Besides, his community support base was fairly weak: General Secretary of the Bernard-Lazare Club, open to all, and counting no more than one hundred current members.

Even when they all work together, these leftist networks do not succeed in really influencing public opinion. With "the caviar left" in a state of rout, "the calf's brain right" reared its head. Claude-Gerard Marcus, an expert on painting, by profession, and a Gaullist by conviction, was first in line in this reconquest. The former national public relations delegate of the RPF (1952) had been a member of the central committee of LICRA for nearly forty years. Former president of the "France-Israel Friendship Group" at the National Assembly, he created and chairs the association "Judaism and Freedom," based on the model of "Socialism and Judaism." A Deputy of Paris, he is considered one of Chirac's indispensable allies, and for a long time he has sat on the Israelite Committee of Social Action of Paris. His zeal in respect to the former mayor of Paris has sometimes been revealed to be excessive. Thus, during a municipal campaign, he wrote to the Jews of the capital a letter in support of Jacques Chirac, addressed: "Dear Co-Religionist" — an initiative considered to be very much out of place, in a community with a strong dislike of databases.

Jacques Chirac, the *Jewish Tribune* noted one month before the presidential election of May 1995, could also count on senior State officials like Jacques Friedmann, the chairman of the UAP, Serge Dassault, his childhood friend, and on all "the beautiful people" of show biz like Rika Zaraï, Vincent Lindon and Michel Boujenah, who added glamour to an evening meeting at the Bouffes du Nord. But they wouldn't have "made" the election for Chirac, any more than Mitterand's networks did before 1981.

On the other hand, it did not escape notice in the community that it was scantly represented within the Juppé government: just one minister (Corinne Lepage, for the Environment), some noted bitterly. The same ones pointed out that they were no more present at the Elysée or Matignon (location of the Prime Minister). That was a big change compared to the Mitterrand era! Some old supports of Edouard Balladur, a great friend of the Pompidou supporter David de Rothschild, however, gave their allegiance after the presidential election. One of these was Jean Kahn, president of the Central Consistory, who was trying to make up for his poor electoral taste in publishing (in *Le Monde*, Summer 1995) a tribune applauding the resumption of nuclear tests.

Active members of the community considered that they should intervene on certain very specific subjects. "On terrorism, for example, the Jewish community has something specific to contribute, because it represents a family of thought that holds a certain memory," explains Solomon Malka, director of *Radio for the Jewish Community*. "It is an influence that goes beyond purely corporatist thinking. Thus, one cannot speak of a Jewish lobby."

"The idea should be discarded," expounds sociologist Daniel Lindenberg in *Passages*. "We, the Jewish intellectuals, should not hesitate to criticize each other." He should feel reassured. The Bosnian question proved, if that was necessary, that the intellectual influence of the Jews is not as monolithic as some would have liked to believe. That Bernard-Henri Lévy sometimes violently opposes Alain Finkielkraut is evidence of that. "It's a different story, that one finds many Jews among the intellectuals, that many old Trotskyites are Jewish, that one finds us among the student leaders of May '68," says one of them. "That has to do with the fact that a generation, naturally inclined by its education toward criticism and reflection, rebelled against the religious and social interdicts that guided our parents. That phenomenon is hardly, after all, different from that which one can witness in the United States among the Asians. A minority, like us, they are standing up and looking to make an impact. It is a phenomenon of generation, and should not be confused with a phenomenon of identity."

The HSP Isn't What It Used To Be

If someday a lay republican Moslem gains sway in France, he will owe his success partly to — imagine! — the Protestant network. Paradoxical? Less than it appears to be. After all, who better than the Huguenots, heirs to a minority culture and uncomfortable with fundamentalism, to give lessons in secularity? The idea of a "Republican" Islamic Institute was even proposed, the first time, at the end of the Eighties by a Protestant politician, Pierre Joxe. At the time, he was Minister for the Interior and for Religion, assisted by the Protestant prefect Alain Boyer. Later, the network of Protestant family associations fired up by a councilor-barrister at the Cour des comptes (French Audit Bureau), Pierre Patrick Kaltenbach (PPK to his friends) started working to convince a core group of Moslems leaders that it would be possible to preserve one's differences while fulfilling one's citizenship irreproachably.

The initiative admirably illustrates the philosophy of the Protestant community that has managed to spread its values across all of French society. "Taking account of differences, to the detriment of unity, is gaining ground everywhere," says journalist Christian Makarian. "It has been the indirect triumph of the spirit of the Reformation." For several decades already, this shows even more in the realm of ideas than in business. The same sensibility, the same state of mind, the same verbal tics — they cultivate their ethical complicity to modernize society, instead of thinking of creating an interdependent diaspora. Thus Family Planning benefited, in the post-war years, from the support of Protestant women's clubs. The association "Happy Maternity," which prefigured the future Family Planning, was created in 1955, with Protestant women first in line: the sociologist Evelyne Sullerot, a pastor's daughter, and Geneviève Monod, Suzanne Duflo and Elisabeth Gruzon, of the Protestant movement "Young Women." The Protestant networks are found more easily in social actvism than in the mythical HSP (High Protestant Society), which isn't what it used to be, and hasn't been for a long time already.

Hatched under the July Monarchy, flourishing at the end of the 19th century, the HSP survived the great crisis of the Thirties with difficulty. The post-war period saw an irremediable decline due to corporate mergers and acquisitions, nationalizations, and some costly managerial blunders. On the Parisian money market, only the clan of Hottinguer, bankers since 1876, remains. On the other hand, Vernes, Mallet, Odier-Bungener, Mirabaud are out. As for the great names of industry (Dolfus Mieg, Kuhlmann, Kronenbourg, Barton and Guestier, Dourthe and Kressman), they have been absorbed into impersonal holding companies, indifferent to religious membership. And one cannot say that Arnaud Leenhardt, vice-president of the CNPF, in charge of the powerful Federation of Metallurgical and Mining Industries, has made a success of "Protestantizing" French corporate ownership. Besides, bosses who go to church do not like to display their religious identity, considering it too private an affair to be brandished like some kind of seal. Has anyone ever heard the Seydoux brothers (Nicolas, the chairman of Gaumont and Jerome, head of Chargeurs Réunies), or Serge Tchuruk (head of Alcatel) make a point of their Protestantism?

Ancestral modesty of the Huguenots? A rigorous tradition that encourages distrust of preferential treatment? Capable of extraordinary generosity in difficult times, molded by the long, painful history of a culture of resistance (they proved it during the Occupation, by hiding nearly 5,000 Jews in the area of Chambon-sur-Lignon alone), the Protestants avidly avoid giving each other a hand when it comes to careers.

There are six Peugeot cousins (five boys and a girl, approaching middle age at the turn of the millennium), all employed in the family company, the only survivor of the industrial dynasties of the Doubs valley; they know something about these traditions. Throughout their youth, they had to endure a harping refrain that the fact of being called Peugeot "imposes more obligations than rights." There was no question of reaching upper management through the magic of the family name alone. One was dispatched to an English subsidiary company that lacked a successor, another interned at Citroën, a third jumped to become deputy manager of a subsidiary company. Not noble stations, but good on-the-ground training, once their diplomas were in their pockets.

The Peugeots have a strong sense of the clan. They play golf, as a family, on the 18 holes created in 1928 in Prunevelle by the patriarch Jean-Pierre III. Jean-Pierre's grandson Eric, 41 years old, is chairman of the Europe Automotive Directorate. He hangs out there with his uncle Roland, 70 years, vice-president of the board of trustees and member of the management committee of the French Golf Federation, and his brother Jean-Philippe, 43 years, head of the international department. Sometimes they play "outside;" but always "between themselves." Bertrand, 73 years, vice-president of the board of trustees, golfs and hunts with Jean-Philippe Hottinguer, associate-manager of the Hottinguer bank, a survivor of the HSP, and with Bertrand Vernes, also a banker, cousin of deceased financier Jean-Marc Vernes, a friend of Chirac.

Losing ground in business (with some rare exceptions), is the Protestant network also losing its political punch? There is no trace of a minister, or an executive assistant, with specific ties to it under the current Chirac team. Only one *éminence grise* emerges: Jerome Monod, chairman of Lyonnaise des Eaux, who always puts his connections at the service of Chirac.

If the Protestants are not full of enthusiasm for the RPR, that is because, throughout history they have forged a culture of resistance. They are hardly "party-liners." And it was the opening of new areas of freedom, like the law of 1901 on freedom of association, and the separation of the Church and the State at the beginnings of the Third Republic, that supported their entry into political life.

The Alsatian Huguenot network was one of most active around Gambetta and Jules Ferry. Ferry was directly subject to their influence via his wife Eugénie Kestner, daughter of Charles Kestner, owner of a prosperous chemical plant and very committed in the political struggle. One of Eugenie's sisters is the wife of Auguste Scheurer, a Protestant friend of Gambetta. One their aunts, Hortense, married the republican deputy and future president of the Council Charles Floquet. Intensely loyal within their clan, the Protestants remain intractably intransigence. For example, Eugenie Kestner-Ferry obstinately refused a religious wedding. This was a demonstration of rare independence of mind at a time when the most savagely anticlerical republicans sometimes accepted this type of concession! Even more, in 1887, she refused Cardinal Lavigerie's offer, promising her the votes of the right-wing members of Parliament in exchange for a nuptial blessing. As an answer, she stood up and showed him the door. . . A few years later, the same network would be mobilized in the defense of a certain Captain Dreyfus.

Protestant influence was noticeable in the early days of the Fifth

Republic. Some Huguenot good fairies took their cue from the Constitution of 1958. A micro-network toiled under the shield of the independent Louis Vallon, a left-leaning Gaullist. At his side were some members of the Calvinist élite such as Paul Bastide, a former member of the Constitutional Council, François Goguel, leading light in political science, and two erudite lawyers, the Donnedieu de Vabres brothers.

But Maurice Couve de Murville, an old veteran of the Quai d'Orsay and General de Gaulle's last Prime Minister, was something of an exception among the political personnel of the era. Moreover, his colleagues, mainly Catholic, liked to tease this spindly and austere man. He was linked to the Protestant upper classes through is wife, Jacqueline Schweisguth, who is an heiress of the Banque de l'Union Parisienne and Banque Mirabaud. "In all his television appearances, he seems to be coming out of a freezer and entering a cold room," laughed the comedian Robert Beauvais, who forecasts in 1976 "the return of Protestantism."[9]

Can one really call it a return when, in 1981, the Huguenots showed up with the new power? "The Socialist party is full of Protestants," Mitterrand had already remarked; "Catholics too, but they are less visible." However, the President did not seem to be complaining about "being surounded" by Protestant collaborators. A son of a minister was working close to him, Christian Sautter, as general secretary associated with the Elysée. Louis Mermaz, the president of the National Assembly, is Protestant. The head of the Socialist Party, Lionel Jospin, and several Ministers also belonged to the Reformed Church: Michel Rocard, Gaston Defferre, Georgina Dufoix, Catherine Lalumière, Catherine Trautman, Nicole Questiaux, George Fillioud, Jean-Pierre Cot, Alain Bombard. . . Some, of course, more transitory than others. "The Eternal Being provided the French Left with Protestant ministers beyond any evangelical or political dreams. Ah! How good is Saint-Barthélemy!" Pierre-Patrick Kaltenbach was ironical in 1994, at the annual meeting of La Force, a Protestant charitable institution.

These ministers didn't find it hard to recruit their colleagues. High public office has long been a haven of the Protestants. Before 1981, the historian Jean-Pierre Richardot affirmed that a quarter of the regional prefects (but only 5% of the sub-prefects!) and that a third of the diplomatic corps attended protestant churches. It is thus hardly surprising that one finds some of these "reformed church" technocrats in the Ministerial cabinets: Louis Schweitzer, the future leader of Renault, as chief of staff to Laurent Fabius; François Scheer, chief of staff to the Minister for the Foreign Affairs Claude Cheysson; and Renaud Vignal, with Jean-Pierre Cot in the Ministry of Cooperation and Development.

Neither did Mitterrand blink when his friend Gaston Defferre chose, upon his arrival at place Beauvau, to name the great Protestant veteran of the Resistance, Lucien Vochel, to the prefecture of Ile-de-France. More amusing, Pierre Joxe, the new man at the Ministry of the Interior in 1984, designated as Vochel's replacement the son of another Huguenot figure from the Resistance, Olivier Philip. And it was another "reformed," Christian Sautter, who took Philip's place in 1991. Is this the story of networks? The rigorous Pierre Joxe always denied it.

Michel Rocard so detests preferential treatments and other privileges that he seemed to be indifferent to the fate of his former team when he had to leave his post as Prime Minister. No emoluments were given to the Huguenot entourage. And while he invited his friend the linguist Pierre Encrevé, a son of pastor, to serve as cultural advisor, it was only to entrust him with the preparation of the Bicentenary, a task that was, frankly, not of much strategic significance. In the same way his friend, the vice-president of Accor, Bernard Westercamp, the "elegant Narwhal" from their days together in scouting, did not consider asking a favor of his old friend from the campfire days, the "erudite Hamster," although he is still close enough to address him as *tu!*

One notable exception: the prefect Christian Blanc, on whom Rocard relied to solve the crisis in Calédonia. The two men had not forgotten that the Protestant missionaries had left traces on "the Caillou." He also appealed to Pastor Jacques Stewart to serve as mediator between the leader of the Caledonian Right, the RPCR Jacques Lafleur, a Protestant parishioner, and the freedom fighter Jean-Marie Tjibaou, a former preacher of the same religion. The Protestant network did not make it as far as the Matignon Accords on its own (the Freemasons were very active), but it was happy to take the opportunity to show its "spirit," without taking sides.

Even more reserved than Rocard on the subject, Lionel Jospin hates being labeled according to his religion. When an Irish journalist asked him during the 1995 presidential campaign what it would mean, if he were elected, to be the first Protestant President of the French Republic, he snapped: "We live in a lay State, my religion does not matter."

Does the extreme Right, which burns everyone, think it can create a breach in this circle? Until his remarriage, the "Breton catho" Le Pen was not much concerned about the Protestants, some of which had however openly flirted with his friend the Protestant Pierre Poujade, spokesman for the small business owners, in the Fifties. But now his second wife Jeanny openly exhibited her membership in the reformed religion, and in the summer of 1995 even attended, together with her extremist husband, the traditional Assembly of the Desert, in the Ardèche, commemorating the martyrdom of the Camisards [*Ed. note*: Calvinist partisans in the 1702 Cévennes uprising]. In his wake Samuel Marshal, son-in-law of the chief and president of the Front National Jeunesse was also supposed to represent the Protestant wing of the movement. This link was reinforced during the winter of 1996 by the creation of an association, L'Entraide Nationale (National Mutual Assistance), a sort of Salvation Army in brown shirts, entrusted to the leadership of "Pastor" Jean-Pierre Blanchard. Quite a curious Pastor, who claims to have been a Maoist in his youth, ordained in the early Nineties by the traditionalist Evangelical Church of Missouri, from which he separated to join that of Wisconsin, which seems to be much more extremist. Needless to say, the Protestant Federation of France does not recognize either of these two "Churches." But the Front National probably hopes to buy cheaply a "good reputation," and the halo effect of being associated, by usurpation, in this case, with the Protestant networks of charity.

Who Goes Hunting?

The Saint-Hubert hunting association in Abreschviller, in the Bas-Rhine region, has long formed a power base that was unrecognized by the Republic. Since Didier Schuller (former RPR general adviser of Clichy, ex-director general of the office of HLM [subsidized housing authority] of the Hauts-de-Seine,) came under suspicion of active corruption, and became a fugitive, they decided to break up. Their heart wasn't in it anymore: they'd just lost their best "shot" and one the their most skillful beaters. Admittedly, a special kind of beater. Schuller had been at the center of a fairly surprising group; specialists in real estate, close to the RPR, they skillfully blended their passion for business and the pleasure of hunting.

All these "concrete-bashers," as the journalists from *Le Canard En-chaîné* (a satirical magazine) Alain Guédé and Herve Liffran[10] so nicely call them, were indeed seen a few months later, between 1994 and 1995, being questioned by a judge from Créteil, Eric Halphen.

Without question, until his legal worries Schuller was the most assiduous hunter of the group. He is a passionate tracker of the stag and wild boar (a pleasure that he inherited from his father and that he pursued during his candidature to the legislature in Belfort in 1978). He would rent some 5,000 acres of Bismarck's old hunting grounds, close to Saverne, and spend all his weekends there. His friends from the Saint-Hubert association, for the most part indebted to him one way or another, would join him there. The construction company bosses who shared the catch with him knew that, during these convivial larks, one might hunt partridge and at the same time contracts. Didn't Schuller directly manage 30,000 residences that had to be renovated and maintained?

Victims of failing memory, many guests no longer remember having taken part in these gatherings. However, they used to come in great numbers to the bountiful game dinners animated by truculent guests, many of whom worked zealously for the Paris City Hall. The first, chairman of the SAR, a painting company serving the city and its HLM office, is one of the heroes of this sulfurous tale. Since he retired to La Santé (a men's prison in Paris) for a few weeks in the summer of 1994, and since he was put under questioning for fraud, his own shooting parties are strangely quiet. Francis Poullain, however, concluded with the ONF (Office national des forêts) a 10-year lease at a rate of about $28,000 for 1700 acres in the Côte-d'Or in the Grand Jailly domain. There he can recall the good old days at leisure with his neighbor, Christian Curtet, another contractor with two sets of books, likewise under judicial inquiry; he no longer makes such a profit from his domain and his gamekeeper.

On the other hand, Patrick Balkany, the former mayor of Levallois-Perret, former President of the HLM Office of the Hauts-de-Seine, in a delicate judicial situation, has disappeared from the vicinity. A big hunter and friend of all these merry men, at the beginning of his "reign" Balkany had annexed a vacation campground ideally placed at the heart of Grand Jailly, and transformed it into a hunting preserve.

As for Jean-Claude Méry, another "intermediary" between the RPR and the building and public works companies (BTP) who was tried and imprisoned at La Santé, he rented by the day (for $10,000 all the same!) a hunting preserve north of the Oise, at the château of Fresneaux-Montchevreuil. There, in addition to certain select elected officials, one could find oneself among future suspects: Christian Curtet again, and Henri Tasi and André Dalzon, two other BTP chiefs. This last, a very accessible fellow, invited the entire delightful bunch to hunt grouse in Scotland where he has some property. "At these hunts," says a BTP owner, "one can find out, among other things, which design office was chosen by the operator and thus have information of the first order."

Criminal conspiracy or hunters' association? Suffice it to say that this nasty amalgam is firmly denounced by "true" hunters.

The "Make Yourself at Home" Brotherhood

And nonetheless! Hunting clubs persist and thrive. "When you spend the day with the guys, all covered with mud, butts in the muck, time goes faster," says Antoine Cohen-Pewter, the former editor of *Plaisirs* hunting magazine.

He himself with four hunter friends founded at the end of 1995 a "Gaston-Phoebus Club" named for the count de Foix, briefly president of the Republic of the Pyrenées and a highly skilled hunter, to bring together the best shots from every profession. Writers like Jean d'Ormesson and Michel Déon mix with the restaurateur Bernard Loiseau, the head of the CNPF Jean Gandois, and the former Minister François Abadie, member of the Constitutional Council. "Fifteen days after its creation," says the founder, "I was getting phone calls for the other members' co-ordinates." Thus a network is born.

Those who were inducted by Jean de Beaumont into the brotherhood of "Mets-toi a l'aise" or, roughly, "Make Yourself at Home," understand this very well. A banker who managed the Rivaud Bank until his 91st birthday with his son-in-law, Edouard de Ribes owns an immense estate at Diebolsheim, in Alsace. Every new guest is welcomed according to a well-established ritual, with the handing-over of a red cord and a badge in the shape of a stag's head, which must be returned after the ceremony! Valéry Giscard d'Estaing, an initiate of the first Club, was there the day of the attack on the synagogue on rue Copernic, when he was so much reproached for not returning to Paris to go to the scene of the drama. An eclectic hunt, where political affiliation does not count, the domain of Diebolsheim also received in the Eighties the brother of the President, Philippe Mitterrand, and the banker Jean-Marc Vernes, both since deceased.

Rare are the businessmen who spontaneously admit to spending a few afternoons per month sacrificing to the gods of game. An associate-manager from Lazard, a leader in the management of personal fortunes, whose diary is full of holes during the season, takes on the air of a startled doe when asked the rate of profitability of such afternoons well-stocked with game. The pâtissier Gaston Lenôtre is one of the rare individuals who acknowledges that if he invites pastry aficionados to his property in Loiret fourteen times a year, it is in the interests of his order book. Equally frank, Patrick Ricard also openly uses his well-stocked estate, close to Rambouillet, to further his public relations efforts.

Would it be appropriate in these times of crisis to go hunting in a less ostentatious way than in the past? Sumptuous hunts where Francis Bouygues or a Marcel Dassault displayed their power seem to belong to another era. Martin Bouygues goes out now in a small group with, among other neighbors, the two sons of Baron Bich, in the paternal fields of Luet in the Sologne. Serge Dassault and his sons receive guests in the property of Coignières. Similarly, Jean-Claude Decaux, father of the roadside bus shelters and the public toilets, hunts discreetly with his friends in Haute-Marne. But the most beautiful property of the Hexagon belongs to an owner unknown to the general public, Jean Leducq, the chairman of Élis. Number one in laundries, he hosts politicians like Giscard d'Estaing and René Monory *incognito*. In the same way, the vice-president of the Interallied club, Edmond de Marcheguay, who is a significant figure in the world of arms deals, and baron Gilbert de Turkheim, President of the National Office of Hunting, are known to take advantage, from time to time, of their hunting contacts. Just like the banker Alain Duménil, who organizes no fewer than twelve hunts a year.

Without question the most discrete hunters of large mammals are a very select network of people who all dream of belonging in "Rowland Ward's records of big game," the international gotha of the best shots. For a long time, their model was Bernard Dumon, owner of the Saint-Louis sugar company, deceased in 1994 in an air crash, on the way to a weekend of hunting in Eastern Europe. Dumon was one of Claude Bébéar's tracking companions in Romania; Bébéar, the chairman of the Axa insurance group, exhibits his trophies in his office: two stuffed antelopes and a panther skin. If he has decided to allocate more time to life (he leaves work on Thursday evenings) it is in order to be able to devote more time to hunting.

The jeweler Alain Boucheron, who shoots Scottish grouse, the Minister Yves Galland, who has rights of exploitation in Central Africa, François Dalle, the former head of L'Oréal and his successor Lindsay Owen-Jones who favors Spanish partridge, Jean de Mouy, chairman of Jean Patou perfumes, who hunts duck in Argentina, Gerard Clayeux, president of an infants' and children's clothing company, who has accumulated more than a hundred trophies, Philippe Delagrange, of the laboratory of the same name, who created in the heart of Texas a ranch where he has introduced rare species, all have shared, and sometimes during the same parties, the same powerful sensations. "That creates a bond," confides one amateur of the safari, "which, it is true, can be quite useful on occasion."

There is no need to go into more precise details. Discretion is the rule among hunters, of pheasant as well as of antelope — even though it is known that Hoechst's takeover of Roussel-Uclaf was decided during a hunt in the Sologne. And that a convenient discussion during a presidential hunt in Rambouillet in 1978, between Giscard d'Estaing and Roger Martin, the president of Saint-Gobain, made it possible for Martin to accelerate his company's dealings with Bull.

The "Crocodile Club"

Heritage of an old world, too élitist according to the new President Jacques Chirac — the presidential hunts were abandoned. Temporarily? In early 1996, the word was out that the former Minister Camille Cabana, charged with managing the domains left fallow, had violated the presidential instruction and invited a well-known insurer. For so long, the hunts of Marly and Rambouillet were useful for the public relations of the State and the members of the Committee of Presidential Hunts.

In this regard, François de Grossouvre, marksman, who orchestrated the presidential hunts under Mitterrand, was one of the keenest. And he had found a weighty ally in the person of Gaston Defferre, another one who was mad about hunting, just like Michel Charasse.

In the very smart hunting grounds of Chambord and Rambouillet, more business plain and simple was being discussed, it seems, than the business of France. Already before the war, one of the most influential hunting clubs briskly mingled business and politics. That was in the Sologne on the property of the Outhenin-Chalandre family, the wealthy industrialists. The son was named Claude, but the father, enamored of hunting, quickly renamed him Hubert, for the patron saint of hunters. "Hubert" thus underwent his apprenticeship under the Third Republic, during a time when the paternal property witnessed a parade of the Presidents of the Council.

"Hubert," who welcomed Leon Blum into the Popular Front, worked for the Intelligence Service during the Occupation, where he indefatigably enriched his network. After the war, he was hired by the American detergent maker Unilever, which in London during the black years was already supplementing the income of close relations of General de Gaulle; then in Paris he launched the "Crocodile Club," named for his chosen mascot.

Thus there were ten unrepentant hunters who would meet once a month for lunch in a particular dining room of the Automobile Club. In this quiet corner, one could meet Jacques Chaban-Delmas who, when the moment came, would entertain his friends at the Hotel of Lassay, Maurice Bourgès-Maunoury and Felix Gaillard, two presidents of the Council, Jacques Maillet, a big shot in the aircraft industry, and Michel Debré, already an impetuous member of Parliament. The journalist Claude Paillat, author of *Les Dossiers secrets de la France contemporaine* (*The Secret Files of Contemporary France*),[11] who knew friend Hubert well, tells how skillfully he used the political network to defend his buddies' interests.

There is no known heir to "the Crocodile Club;" but there are, all the same, very "political" hunts organized locally by the departmental federations. "Since 1942, they have been regulated under the 1901 law on associations," explains a specialist. "They have a monopoly, since they receive all the hunters' contributions. Their presidents are local small landowners who, every year, organize one élite hunt with the members of Parliament from the area, the prefect, and other notables. They are powerful electoral networks. More than one senator owes his election to them."

"Handicaps" Transformed into Assets

Are the bonds woven at hunting any tighter than those of golf? "Splashing around together in the mud, and feasting then, after the effort — that creates a feeling of unity that has to be far stronger than anything created by concentrating together on a green." This banker and huntsman scornfully adds, "Golf is hunting, for the poor." That may be a slightly premature dismissal, for golf, practiced on a certain level and in certain company, creates a climate of trust at the very least.

"Not under just any conditions, nor in any setting," a renowned golfer clarifies. "Many play golf with only one aim, that of belonging to a network. They vainly claim that they chose this sport in order to enjoy walking and getting out in nature; no one believes them. Similarly, the proverb that says, 'They talk about golf in the office and talk about business on the greens,' is completely false. It was out of question to talk with Mitterrand about anything but golf while we were out on the course. What is funny, is that this sport often makes it possible to make contacts at so high a level that they are useless! It is not by playing golf with the entourage of the king of Morocco, or even with the king himself, that you will be able to make money!"

But the magic is still there. What a sudden fascination that small white ball took on after Mitterrand's election! Until then, his golf network was limited to some close relations like his former chief of staff of the Ministries for the 4th Republic, André Rousselet, who got rich in the taxi business, or Doctor Laurent Raillard, a radiologist whom he had met in the Sixties in Hossegor. He used to play sometimes at Chantaco, a golfer's paradise where he crossed paths with Jacques Chaban-Delmas and his wife Micheline. But that was not for public consumption. In August, 1965, he asked the political journalists — who had descended upon him to sound him out on his presidential intentions — not to mention in their articles his practice of this "rich man's sport"!

Once elected to the Elysée, the neophytes were seen running, persuaded that a "handicap" would be an additional asset in getting closer to the Prince. Jacques Attali, however well-placed already in the offices of the Palace, undertook to learn to "putt" correctly and the lawyer George Kiejman trained by panting along behind the President's golf cart. Golf-playing business leaders tried to play on the same courses as the President. It was a waste of time and effort: he officiated Monday afternoons on a course that was closed to the public.

"In any event," our golfer adds, "this sport is not sufficient in itself as a network. It is something that caps off other memberships." For example: members of the "Trophy of the Presidents," which for ten years has brought together a score of heads of large enterprises. All belong, more or less, to other more or less fashionable, more or less élitist brotherhoods. But it does not displease to them to be recognized together for their sporting excellence.

The famous Basque player Pascassio originated this trophy; he created it with some of his "students" like Gerard Pélisson, co-founder of the Accor group, and Jerome Seydoux, the owner of the Chargeurs Réunis (handicap 18). These two followers took up the sport with such relish that they bought together a private course in Médoc, close to Bordeaux.

These golfing corporate chairmen often play among themselves, but the whole group meets each year for a weekend, generally in Basque Country. There, among others, in addition to Pélisson and Seydoux, you can find Christian Bregou (CEP Communication), David de Rothschild (the bank), Kléber Beauvillain (Hewlett Packard), André Rousselet (ex-Canal Plus TV), François Hanot (French Cement), and so on.

For their tenth anniversary, in September 1995, they organized a weekend at Turnberry, in Scotland. All very fit, they even had fun in the evening like schoolboys, and the majority did not hesitate to dine in kilts. Suffice it to say that that year's winner, Jean-Michel Andrieu, president of the Board of Directors of Auguste Thouard, was duly celebrated. Business wasn't much discussed, those sordid contingencies were postponed to a later date.

Ultimate chic this club may be, but it is no rival in any sense to another network, to which all these chairmen dream of belonging one day: "The Royal and Ancient St. Andrews," in Scotland. 1,800 members from the whole world, of which six to seven Frenchmen (club presidents and a specialized journalist, André-Jean Lafaurie) have the badge of honor enabling them to play at this Mecca of the golf world. It is forbidden to mention this membership on one's calling card under penalty of ejection. The future "elect" is brought in by two godfathers (to present one's own candidature would be in the worst of taste) but two years may pass before anyone notifies you very officially of your admission. Meanwhile, "one" receives information and "one" deliberates. To be a member of St. Andrews, incidentally, means to discharge an annual contribution of 160 pounds sterling, to have the right to buy the few "collateral products" from the club, such as a tie with the insignia of St-Andrew's cross, and to receive in one's turn the list of future candidates, upon whom one must deliver his opinion in a well-argued letter!

At its origins, golf was an offshoot of freemasonry. This sport, of Dutch origin, was adopted in about 1500 AD by Scots freemasons of Edinburgh. And not everyone has lost sight of this fraternal heritage.

Chapter 3

SOCIALIZING TOGETHER

In their university jargon, the sociologists speak of the "*entre-soi*" (roughly, what goes on when people feel they are "among their own,") to decode the little understandings among certain social groups. "Among one's own"? A delicious art, cultivated by a few hundred "downtown dinners," pillars of the chic salons and clubs. And let's not forget those whose birth predisposed them to this know-how: the aristocrats. They always find time for a lunch or a dinner, faithful to a very French tradition of the table.

At these very refined meals, served by lackeys in livery, friends from the same corporation, interested gastronomists, weave bonds that are especially invaluable since they are durable.

At the top of the social scale, an abstract network regularly gathers, in the best places, between 200 and 300 people, government figures, corporate directors, heirs to famous dynasties. These "convicts of mondanity" receive and are received in turn. "The solidarity of the dinners downtown are the most solid that I know," says a high-ranking government official who is integrated in the circuit. "When you meet somebody at a dinner at least once a month, it is very difficult to be annoyed with him. These shared reunions have often allowed me to resolve some intractable problems. Conversely, I have sometimes had to give in, sometimes against my convictions, in order not to cross one of my social relations with whom I was in negotiation."

These evening dealings are all the more effective since they are above suspicion. "Maybe you wouldn't imagine, since Combray, that Charles Swann could attend so many influential salons in Paris, so many elegant people following the example of the Guermantes, so distant, so inaccessible?" muses a hostess. "Today, a certain 'upper crust' still lives in community, sheltered from the public view, as in the time of Proust."

One's connections are thus only more indecipherable. In the summer of 1996, the government and the Elysée were struggling to save the company Air Liberté, dramatically overdrawn. However, the principal shareholder of Air Liberté was none other than the Rivaud Bank, which was also the administrator of finances for the RPR. There you have a preliminary explanation for the governmental zeal. But, in addition, Rivaud maintained a social network where a recruit of considerable weight, Bernadette Chirac, was active.

The wife of the President has long been assiduous in her attendance of the dinners given at the rue de la Bienfaisance, at the Viscount de Ribes', who was owner of the Rivaud group until the autumn of 1996. His wife Jacqueline is among the most revered hostesses of Paris. "One has the impression of dining in the Louvre museum and one meets unexpected characters, like the young archduke of Austria. It is terribly chic," says a guest, conquered. Terribly chic also when a few dozen privileged people received a card inviting them for June 19, 1996, in the evening, with only this inscription: "To dine." Thereafter, an assistant called to specify, by telephone, that it was a birthday celebration for Bernadette Chirac. "It's natural," comments one regular, "the Ribes specialize in birthdays!" Too bad! The government's efforts in favor of Air Liberté were not enough. But perhaps it would have not existed without these social favors.

Each dinner has its own particular "slot." Among those "not to be missed" are a few renowned hostesses, all of whom have reached a respectable age and who perpetuate a certain tradition within the "*entre-soi.*"

Colette Taittinger, wife of Pierre Jacquin de Margerie, and sister of Jean, former Minister of Justice under George Pompidou, learned how to host during her childhood. It was enough for the youngest in the family to observe her mother Anne-Marie create the best children's parties in the 16th district. She herself is bringing along a few young women from the good society, whom she intends to initiate into the charms and the constraints of the trade, teaching them, for example, that one never places two people together at table without good reason.

The family patrimony brings her an invaluable technical aid. Colette de Margerie does not receive at her own home, but at the Hotel Crillon, which her Patrice son directs — unless she is inviting 300 people to a preview organized due to her efforts for the release of the film *Beaumarchais...*

Heiress of the cosmetic group L'Oréal, Liliane Bettencourt belongs to the same generation. She continues to work, at a less hectic pace than earlier, in her residence in Neuilly; she puts on small dinners that seldom count more than ten place settings. In the stunning home that she inherited from her father, the very controversial Eugene Schueller,[1] leaders of the Left and Right meet: her husband André Bettencourt, a childhood friend of Mitterrand, was also a Minister under General de Gaulle.

Claude Pompidou also received many guests, in her apartment on the Quai de Béthune, even after her husband's death. In addition to meals centered around modern art, she made a speciality of dinners of reconciliation, particularly to the benefit of Chirac.

Another legendary figure of this All-Paris network is Jacqueline Delubac, the former wife of Sacha Guitry. She remains an esteemed hostess of the artistic milieux and show business and does not hesitate to approach the edges of the political. Thus she organized a soirée, at the beginning of 1996, to celebrate Jean-Jacques Aillagon's appointment as head of Beaubourg.

Among the "grandmothers," as the diners call them with respect and affection, let us also mention Simone del Duca, who "made many academicians" thanks to her select dinners. The wife of the duke of Luynes, she ostentatiously receives visitors in batches of 150 people, in her château of Dampierre, and follows two basic rules: small tables, and no politicians.

But the dinner circuit is pitiless. The least error of taste is watched for, repeated and amplified. The art of receiving, so essential if one wishes to expand one's address book, also requires a patina — on the furniture as well as in manners. "The advantage of the dinners organized by the top people is that good wines are drunk there, because they all bought from prestigious vintages," says an old veteran of the social game, a pitiless arbiter of elegance. "The disadvantage is that they over-do it. At Claude Bébéar's events (the head of Axa, whose extraordinary rise was so impressive), one finds oneself among 120 guests, in the midst of furniture that is too gilded, with paintings that match the cabinets. All that gives the feeling of the impersonal work of a hired decorator. And, moreover, there are too many people."

Ah! The experienced diner then evokes, with tremors in his voice, the finesse of the Croissets and the Noailles. Hélie de Noailles, duke of Ayen, ENA alumnus and diplomat, receives according to the great tradition. Charles Wiener de Croisset, aristocrat and finance inspector, chairman of the CCF, impresses Parisian society with the quality of his salon. This supporter of Balladur hosted many events in service of the former Prime Minister, when the latter believed in his presidential destiny. But Chirac's victory did not tarnish his fashionable star. Russian imperial-style service, French aristocratic-style conversation, furniture from the 18th century, and no more than twenty people at the table: this is the last word in dinner parties; a summit one cannot hope to reach, in the experts' opinion, before the third generation.

Only a chief in residence is lacking, ensure the most demanding, for the Croissets' dinners to become the absolute reference point. But that vestige of the old times is hardly found anymore except at the Rothschilds', a high point in the social world. The baron Elie and his wife Liliane, in their private mansion of Saint-Philippe du Roule, cultivate the intellectual and artistic networks. At the David-Weills', on rue Saint-Guillaume, Hélène receives without her husband Michel. Moreover, the business connections of Lazard Bank, which he directs, are less represented there than the lions of modern art. Antoine Gallimard for publishing, Claude Imbert for the press, Karl Lagerfeld for fashion, Tony Dreyfus for the political sector and business, also count among the distinguished hosts whom the diners, from every sphere mingled together, like to honor at the table.

When it comes to eclecticism, conviviality, and relaxation, one of the most sought after invitations, in recent years, remains the cinema evening organized at the top of the RTL buildings (Radio/Television Luxembourg) sometimes by Jacques Rigaud, the owner of the CLT (Luxembourg Telecommunication Company), sometimes by the station director Philippe Labro. It is not the film preview that delights the fifty guests so much as the scientific blend of leaders from all walks of

life, so skillfully realized by the master of the house, who flits from table to table with the apparent ease of the true sophisticates. The regulars, like the writer and literary columnist (at *Le Point*) Marc Lambron,
the historians Jean Tulard and Jean-Noël Jeanneney, the writer Roger
Peyrefitte, the administration official and banking leader Simon Nora,
and Tony Dreyfus know that the menu hardly varies from one meeting
to another: a meat dish, a soufflé and dessert. They taste it with some
"intermittent guests": Louis Schweitzer, the owner of Renault, Renaud
Denoix de Saint-Marc, former General Secretary of the government and
colleague of Jacques Rigaud at the Conseil d'État,* but also the former
Communist Minister for Health Jack Ralite.

Fundamental to the maintenance of an elitist network, these dinners are almost magical in that they appear to be neither codified nor
institutionalized. Nobody is registered, nobody is excluded . . . seemingly. They have nothing in common with the innumerable clubs that
abound everywhere in France and especially in the capital. Nothing,
except that the majority of them likewise formalize their meetings
around a meal.

A Place At the Table

There is even one that claims gastronomy as its reason for being.
The Club of the Hundred applies, as its name indicates, a pitiless *numerus clausus*. As with the Academy, only the death of a current member
releases a place at the table. They meet at Maxim's each Thursday at
12:30 precisely, except once a month, when one of the members invites
the others to a place of his choice. The person who was brought in as
number 100 in the 1970's is still today in the phalanx of the group's remaining twenty original members.

Originally a loosely structured group when it was created in 1912,
the Club has become very select today. While the applicant must always pass "a great gastronomical oral examination" before a commission of fifteen members, his titles of glory and his sponsors count as
much as the sureness of his palate. Having crossed this distinguished
barrier, all one has to do is come up with a contribution of $650 a year
plus the price of the meals, which are "high enough so that one could

---

*The 200-member Council of State serves as the highest court to which legal matters can
be referred, and as the consultative body to which the government submits bills before
they are presented for examination by the Conseil des Ministres.

say, without having his head chopped off, that they are sometimes disgusting," jokes a member.

Who are the happy chosen? Politicians like Raymond Bars, Jean François-Poncet, Jean-Pierre Soisson and Pierre Messmer, "a young recruit" from 1996; two Rothschilds, Edmond and Elie; a few aristocrats, like the duke of Luynes and the count de Fels, who also receives sumptuously in his château de Voisin, close to Rambouillet; the head of Lazard, Michel David-Weill, and that of Renault, Louis Schweitzer.

The Club of the Hundred was infiltrated recently by a network that is on its way up in the business world, "Bébéar's Gang." In addition to the chairman of Axa himself, his friends Jean-Rene Fourtou from Rhône-Poulenc, Didier Pineau-Valencienne of Schneider, Jean-Louis Beffa of Saint-Gobain, Pierre Dauzier, head of Havas and godfather of the Corrézian network, have won their napkin rings there.

The society man the Viscount of Ribes mixes with very social Jean-Marc Simon, of the Accor group. Two chefs, Paul Bocuse and Joel Robuchon, three gastronomy journalists, Philippe Bouvard, Jean Ferniot and Claude Imbert, not to mention the very gourmet Jean-François Revel, contribute their knowledge of good fare to the assembly, where also sits a doctor who is much in vogue with the elegant society, Jean-François Lemaire, the art appraiser Jacques Tajan, and the couturier Pierre Cardin, who receives at his own place within the walls of Maxim's.

Does the list exclude only women? They are excluded from it since 1920 for the reason that only one ever recruited, a journalist, was such a bore (say the men) that it was necessary to modify the statutes not to put endanger the serenity and the permanence of the institution. Only that!

Those who are distressed by such ostracism can join a more recent institution, less prestigious but nevertheless promising: "the Bistrot." Its founder was not just anyone. A goldsmith when it comes to networks, George Bérard-Quélin, director-founder of many confidential meetings, a freemason, and a very highly respected constitutional adviser of the governments of the 4th Republic, also initiated the very famous and very serious "Century." He was the first president of the "Bistrot," which sees itself as the direct competitor of the Club of the Hundred. This competition does not prevent 20 of its 50 members from belonging to both. Such is the case of current president Jean-Marc Simon and his predecessor Jacques Tajan.

Among the women, in addition to Corinne Fabre (of the laboratories of the same name) and the journalist Anita Hausser, the magistrate Danièle Burguburu plays the role of muse. Because the club was very close to Mitterrand, they used to meet in establishments that the former President frequented, like "Chez Lulu," "Le Pichet" or the seafood restaurants "Divellec" and "Le Duc." The table companions are now looking for new sources of inspiration.

But not all the clubs (candidates should bear this in mind!) are necessarily connected with a network. Thus fashionable establishments like the "Jockey Club." Do people recognize each other there or help each other out because they are members or, more simply, because they are part of the aristocracy?

As for the "Century," it appeals more to prestige than to a feeling of common membership which its associates might feel. They are certainly very select, but there are so many: approximately 400 members of the *nomenklatura* invited to meet on the third Wednesday of the month, in the salons of the Automobile Club of France, on place de la Concorde. Business leaders Ambroise Roux, Claude Bébéar and Jerome Monod, the banker Michel David-Weill, the politicians Jacques Toubon and Laurent Fabius, academics including Olivier Duhamel and Luc Ferry, government officials like Marceau Long, telecrats Jean Drucker and Patrick Poivre of Arvor. Plus a handful of women, welcome in the club, like the journalist Michèle Cotta, the great hope of the Socialist party Martine Aubry, and Daniele Burguburu, definitely omnipresent. The aperitif, where contacts are made, is the strategic moment of the evening since it allows everyone one to navigate through the crowd at will, before being seated at a table of eight.

As the price one pays for success, the "Century" has been copied. Marc Ladreit de Lacharrière, the ENA alum who is chairman of FI-MALAC bought the *Revue des Deux Mondes* — as much out of a taste for intellectual speculation as the desire to weave a relational matrix operating to his own benefit. The dinners which he gives at Royal Monceau or the Plaza-Athenéum under this elegant patronage lack none of the formalism of its precedents: a meal with assigned places, and each table chaired by a foreign ambassador in France, with a guest of honor invited to make a speech (only very prominent ones). But the guests are always the same ones, as we have already seen at Club of the Hundred, the "Century" and elsewhere.

This dinner circuit, where people keep on meeting each other, as if by mere chance, also attracts younger people. Too tender of age to belong to the true coteries, some of them have tried to imitate their style. They were hardly in their thirties when they decided, in 1990, to found the "Banquet." That may be a gastronomical or philosophical reference, as you choose. Young ENA and École Polytechnique alumni, rising executives, parliamentary deputies, journalists, forty of them meet on the second Wednesday of the month (children's day!) for dinner at Edgard, one of the most famous politico-media eateries of the Right Bank. This "Mickey Mouse Club" of influence tries to do everything like the big ones: tables of eight, the ritual of induction, and of course the obligatory practice of giving each other a hand. While they have not made it to the top yet, they are on their way. The journalists Claude Askolovitch, Christophe Barbier and Thierry Portes are climbing through the hierarchy at *L'Évènement du Jeudi*, *L'Express* and *Le Figaro*. Jean-François Copé and François Cornut-Nice form the relief guard of the young deputies under Chirac. The X-Bridges (a prestigious group from the École Polytechnique) Edouard Sauvage manages regional planning in Alain Juppé's cabinet while the financier François Werner directs Guy Drut's cabinet. The general idea is rather simple: the journalist talks about the elected official, who gives information to the journalist; the ministerial adviser delivers some information to the former, and moreover expects to retire some day in the private sector thanks to his friends who work there already. Apparently, every alternative is possible in this Kamasutra of success!

Hen and Chicks

Not everybody spends time with his peers because of the "mirror effect" analyzed by the philosopher René Girard, wherein people of the same social echelon recognize each other due to a kind of sociability of vanity. On the chessboard of conviviality, "social debtors" are not the only players. Other strong connections are forged by sharing experiences and critical moments.

Thus, veterans of certain ministerial cabinets take pleasure (and sometimes interest) in eating together. They worked hard, and withstood for better or worse the forced departure from their gilded offices. After saying good-bye to the doormen, some continue to keep the flame alive.

By order of seniority, the ex-collaborators of the Gaullist minister Olivier Guichard founded the "109," which still functions. Those from Simone Veil, during Giscard d'Estaing's period, remember together, more than 20 years later, the pitched battles over the abortion law. Jacques Delors brings together the Cleisthenes Club (for the father of Athenian democracy, if you please); his daughter Martine Aubry harbors "the Chicks of the Châtelet"; the "Friends of Béré Club" has outlived the former Prime Minister and Cabaroc (a sly abbreviation of "cabinet of Rocard") was created shortly after shattering resignation of the Agriculture Minister in 1985.

In addition to the routine mutual aid, it happens that these gatherings affect the country's businesses. Thus, René Monory, the president of the Senate, still brings together his chiefs of staff twice a month. Among them are Michel Pébereau, the chairman of BNP, and Jean-Jacques Bonnaud, former president of GAN. Bonnaud, since the beginning of 1996, has been the object of insistent pressures from Juppé, who wanted to fix up his deputy chief of staff, the comptroller Pierre-Mathieu Duhamel, as head of the CIC (Industrial and Commercial Credit), a subsidiary of GAN. "If this attempt to force his way in failed," explains a high-ranking civil servant from Bercy (the Ministry of Finance), "it is mainly because Bonnaud, who did not want to give in and who had the law on his side, benefited from Monory's support. The President of the Senate had no trouble getting a message to Juppé that this matter, which was starting to make noise in the newspapers, could very well turn ugly." The irony is that it was another network, resulting from the Juppé cabinet at the Budget office, between 1986 and 1988, that had been working secretly to set this up. Pierre-Mathieu Duhamel belonged to the first team under the orders of the auditor Daniel Bouton, who had become number two at Société Générale, a bank that had been eying the CIC for a long time.

This kind of little coteries, half "a bunch of pals," half corporate network, frequently exists within the Administration. One example is the police force, where forty young police chiefs founded, in the Eighties, the Poularde club (the Hen), named for the restaurant where they used to meet early on. Since then, many have achieved important positions, like Claude Cancès, ex-director of the Parisian Criminal Investigation Department, or Ange Mancini, the former number two of the national Police Judiciaire. A competing "boutique" was created early in the Nineties under the wing of the general controller Delebois. This police officer, close to Charles Pasqua, acquired minor but unwelcome notoriety in the course of his career; he was implicated, in 1973, in the incident with the microphones posted at *Le Canard Enchaîné*, then, in 1986, for having given to Yves Chalier, fugitive chief of staff of Christian Nucci,[2] a fake passport for Brazil. Jacques Delebois is the inspiration of the "Club of Vaupalière," which brings together police officers, a member of the prefectoral, and a former gendarme in the buildings of the Military Club, in Paris. Well! Some of its members, unhappy rivals of those of "The Poularde," started to make up files on the head of Renseignements généraux, Yves Bertrand, and on how the organization was being managed (poorly, in their view). Scandal, investigation of the IGPN (police disciplinary body), dismissal: Vaupalière is only a shadow of itself these days.

These not very glorious internal fights should not, however, obscure those networks where friendship and conviviality form the principal common cement, the little hand-shakes only being frosting on the cake. "Feet in the Water" is one. This honorable association, whose statutes are duly registered with the prefecture, was formed in 1987. It owes its name to a restaurant located on the Ile de la Jatte, in the west of Paris, where the dinners began in a spontaneous way around the owner, who was also in advertising. Now there are 25 who attend, among them Michel Charasse, the former socialist Minister Louis Mexandeau, the former Budget Director Isabelle Bouillot, the journalist Philippe Tesson, Isabelle Ockrent, director of the communication of SEITA, the lawyer from S.O.S Racism Francis Terquem, the advertising executive from Chirac's camp Bernard Brochand, and the Life President, Françoise Sampermans, former chairman of Générale Occidentale (a subsidiary of Alcatel, which owned in particular *L'Express* and *Le Point*) and director of the French subsidiary company of the Canadian paper group Québecor. "We meet once a month for dinner, with no other agenda than that of having a good laugh," she explains. "We are among the few to respect male-female parity, and left-right equilibrium. For the Chirac-Jospin debate, during the presidential elections, we put the Right on one side, the Left on the other, the TV in the middle. It was great." The criteria for admission, according to the president, are: to be convivial, not to have too great an ego, not to specialize in fashionable calumny.

From the most frivolous to the most serious, all these convivial Clubs have something in common: they are artificial. All were created by the will, the ambition, the spirit of fidelity, by one or many individuals. However, there is a network whose composition relies only on destiny: to belong to it, all you have to do is be born there!

A Mafia by Birth

She smokes a cigar, rides a Harley Davidson, and ensures that the fashionable news columns have plenty to write about in specialty magazines. Hardly thirty years old, she created her club, "Le Tonnerre" ("Thunder"), with a rich membership of 150 selected from among the pillars of Parisian social life. Even if the image she gives hardly enchants most of her peers, who are often more at ease than she is with the details of etiquette, Hermine de Clermont-Tonnerre takes advantage of a form of capital that is embodied in the particle "de" in her family name.

In spite of the hard laws of modern capitalism, which have forced the landed gentry into the labor force, in spite of the easing of manners, which often contravenes their codes of propriety and honor, the aristocrats are still distinguished. "We seem like troglodytes," teases Henri-François de Breteuil, marquis and president of "Historical Residence," an association that protects the owners of historic buildings.[3] "The grounds aren't worth much anymore, the châteaux are hired out for weddings and banquets, but there remains the social capital, i.e. the network. And that network, registered in time and space, is worth all the others combined. For example: what did the baroness of - - - do, when her son, back from performing his national service on a foreign aid program, started to look for work? She gave three dinners a week. Her son was quickly engaged by someone high up at BTP. But he was vegetating a little in south-western France. By chance, he found himself (during a wedding) sitting beside his president. And soon found himself named, as he had dreamed, to go to South East Asia." There is an almost innate sense of mutual aid that Laure de Beauvau-Craon, president de Sotheby's France, does not disavow. He acknowledges that he readily recruits trainees of noble origin and is devoted to help any young person who has been recommended to him by friends.

It is "distinction," to use an expression dear to sociologist Pierre Bourdieu, that founds the network, a matrix all the richer since these well-born people have opulent "social capital." This impalpable and nevertheless essential patrimony is defined by the sociologist as "the whole of the current or potential resources that are related to the possession of a *durable network of relations,* institutionalized to some extent, of acquaintance or recognition."[4]

Applied to the aristocracy, the concept of "social capital" is a dream concept. Even if the most famous salons of the interval between the wars, like those of Marie-Laure de Noailles or Edmée de La Rochefoucauld have no modern successors, the art of cultivating one's relationships remains the principal duty those whose compound names indicate their aristocratic heritage. Still, is advisable to make sure of the nature of the aforementioned particle.

Among the aristocrats, how many divisions are there? Would there be just over 2,000 families, as is claimed by the scrupulous, even suspicious homologation of the Association of Mutual Aid of the French nobility (ANF)? Or between 3,000 and 4,000 families, as maintains the "Catalogue of French Nobility," which states that 6,000 others, although equipped with the particle "de", cannot claim the quality of nobility? The unit that is counted, in any case, is not the individual but the family. Each individual is indeed only one link in the chain. "At the same time," explains the sociologist Eric Mension-Rigau, author of *Aristocrates et grands bourgeois,*[5] "the individual is embraced in the complex network of cousins and alliances."

The extended family thus represents the heart of this "social capital," whose contours were drawn a long time back by meticulously contracted matrimonial alliances. Where one resides, where one socializes, from the château to the beautiful Parisian apartment, vast enough to be able to receive guests and consolidate social capital, all depend on the marital conditions. "In Bordeaux, depending on whether they are involved in the wine or pine trade, the families have a château in the vineyard or a beautiful residence in the forest of the Landes," note the sociologists Michel Pinçon and Monique Pinçon-Charlot, authors of *Grand Fortunes*[6]. But they also have a private mansion or a vast apartment close to the Park or on Xavier Arnozan Court, and a villa in Arcachon or at Cap-Ferrat, as well as a country cottage in the Pyrenées, for winter sports. This double or triple territoriality is very much a component of a dominant position. To mark one's place in the social space seems to require that one be able to mark it in geographical space as well." According to this pair of sociologists, who have been studying the codes and rituals of the "great families" for a long time, we would thus be witnessing a kind of "collectivization" of the patrimonial real estate, placed at the service of the extended family network. These broad spaces also contribute to guaranteeing the integrity of the clan, by keeping a close eye, for example, on the children's social contacts. (*Grand Fortunes* was translated by Algora Publishing in 1998).

However, there are places for establishing relationships. The Jockey Club, for example, is the only worldly institution made up almost exclusively of authentic aristocrats: no fewer than 13 La Rochefoucaulds, 12 Dampierres, 7 Broglies and 6 Polignacs are regulars there! Initially created in France to encourage the improvement of the equine race, the Jockey (the "Club," say the initiates) functions like the English clubs: ladies are not allowed, although they have a reserved platform at the hippodromes of Longchamp, Chantilly and Deauville; etiquette is important, and courtesy requires that one not conduct business at this place, located at 2 rue Rabelais, in the 8th arrondissment of Paris.

This is a place where, to quote one of the "house" editorials,[7] "diplomas, decorations, talents and careers are not always the necessary nor sufficient passports to be allowed in."

Admission, indeed, requires far more: to be recognized by the some 1,100 members who are up to date with their dues. "A fellow who is rather well-known in this milieu asked to be presented to the Jockey," one of the members told us. "He said he knows many people there. Somebody whom he believed he could choose as a godfather answered him: 'My dear friend, individually, everyone will be for you, but collectively everyone will be against.' This person absolutely did not make the grade. Somebody who is socially ambitious is carefully drawn aside, for he will not contribute anything. The hive supposes that each bee brings pollen, not that she takes pollen from the others."

But among well-bred people, there is no question of subjecting an applicant to the humiliation of a rejection. Thus one only introduces candidates who are sure to be adopted, at the conclusion of a pitiless selection process. A negative vote expressed by a black ball cancels five positive votes expressed by a white ball. It is also a decisive means for the "hive" to maintain the quality of its bees. The others, all the others, have no chance of ever being able to list, after their name, in the "*Bottin mondain*" ("the Book," to initiates; the equivalent of the *Social Register* in the U.S.) the prestigious and distinctive letter "J."

What the Jockey Club carries out in a gentle way, the ANF carries out with willful brutality. Created in 1932 by some aristocrats anxious about the possible extinction of the species, this association intends "to ensure the maintenance and the respect of laws, rules and uses which control the nobility." While its primary vocation consists in "bringing material and moral aid to its members," still it is necessary that those are carefully selected. Therefore a significant part of the association's activity turns around authentication. A very formal "Commission of Evidence" attentively examines the affidavits of filiation provided by each applicant and requires the sponsorship of four members including two who hail from the same area as the candidate.

Once all these unpleasant obstacles are passed, the applicant can benefit from the solidarity institutionalized by the ANF. That is a moral comfort, of course, but there is also real material assistance. One of the more folkloric lucky finds is called "the cloakroom." This is a collection of used clothing given by most privileged. But this very smart attic of Emmaüs has certain characteristics suitable for the class to which it is addressed: one finds there tailor-made suits and cocktail dresses carrying the tag of the great couturiers, as well as tuxedos and jackets. In short, all the accessories essential to continue to devote oneself to the collective and deliciously restricted art of l'entre-soi.

And what an *entre-soi*! A concentration of everyone who counts and everyone who knows everything that counts. The duke of Brissac appears emblematic of the aristocracy that adapted to its time and knew how to widen its networks without derogating. An alum of the École Polytechnique, he graduated in too poor a rank to be able to get into the great corps. Cossé-Brissac then married May Schneider, heiress of the ironmasters' family. He made a career within the group of Creusot, where he was particularly successful in directing all the high class public relations.

For the Duke de Brissac collects relations; the habit runs in the family and he was trained to do it. "The cruise on *Achilleus*, organized by an American journalist, in which the Duke de Brissac agreed to participate in 1955, undoubtedly represents and extreme example of these artificially arranged 'chance' meetings that are so knowingly planned," notes sociologist Monique de Saint Martin in her very well-documented book on *L'Espace de la noblesse* (*Among the Nobility*).[8] This two-week tour of the Mediterranean was the initiative of the Greek ship-owner Stavros Niarchos, who took care of travel expenses in exchange for the privilege of sailing in the company of all the European and American "upper crust."

Among the Frenchmen, the Duke de Brissac was pleased to find the former president of the Council Paul Reynaud, whom he had met on several occasions in the 1930's. He also knew the Countess of Contades, who would become his elder son's mother-in-law; and the Baron de Cabrol, a cousin whose wife excels in organizing charity balls. As for that promising young couple, the Viscount and the Viscountess de Ribes, the Duke knows them very well indeed. The Viscount is none other than his nephew; he made a good match by marrying Jacqueline de la Bonninière de Beaumont, daughter of Jean de Beaumont, great leader of the enigmatic Rivaud Bank, president of the Club Interallié and himself a cousin of the Duke!

Who would be, today, the guests of such a cruise? In the 1980s, perhaps it would have been some members of the informal Association of the Friends of Canisy, created in 1982 by Denis de Kergorlay, and since gone by the wayside due to the lassitude of its promoter and especially of his wife. A graduate of Columbia University, Denis de Kergorlay was a treasurer of Doctors Without Borders when he undertook to organize some very posh gatherings at his château of Canisy, on the English Channel. The 17th century residence, refitted by his parents, counts more than 50 rooms and is surrounded by a park of approximately 1200 acres. Over the weekend, the "friends of Canisy" — lawyers, writers, artists, businessmen, high-ranking public officials, and politicians — gather at the château for a consideration of a modest bit of support for the operating costs. The journalists Jean Bothorel and Patrick Poivre d'Arvor come as neighbors, just like the Breton Jean de Kervasdoué, at the time the director of the hospitals. Thanks to this last, Denis de Kergorlay soon hosted all of "Fabius' gang:" Maurice Bennassayag, Serge Moati, Gerard Unger and Henri Weber, all delighted to play the nobs for a weekend. On the Right, regulars at these very cohabitationist weekends mix side by side with members of the UDF. Bruno Durieux and François d'Aubert, a neighbor from Mayenne, mingle readily with these country weekends.

Canisy illustrates rather accurately one of the renewed vocations of the aristocrats: to diversify their "social capital" while preserving, as far as possible, the specificity of the caste. In other words, to mix without demeaning oneself.

Luxuries, Delicacies, and Antiques

A wife, or a new roof for the château: the "barter" is never stated in such straightforward terms. But all the same, for centuries the aristocracy has followed the practice of joining forces with those families of the grande bourgeoisie that are equipped with an enviable patrimony, exchanging social capital against economic capital.

It's an old tradition. Colbert, son of a rich clothier from Rheims, succeeded in "placing" several of his daughters in the best of all possible aristocratic worlds, respectively marrying the Duke de Chevreuse, the Duke de Beauvilliers and the Duke de Mortemart, nephew of Mme. de Montespan.

Even if the rule is not infallible, in fact generally still today the sons are matched with commoners: the name, as well as appearances, remain intact even if nobody is fooled. During his research, sociologist Eric Mension-Rigau was able to draw up a list of the bourgeois families that the aristocracy regards as honorable and worthy of incorporating into the network.

One finds there in particular the Bizots, a Lyons family that for generations has been established in banking (including Jean-François Bizot, the former head of *L'Actuel*), the Cartier-Bressons, whose fortune comes from textiles, the Fenailles, prosperous thanks to oil, the Firino-Martells and their famous Cognac, the Georges-Picots, with more diversified activities, the Meuniers of chocolate renown, the Say sugar family and the Mansets of Bordeaux. Not to mention the bourgeois families that have probably contributed the most to reinflating the great and noble dynasties: the Wendels and Schneiders, legendary ironmasters, as well as the Rothschilds.

These are extremely useful alliances when one wishes to increase one's professional opportunities. Aristocrats co-opted by the bourgeoisie have thus little by little garnered seats on various boards of directors. Even though the Board of the Saint-Cyr military academy, extraordinarily interdependent in all ways, continues to comprise a statistically crushing number of names with particles, the professional ties of the aristocracy are indeed seriously diversified.

In the sphere of diplomacy, the tradition is maintained over the course of the various governments. Continuing the Jacquin de Margerie dynasty as ambassadors of France, President Chirac named as ambassador to Washington, the most envied post, François Bujon de l'Estang, and the General Secretary of the Elysée, Dominique de Galouzeau de Villepin, comes from the Quai d'Orsay. *Noblesse oblige.*

But never, to tell the truth, was the "petty nobility" network so active and so well-represented as during the short reign of Edouard Balladur in Matignon, between 1993 and 1995. Just consider: Olivier Costa de Beauregard, technical adviser in charge of housing; Victoire de La Génière for the press service; Thierry de Mazancourt for industry, crafts and trade, Bernard de Montferrand, special adviser, Anne de Danne for health, the family and the city (suburbs included), Yves-Thibaut de Silguy, responsible for Community questions (he also would become European police chief in Brussels).

In political life itself, the aristocrats' linkages are slack enough. Admittedly, the Duke Josselin de Rohan, senator of Morbihan, chairs the RPR group at the High Assembly. And he is quite capable, when the occasion warrants, of keeping an ear cocked for any requests presented by one of his many cousins.

In the public sector, it is rather the mandates of local councilors that most inspire the nobles. This is apparently a vestige of certain aspects of feudality. At the national level, they prefer high administration posts. A study carried out by the European Sociology Center at the beginning of the 1970's thus counted 12% of the chief comptrollers' names as having the critical particle.

In the private sector, banking is the preferred field, but it seems to be standing still vis-à-vis some modern trades related to communication. The art of managing one's address book, making conversation, and receive guests properly, accounts for a good deal in the trades of representation. Renaud de Clermont-Tonnerre, after having directed *Point de vue/ Images du Monde* for many years, became president of *Avenir Havas Media* while Jean de Yturbe chairs the Ted Bates advertising firm.

But it is especially in the luxury industries that a good-sounding name wins all the votes. At Chanel, communications pass through the very elegant Marie-Louise de Clermont-Tonnerre, while for the longest time Ines de Fressange embodied the house's image. Daphne de Saint-Marceaux, like Laure de Fels, handle public relations for the American company Estée Lauder. Eliane de Béraudière, at Dior, and Elisabeth de Hennezel, for Guerlain, "sell" perfume, while Anne de La Rochefoucauld specializes in champagne.

The career of press attaché, therefore, goes well with a particle. If Ghislaine de la Serre seems to represent a more commonplace brand, in Martini Rossi, the appearance is misleading. Indeed, the brand has a prestigious terrace on the Champs-Elysées, where grand cocktail parties can be organized.

Luxury. . . and antiquities. How can you find a better expert than someone who was immersed, since his or her tenderest childhood, in the milieu of "beautiful things?" And what would be better suited to the image of a big antiques dealer than to be able to display a name that has a patina, just like the objects that he offers for sale? Laure de Beauvau-Craon, president of Sotheby's France, recognizes this tendency without hesitation. The princess invented, if one dares to say, "aristocratic *pantouflage*" (the art of leaving a civil service post for an advantageous post in the private sector). Former president of "Historic Residence," which represents the interests of 2,000 châteaux in France, she was as well positioned as one can be to know the highlights of a patrimony from which the less flourishing owners are sometimes constrained to separate. And they separate, preferably, through the discrete services of Sotheby's.

Christie's, the other the great world player in the art market, also invests in the social network. In 1990, the house engaged Emmanuel Jacquin de Margerie, former French ambassador in Washington, ex-director of the Museums of France, and especially a descendant of one of the greatest French families, as patriarch of its "European" branch. Christie's also recruited among its top executives the Viscount Thierry Roy de Lachaise, who was requested to mention his noble title on the catalogues!

The best names from the *Bottin mondain* are listed one after another at the receptions organized to make people more familiar with the Anglo-Saxon house. One such reception, organized in Provence during the summer of 1995, brought together Prince Charles-Louis de Mérode, Bertrand de Vigneau, the Princess Charlotte de Croÿ, Olivier and Bruno Latil d'Albertas, as well as the inevitable Jonkheer Daniel Cordon of Lichtbuer.

"Being a member of a great family, having a strongly integrated network of relations, becomes a particularly effective guarantee against the threats of demotion or of loss of position," says Monique de Saint Martin. "The well-governed management of relations makes it possible for the descendants of the nobility to avoid decline more surely than having a diploma or an academic title."

Of all the adepts of the *entre-soi*, the aristocrats benefit from a considerable privilege: they belong to the same social network, effective, diversified, and lasting, from their first to their last breath.

Chapter 4

MAKING A CAREER

This is the story of an elevator. But it only goes in one direction: always up. The image is as old as social ambition. Not being a hypocrite, the prefect Paul Camous, a great figure in the Parisian networks, aptly named a small club founded by his efforts, "The Elevator." This was during the flourishing 4th Republic. The graduating classes from the ENA (École national d'administration) gave the nation the illusion that they had embraced the Oh!-So-disinterested religion of the sacrosanct "public service." High-ranking civil servants, conversing with corporate leaders and elected officials, had this subliminal maxim in their heads: networks are good for the career.

Does anybody still remember the impassioned remarks of the founder of the ENA, Michel Debré, during his inauguration in 1946? Far from "social elevators," this fiery member of the Conseil d'État evoked "the moral objective" of the training, "the meaning of the State" and "the constraints of the trade."

The lyricism was sincere, and in the first years had a certain correspondence with reality. The idea of hopping around amongst the groggy and stumbling mortals in the private sector did not occur to the first graduates. Even the élite of the élite, the financial inspectorate, had not begun searching out positions in the financial sector. It was a question of rebuilding France.

A half-century later, reality no longer matches the noble principles hammered out by Debré. One of the old boys from the ENA, Jean-
Michel Gaillard, magistrate at the Court of Auditors, former adviser to
Mitterrand in the Elysée, worried: "In 1994, 60% of ENA alumni between the age of 25 and 40 plan to leave the public service."

They were no longer seeking only to advance within public administration. They also wanted to *"pantoufler,"* to make the jump to lucrative jobs in the private sector, to cross the threshold into the corporate world, the natural environment for competition and its material
advantages. To succeed in this mutation, the best approach is not inevitably a straight line, but via the network.

There is a very selective network that hardly concerns the
"average" ENA alumnus. Indeed, upon leaving the school, after a pitiless
battle for jobs, all and sundry go their separate ways and seldom meet,
unless they share particular affinities. There are, of course, exceptions.
Thus there are some celebrities of the "Robespierre" class, who left the
school in 1970. A small group of people, of varied political persuasions,
still meets regularly, twenty-five years afterwards, and is ready to give
each other a hand. Philippe Séguin, president of the National Assembly, Jacques Attali, Marc Ladreit de Lacharrière, chair of FIMALAC,
Étienne Pflimlin, banker, and Philippe Lagayette, general manager of
the Caisse des depots et consignations (which funds French public
works and housing), never broke off with each other. A few years ago
Marc de Lacharrière, a wealthy capitalist, bought the right-wing
weekly magazine *Valeurs actuelles* in order to use it to promote the ideas
defended by Philippe Séguin. In 1995, the president of the National Assembly even engaged in his staff an alumnus of the École Normale
Supérieure, Nicolas Baverez, who was accustomed to writing speeches
and interviews for Philippe Séguin.

Such proximity is a dream for the ordinary ENA alumnus, who
usually can't get very far in these circles. He is often "confined" to tasks
comparable to those of someone working in the private sector. The
mandarins, who came out in the first ranks, look at him more with con-
tempt than with mutual recognition.

"Job offers published in the ENA bulletin? They don't do a thing
for me!" exclaims a woman who did well in the triage. "I never benefited from the ENA as a network. The only network that truly works
for 'the old boys' from the ENA is the one for the finance inspectors."

Are the Council of State and the Court of Auditors, such august bodies, simply a larger-scale depiction of careerist connections? "At the Council of State," continues our interlocutress, "they are hedonists who prefer to spend their time with literature rather than maximizing cash-flow. I don't know of a single company that they have colonized." And at the Court of Auditors, the original locus of this expertise in estab-lishing elite fiefdoms? "They have the image of hard-working drones. Hardly what the leaders dream of."

Thus remains only the financial inspectorate. The "Inspection"! Its regular meetings, its dinners, its private directory that everyone keeps in hand's reach: now, that's the way to cement an indestructible solidarity. The more so as any young inspector is taken in hand from the first day. Two years of "making the rounds," of going off in a team to verify some dark provincial disbursement office, under the aegis of one of the great veterans of the corps creates a feeling of complicity and supports the team spirit.

In order to keep the system securely locked, a "head of depart-ment" devotes himself at least as much to managing his flocks' careers as to keeping up with the daily reports and missions. Installed at Bercy, he sees to everything that concerns the some 320 members of the active body, of which only 70 belong to the service, strictly speaking. The others therefore are not forgotten; quite to the contrary. The wor-thy head of department takes care that such and such position devolves to one of his, or on the contrary, he takes pains to discourage one of his protégés from accepting a job that is considered to be not very worthy of an inspector. For the law of the network holds that the dishonor or glory of one reflects on all the others. Together with the Mining Corps, where the best "X" graduates go (*Trans. note:* The École polytechnique is known as "X"), "the Inspection" is the only official place where a high-ranking civil servant has as an official and nearly exclusive task to guide his colleagues toward the professional route most advantageous for him.

"It is the position and the competence of each member that makes the Inspectorate a recognized body," explains Philippe Jaffré, chairman of Elf Aquitaine. Therefore, every position that is released is consid-ered. If it appears worthy of a finance inspector, then they put someone there. "I have sometimes had to recruit for American companies estab-lishing themselves in France and wishing to engage a high-ranking offi-cial to handle the public relations," says a Parisian headhunter. "When I contact an inspector for a position, I know that within three days, the head of the agency will have taken the matter in hand, and suggested his own candidates to my client."

To preserve the reputation of the body also means coming to the help of a threatened member, despite any political divergence. Early in 1994, Patrick Careil, an inspector and pro-Fabius, knew that Balladur's government was getting ready to sack him as chairman of the Hervet Bank. Its financial results were pitiful. But say! He is a finance inspector. So quite naturally he appealed to four inspectors to save him. Jean-Claude Trichet, governor of the Bank of France, Charles de Croisset, chairman of the Commercial Credit of France, Jaffré, chairman of Elf and Pébereau, chairman of BNP, all in the Balladur camp, got together privately to concoct a "rescue plan" for the Fabiusian Patrick Careil. For the honor of the corps!

A few months later, another member of the brotherhood likewise succeeded in saving his position thanks to some well-placed friends. Jean Farge, former director of the Public Accounts, former Secretary of State for Health in Raymond Barre's government, was heading comfortably for the end of his career as head of the PMU (the French betting authority). In 1995, at the age of 67, he could have claimed a well-deserved retirement. But he didn't seem to be aging. However, the Française des Jeux, which had interests in the PMU, would have like to see him retire as soon as possible.

The position, at the time, should have redounded to Pierre Charron, former collaborator of Jacques Chaban-Delmas, then of Jacques Chirac, and president of France-Gallop. However! It was the chief of staff to the Budget Minister Nicolas Sarkozy who subverted the operation, in solidarity with Jean Farge, his colleague from the Inspection. Hanging on beyond all reason, Farge put up quite a resistance. The decree modifying the operation of the PMU was delayed. Three general meetings were cancelled. This, in effect, prevented his dismissal. To an astonished interlocutor, Farge answered: "I have the Inspectorate with me."

In addition, a year later the corps, which indeed obstinately supports its protégés, successfully barred the road to another potential successor as the head of the PMU. The candidate favored by the Finance Minister Jean Arthuis has the flaw of not belonging to the brotherhood. "As long as a general meeting has not kicked me out and my administrative hierarchy has not asked that I leave this post," Farge specified publicly on February 5, 1997, "I regard myself as the sole general administrator of the PMU." In early March, at the age of 69, he gave up his position to a man chosen from within the "seraglio," Bertrand Bélinguier.

Such behavior can be breathtakingly blunt. It is the simple result of a system where some 300 Mister So-and-So's, and a few ladies consider themselves better than the others, because they did well at school once upon a time. Thus, Jean-Claude Trichet, when he was Director of the Treasury, referred to his "thoroughbreds" when talking about the financial inspectors working under his orders. "They have a fantastic cheek, with this superiority complex," notes one ENA alumnus who is at the Ministry of Finance but who is not a member of the group. "These types are always ready to trample on anybody to get what they want, and they don't feel the least bit of shame."

A Very Small World

The banking and insurance sectors are now almost thoroughly taken over by these "thoroughbreds." Who is chairman of BNP? Michel Pébereau, finance inspector. Chairman of Société Générale? Marc Viénot, finance inspector, assisted by Jean-Paul Delacour, finance inspector, and Daniel Bouton, finance inspector. Commercial Credit of France? Charles de Croisset, finance inspector. Crédit du Nord? Philippe Toussaint, finance inspector. SME Infrastructure? Jacques-Henri David, finance inspector. Crédit Lyonnais? Its number two, Pascal Lamy, is a finance inspector. Not to mention the many inspectors who contributed to destruction of Crédit Foncier.

The Finance inspectorate is aided and abetted by the Treasury. This prestigious office, which governs the Finance Ministry, developed mythological qualities thanks to the power that it exerted over the banks for so many years, given that it determined the monetary policy. Times have changed, a little. The Treasury has lost some of its aura since several large banks were privatized and the Bank of France gained some independence. But what difference does that really make? Jean-Claude Trichet, governor of the Bank of France, is a finance inspector, as is the deputy governor Hervé Hannoun.

Masters of the franc, if not Masters of the Universe, these powerful men have, however, experienced some setbacks since the arrival of Jacques Chirac in the Elysée —for example Trichet, who saw himself as the agent of the politically correct line ("the only way. . .") with regard to Balladur's shock program. When he went in for the first time to give Chirac the Bank of France's annual report, he began a speech that expounded upon his achievements and his plans; the President interrupted him and said, in so many words, "Mister Governor, I do not doubt that your monetary policy is excellent, since I hear, here and there, that it is the only one conceivable. Now, we have approximately fifteen minutes remaining in this interview. I would like you to explain to me what you have done, as Director of the Treasury for Crédit Lyonnais, and as Bank of France governor for Crédit Foncier, so that these two major financial catastrophes will not turn out to be more disastrous still."

What an ambiance! Trichet was all the more concerned by the presidential irony since it related to one of the worst messes in the history of the Inspectorate. At the heart of the Crédit Lyonnais matter was Jean-Yves Haberer, who was both a finance inspector and a former director of the Treasury like Trichet.

It was Haberer who institutionalized the career network among the "Treasury guys." "As head of the Treasury, Haberer acted like a shepherd anxious to take care of every member of his flock," says another finance inspector, "a critical tendency. When a bank director came to ask his assistance, Haberer was accommodating — provided that the beggar offered to hire one of his protégés. Thus he wove a whole grid throughout the major companies."

Haberer's conduct with regard to the network is all the more interesting when one stops to realize that under his reign, Crédit Lyonnais would lose tens of billions of francs, and would arrive at a state of virtual bankruptcy without the State, as owner of the bank, seeming to worry overmuch for several years. "How could it have been otherwise?" asks one of the magistrates of the Court of Auditors who took part in auditing the Lyonnais during the scandal. "The people at the Treasury who were responsible for governing this bank had only three principal career outlets: Crédit Lyonnais, BNP and Société Générale. How can anyone imagine that under these conditions, the Treasury guys would be merciless?"

Let us add that the president of the Banking Commission, charged with overseeing the proper operation of the credit institutions, was at that time the finance inspector Jacques de Larosière. And that the president of the COB (the Stock Exchange Commission, responsible for keeping an eye on every enterprise that was more or less financed by public funds), that Jean Saint-Geours, another finance inspector, had, in a former life, presided over the destiny of the Lyonnais which he had left in a none too glorious condition. That the general manager of the same COB, Pierre Fleuriaux, belonged to the same corps. And that, of course, the president of the French Banking Association (AFB), the representative organization of the profession, is traditionally a finance inspector, too.

Would the Lyonnais disaster have been as severe if the faulty chairman's "comrades" hadn't trusted the supervisory authorities? Perhaps the career and supremacy networks built at the Finance Inspectorate are not enough to explain everything. They do clarify, nevertheless, and very sharply, the practices of a very small world that is very sure of itself.

When Haberer took up the reins of Crédit Lyonnais, in 1988, he was filled with an irrepressible spirit of revenge. The Right, having returned for two years of governmental cohabitation in March 1986, had dared to make him an unacceptable affront. They dismissed him from Paribas Bank, which the Left had offered to him in 1982! They did that to him, the former director of the Treasury, one of the most powerful men in France!

In this year of 1988, professional life was thus smiling again on the finance inspector. Here was his opportunity to give the place de Paris a lesson in financial creativity! Haberer set out to make his the largest bank in the country, and why not, he boasted to his friends, the biggest in the world? His objective: to grow at any cost. His method: the industrial bank, inspired by the German system where all the great industrial groups are dependent upon financial institutions. But Haberer wanted to do in a few years what his German fellow-members had taken decades to build. He was encouraged in this by his supervisory Minister, Pierre Bérégovoy, who was only too glad to see a banker who was ready to invest all out, and very inclined to support the friends of the people in power.

The parliamentary board of inquiry was finally established in October 1994, a month after the extent of the damage was revealed. During some of the hearings, they thought they must be dreaming. One spring day, the Honorable Members were questioning Haberer. This was during the full fury of the storm, since the interested party had just been dismissed by Crédit National, where the State had initially tried to fix him up again, so as not to make waves. Haberer confessed that day to a disturbing little game he like to play on his competitors: "I had fun once, announcing our semi-annual results as 1,610 million, in reference to the date that Henri IV died, in 1610. I was delighted to see that BNP, which always wanted to be better than us, came out with its accounts one week later and showed 1,611." That is how a senior State official amused himself! Such an irresponsible child, he practically played darts to decide what financial results he would post!

It would take time to discover all the facets of the greatest banking scandal of the post-war period. The phrase, "You can't do that to a former Treasury Director," did someone really say that, in response to a note written by a government commissioner to his higher-ups? The experts from the Equinoxe group wondered. His career in the administration got Mr. Haberer more indulgence than he would have enjoyed as the head of a major corporation. "This not very pleasing phrase was not uttered by irresponsible hooligans but by high administration officials and politicians who were determined "to examine what the parliamentary board of inquiry did not know, did not want to, or could not say." In their conclusions, these experts stated that "the crisis at Crédit Lyonnais is not a crisis proper to Crédit Lyonnais. It is a crisis of the Administration of Finances, a closed system of power, sure of itself to the point of excluding any possibility of error on the part of one of its members."

Little Bankruptcies Between Friends

Caste, network, complicity. This quite French trilogy keeps cropping up any time the Lyonnais scandal is mentioned. In October 1995, the members of Parliament approved the bank's rescue plan, which envisaged writing off some $22 billion in "compromised" credits. RPR Deputy Gilles Carrez then questioned the fragility of the oversight provisions, which he to the omnipotence of these career networks.

Could something have been done, sooner and faster? In its very severe report, the Court of Auditors stated that the governing board's first concerns must have been piqued in 1989. Moreover, that was when François d'Aubert, the great eliminator of public bureaucratic waste and covert financings, called for a parliamentary inquiry. He had to wait five more years before being able to allow his curiosity to run free.

There was talk of a parliamentary inquiry again in 1992. This time, maneuvers were being made at the Senate under the direction of Charles Pasqua, president of the RPR group. He stubbornly insisted that he would attain his objective, up until the very moment when he gave up. It was a short interview with Jean-Maxime Lévêque that made him change his mind. This finance inspector was Haberer's predecessor as head of Crédit Lyonnais. President of the CCF (Commercial Credit of France) when the Left took power, in 1981, he resigned suddenly before heading up a crusade against the nationalization of industry. This was enough to make of him a close friend of the RPR. And he had another bond with Pasqua: in his early youth he was active in the Resistance, as a young recruit of the Leclerc division.

Exit, board of inquiry. In addition to the solidarity between finance inspectors that bound Lévêque to his successor, he had a less admissible reason for wanting to stifle this parliamentary initiative. A reason that can be read in four letters: IBSA.

International Bankers S.A. (IBSA) is a financial company that was created in 1983 in Luxembourg, using Arab capital, by Jean-Maxime Lévêque after his departure with fanfare from the nationalized CCF. After a promising beginning, International Bankers suffered a series of disastrous "blows," including the massive support they gave to Sylvain Lévêque, nephew of the boss, who dreamed of becoming the king of Parisian breweries. And, more serious, International Bankers endured colossal losses on the real estate market: three-quarters of a billion dollars in dubious loans!

It was up to the Lyonnais to fill these financial holes. For in 1989, Jean-Yves Haberer agreed, at the request of his predecessor and former colleague from the Inspectorate Jean-Maxime Lévêque, to take on of 25% of this holding by the nationalized bank that he directed. This 25% put Crédit Lyonnais in the position of "principal shareholder." During a hearing before the parliamentary inquiry board, June 16, 1994, once the scandal had been revealed, the new chairman of Crédit Lyonnais (an X alum) Jean Peyrelevade described clinically and freely this sad episode in the life of a bank. "The initial error in taking on IBSA was a strategic error, the reasons for which... escape me.... The fact is that, for all the deals that were made or approved at the highest level of Crédit Lyonnais, they always had good information. . . .When you are involved in a bank such as IBSA that has behaved as badly as I see today, and when you are a minority shareholder, you have no control and can't do anything at all to set things right. . . . What still astonishes me is the precipitousness with which Crédit Lyonnais — nothing forced it — dove into this mess."

An illuminating dialogue between Peyrelevade and Philippe Séguin (who chairs the commission) then follows:

Séguin: You have an explanation for this precipitousness. . .

Peyrelevade: My interpretation is completely innocent, Mr. President.

Séguin: Innocent?

Peyrelevade: Relatively. Let us say mischievous. I think that it is a matter of friendly Parisian complicity between finance inspectors."

A complicity that Haberer, questioned, next, about his successor, asserts almost cynically. He went as far as to point out to the parliamentary board of inquiry: "Jean Peyrelevade hasn't even been passed by the ENA"! When Séguin asked about ways to address the public's interest in the commission's proceedings, the former chairman of Crédit Lyonnais answered: "I think that you could make two products: a small three-page report for the public and a longer report for the government. For the public, I do not believe it is necessary to go into too much detail."

Three pages for over $8 billion! An astonishing ratio! Should this be read as contempt for Joe Blow, the average citizen, or a touching concern to spare the nerves of the taxpayer who would have to cough up some $300 per household to erase Haberer's incompetence? The feeling of belonging to a higher, intellectually infallible species is so strong that it led Jean-Claude Trichet to confess before the members of Parliament, in connection with Haberer, his distant predecessor in the management of the Treasury: "*A priori*, it is true, the idea that he could be so tragically mistaken, that he could say anything that would turn out to be false, that was a shock for me, almost a cultural shock."

Haberer, however, did not escape from the terrible scandal. In playing too much on the networks of friendship in high public office, the former chairman of Crédit Lyonnais allowed his case worsen to such an extent that it was no longer salvageable. Cruel destiny for one who had declared in the *Financial Times* in 1983, during the height of his glory at the helm of Paribas: "The day I entered the Treasury, I knew in any event that I would end up directing a bank. To go from the State service to the head of a big bank is not unusual in France."[2] To get kicked out is far more unusual, indeed.

The "Miners" Are Always There, in the Background

The same principle of impunity holds true for the X-Mines. They are the lords of the École polytechnique (Polytechnic School), as the finance inspectors are those of the ENA. Only a measly fifteen happy candidates make the grade each year, expanding the demanding ranks of the legendary Mining Corps. They graduated among the first in their class at X or, in the case of two individuals, at the École Normale Supérieure. But with the last mines being closed and with the rout of the iron and steel industry, then the domination of the tertiary sector, their traditional bastions have been weakened.

After largely contributing to the downfall of Creusot-Loire in the early 1980's, they certainly saved their honor thanks to Usinor. It was one of this gang, Francis Mer, who made it possible for that iron and steel entity to become miraculously profitable once again. But, in a terrible affront, Elf, heartland of the mining engineers, escaped from the Corps some ten years ago. "The miners" can certainly be found at Elf by the dozen. But the president is not one of theirs! This mishap began in 1977, when Valéry Giscard d'Estaing had the impertinence to entrust Elf's destiny to the finance inspector Albin Chalandon, whom the X-Mines then badgered and discredited relentlessly. They had to wait until 1983 to get one of their own again, in the person of Michel Pecqueur.

This was a respite of short duration. While he was Prime Minister, the finance inspector Michel Rocard broke the rule once again by replacing the X-Mines Pecqueur with the "autodidact" Loïk Floch-Prigent, graduate of a modest engineering school. Three years later, as a State Councilor, Edouard Balladur multiplied this humiliation ten times over by naming the finance inspector Philippe Jaffré to succeed Floch-Prigent and to undertake the company's privatization. As troubles never come singly, the new president, barely installed, decided that the high-ranking civil servants working at Elf would have to resign from their original positions. This was total nonsense in the eyes of senior officials accustomed to the joys of the cohabitation between the State and the private sector! With bad (very bad) grace, it was however necessary to comply, and to the give up the comfort of having a ready return ticket to life in the administration in the event of career turbulence.

"One of us has been cut down. One of us will replace him." With these words, worthy of the heroes of Alexandre Dumas, a representative of the Mining Corps commented on the 1986 assassination of his comrade George Besse, chairman of Renault, by the group Direct Action. His prophecy was carried out. The X-Mines George Besse was succeeded at Renault by the X-Mines Raymond Lévy. But, for the miners, this was a kind of swan song. Having reached the mandatory retirement age, Lévy had to give up his position in 1992. He was replaced by the former cabinet director for Laurent Fabius at Matignon, Louis Schweitzer. This finance inspector soon decided to separate from the owner of RVI (Renault Véhicules Industrial), Jean-Pierre Capron, an X-Mines who had been co-opted by Lévy.

But, in the Corps' mythology, the great failure was the SNCF. For more than ten years now, the public company has not been controlled by an engineer from the Mining Corps, as had so long been the tradition. The trains, however, continue to run! But in 1994, the X-Mines Raymond Lévy had still not swallowed the ousting of his comrade Jean Dupuy, an X-Mines who was given the boot during the big train strike in the winter of 1986. "Jean Dupuy made the TGV. He was driven out from the CEO's spot at SNCF because he didn't express himself well on television."[3]

There is only one occasion where the finance inspectors and the engineers from the Mining Corps, merciless rivals, joined forces. In 1986, the new Minister of Industry Alain Madelin decided to reform his dusty administration. He called in the head of the national industries agency (the DGI), a den of X-Mines, the international manager Jacques Maisonrouge, who was once the number three man at IBM. The devil incarnate, for the civil servants of rue de Grenelle!

Maisonrouge however was able to resist all the attempts at destabilization during his career at IBM, which is no ladies' sewing circle. But with the DGI, he withstood only eleven months before calling a time out. He wanted quite simply to reorganize the administration, a reform that could have put the Finance Ministry in the shade. The holy alliance of the two great State agencies soon set straight these intolerable modernization plans. Maisonrouge left his post in 1987 to Jean-François Saglio, a member of the Mining Corps, coming straight from Elf. The situation was under control again. "To do well in the world outside, we need to start from solid positions. The more high positions we hold within the administration, the more public or private companies the members of the Corps will be able to supervise in the name of the State; and the more relationships we maintain at a suitable level, the more abundant the opportunities for "remunerative *pantouflage*'" This excellent advice on the geopolitics of career networks was given more than 20 years ago in an acid book, *The Polytechnic "Mafia"*, written by two X's.[4]

Only one of them, Jacques Kosciusko-Morizet, had the courage to sign the work. His very discreet co-author surely knew that to expose himself thus was not the fastest way toward a beautiful career. Wise intuition! Peyrelevade, since we are talking about him, collected prestigious chairmans' seats in the public sector.

"The strength of the X's," continued these perspicacious authors, "comes not only from their close friendly solidarity but especially from the fact that they have succeeded in convincing people of the underhand effectiveness of the network." What is true for X is necessarily so for the X-Mines. For the Corps resembles a cult, more or less, founded on the shared belief in the undeniable superiority of its members over the rest of humanity. The Corps has its president, currently Jean Syrota, chairman of the COGEMA, a great stronghold of the brotherhood; but it also has a guru, yesterday Pierre Guillaumat, the founder of Elf, today André Giraud, former Minister of Defense and Industry. It also has an association, chaired by Raymond Lévy. He, one of the Corps' most active "voices," is illustrious in the family replication of careers. His eldest son, David, is an engineer in the Mining Corps, whose territory he defends in the military-industrial sector in the office of Defense Minister Charles Millon. Lévy's three other children are also alums of the École Polytechnique, but "only" of the Bridges and Highways Corps.

"The Corps is less rigid than people think," says Anne Lauvergeon, the very cordial vice-president of the association. Her style contrasts, indeed, with the taste for secrecy cultivated by most of her male colleagues. "The best proof of this mobility is the nomadic spirit that exists among us. The Corps has lost its traditional strongholds, and it has conquered new ones. What remains is the Corps' capacity to react, proposing a candidate as soon as a position becomes available."

Lauvergeon is a typical example of the new conquerors. As former number two in the Elysée under Mitterrand, she rebounded as associate-manager at Lazard Bank before becoming assistant general director of the "telecommunications" branch of Alcatel.

However, most of the mining engineers prefer to stick to their own turf. Jean-Louis Beffa, at Saint-Gobain, thus hired Robert Pistre, former leader of the Corps and the confidant of a number of his juniors. At Pechiney, Jean-Louis Vinciguerra, Jean Gandois's heir apparent, never reached the chairman's seat that had been promised to him. Since he had only the tenuous security conferred by degrees from Science Po (the top French school for political science) and Harvard, in 1995 the Mining Corps managed to snap up this post for one of its own, Jean-Pierre Rodier.

Jean-Luc Lagardère always compensated for his weak ties with the business circles by placing an unequalled proportion of X-Mines on his staff: Jean-Pierre Souviron, former general director of Industry, Jean-Bernard Lévy, a close relation of Gerard Longuet, and Noël Forgeard. Lagardère accelerated things by luring the two gurus of the Mining Corps, the former minister André Giraud and the former head of Renault, Raymond Lévy. And the vice-president of his group is none other than Bernard Esambert, the former adviser to George Pompidou, an X-Mines too. Quite the personal army to have, when one works in the arms sector and wants to get government orders.

This almost mythical prestige that surrounds the Mining Corps tarnishes that of the other engineering corps coming out of X. The X-Bridges, however, are no slouches. With Ambroise Roux, George Pébereau and Pierre Suard, a dynasty of engineers has come out of their ranks and reigned over Alcatel-Alsthom for years. It was good time, when the Compagnie générale des Eaux (CGE, the Water Company) was directed by X-Bridges Guy Dejouany and EDF was headed up by several of his colleagues. Now the chairman of CGE is the finance inspector Jean-Marie Messier, while EDF is controlled by the centrist academic Edmond Alphandéry.

Finally we have the X-Telecom, thanks to their sector's growth, and the X-ENSAE, who influence economic policy by the means of their bastion, INSEE, which ensures the future of the École Polytechnique. A sign of the times? In 1993, for the first time, most of the pupils who were admitted to both X and the École Normale Supérieure chose the second one. Only 4 out of 36 bet on Polytechnique. The others preferred the austere tradition of research over the promising prospects for catapulting into the private sector.

The alumni of the École Normale Supérieure (ENS), however, are not remarkable for their aptitudes as regards mutual support. Is this the result of training in intellectual labor as a recluse? Certainly, ENS alumni turn up in a disproportionate number in certain coteries, like the entourage of cardinal Lustiger.[5] But even when one of their own, George Pompidou, reached the supreme office, hardly stirred any new currents in the careers of these admittedly quite full heads. Still, the former President, nostalgic for his youth, liked to bring together comrades from his class like the writer Roger Ikor, the State Councilor Roger Grégoire, the ambassador of France René Trotobas and the finance inspector Philippe de Montrémy.

Solidarity among the ENS alumni, finally, really had its hour of glory only once. But on what an occasion! In 1963, France discovered that one of its brilliant scholars, Georges Pâques, had been a spy for nineteen years in the service of the Soviet Union. Technical Adviser in many ministerial cabinets, he worked his way, at the request of his clandestine employers, into national defense until he became assistant chief of the NATO press service. That would be a station that would not enable him to deliver the secret code for the atomic bomb, but would all the same enable him to provide various biographical files, some confidential classified reports as well as organizational charts, and so on.

Even prior to his trial before the State Security Court, in July 1964, Pâques received the support of some former school-fellows on the right as well as the left, from Pierre Boutang to Maurice Clavel. "Seldom has the *espirit de corps* come into play, in a matter of this importance, with such speed and such unanimity," said the astonished writer Pierre Assouline.[5] The informal association of people from rue d'Ulm have formed a bloc, jointly, around one as of theirs who has been "wrongfully" condemned by society."

Indeed. The friends from Ulm Street stepped forward, one after the other, as witnesses at the bar. They made a huge effort to save their comrade's neck. Maurice Clavel waxed lyrical to evoke the complexity of the human heart. The philosopher Jean-Toussaint Desanti pleaded the pacifist fiber of a man obsessed by the American hegemonic will. Pierre Boutang cites as extenuating circumstances his keeping company with "imbeciles" meaning the political personnel of the 4th Republic.

Pâques escaped the firing squad and was condemned to criminal detention in perpetuity. Even after the sentence was pronounced, the Pâques enigma continued to mobilize the alumni network of the École Normale Supérieure. Another school-fellow, the former minister Michel Soulié, who continued to defend Pâques in the press, tried to understand the incomprehensible treason. "I cannot keep myself from thinking that he was especially impelled by the desire to make a little difference in history. It is this ambition, disappointed by an honorable but not earth-shaking career, that I see as the deepest root of his treason."

Epilogue. In 1970, that is to say six years after his sentencing, Pâques got a conditional discharge. This was an exceptional measure of leniency, which he owes to President George Pompidou, Class of 1931, École Normale Supérieure.

The Detergent Gang

The finance inspectors, fortunately, have not infiltrated every industry. Wholesale distribution, light industry and, to a lesser extent, management consulting, have remained for the most part *terra incognita* for the networks.

On these virgin lands where no ENA colonization has made its mark, other brigades, less well-recognized but still very powerful, are at work! The most effective clans are not always the one we may think. Thus, the graduates of HEC (*Hautes études commerciales*, a management and business school), the ESSEC (*École supérieure des sciences économique et commerciales*, similar) and Co Sup do not, contrary to some people's fantasies, have a very solid structure: just an association, a directory, a matchmaking bulletin, nothing more. Some prominent retirees, happy to have come up with a way to pass the time, work away in the shadows. One of them, coming out of the ESSEC, discreetly telephones job recruiters to propose a list of alumni to them as soon as a good position is offered. "But that doesn't go very far," says a headhunter. "It's nothing compared to the extraordinary organization of the Procterians."

Did you say "Procterian"? A "Procterian" is, quite simply, an executive who has taken classes at the famous American multinational, Procter & Gamble. In 1975, a veteran of the house, Mireille Bouisset, launched the "Procterian Club." This brotherhood of ex-P&G'ers, an association of a new kind in France, started with 70 people. Twenty years later it has 450, many of whom have succeeded to build a very handsome career. Thanks to this influential secret society? Not only, they chorus. Solidarity, however, is an integral part of their style.

Procter & Gamble is a little like the Finance Inspectorate of the private sector, with American characteristics and a vocation for marketing. Usually, one gets in after brilliant studies, with the feeling that the company selected you from among the best of your school. Then begins a hard training period in which one learns to conform to the house rules, which leave little to the imagination. Obedience to the twelve commandments concocted by the headquarters in Cincinnati, Ohio (pleasantly known as "the Kremlin," training in productivity, praise of professionalism, and starting at the bottom of the ladder (albeit for only a few months), these are the basic realities of the company.

Before being able to manage the launching of big products like Pampers diapers, Ariel detergent or the cleanser Mr. Clean, the young graduate must start in the trenches. The probationary period strongly resembles that of "making the rounds" with the finance inspectors. It infuses the beings who experience it with a feeling of complicity based on the nostalgia for these years of initiation, which will mark a whole life and will give rise to a vigorous superiority complex.

All the conditions are then met to generate solid career support. For P & G, like the Finance Inspectorate, is one of the best calling cards. And at P & G, as at the Finance Inspectorate, job offers are constantly flowing in — often thanks to former employees.

About 20 Procterians got into the Jacques Vabre company. The marketing director of P & G France, François Steeg, was hired away to launch the coffee brand in France in the 1970's. His first reflex? To recruit among the élite troops in the detergent, diapers and cleansers world. The imitation is so pronounced   that the internal documents, right down to the envelopes, are certified copies of the ones they knew at P & G.

His second move? To entrust the advertising campaign to Bernard Brochand, a P & G veteran who headed off into publicity. Jacques Vabre headquarters had no complaints about this spirit of co-optation, since the advertising executive invented the marketing concept of the "Gringo," which was a success for many years.

When he worked at P & G, Brochand helped launch one of the firm's best-selling products, Ariel, in the company of three other promising young people: Jean-Claude Boulet, Alain Cayzac and Jean-Michel Goudard. One evening, after an already full day of business, the four accomplices went to a small advertising agency on the Champs-Elysée to learn about the trade, still new in France, called "advertising." When he was set to create his own agency, he landed his first accounts among other P & G alums, especially with Lesieur, another hospitable domain for the former detergent men. Jean-Michel Goudard, likewise tempted by the advertising adventure, joined Young and Rubicam, which was managed by his colleague Jean-Claude Boulet. Business went well — thanks to a big advertiser named P & G. A few years later, Goudard assembled his own structure in association with the fourth musketeers from the Ariel episode, Alain Cayzac. They would become the "C" and "G" of the agency RSCG, together with Roux and Séguéla. Jean-Michel Goudard would also pick Bernard Brochand, years later, to advise candidate Chirac during the presidential campaign.

The colonization turned out to be less profitable in the agro-alimentary sector. Early in the 1980's, Pierre Dupasquier, ex-rising star at P & G, became chairman of Gervais-Danone, a subsidiary of BSN and began recruiting from his old fish pond. Very quickly, all the strategic posts were occupied by Procterians, from research and development to sales, distribution and general management. As a rule, this tight a formation is not to everyone's taste. Waiting in ambush was a rival band made up of Colgate veterans (P & G's competitor) who were enraged to see the headquarters monopolized by Procterians.

They did not have to wait for long. Following a falling out with Antoine Riboud, chairman of BSN, Pierre Dupasquier left to join Johnson + Johnson France; they had been offering him the top spot in its French subsidiary for a long time. In a few months, the transfer of the Procterian team from Gervais-Danone to Johnson + Johnson was organized. Colgate rubbed their hands. The openings created by these departures allowed them infiltrate Gervais-Danone.

But what these darlings of marketing like best is the luxury industry. Yesterday in the hands of artisans, today it is in the hands of big companies looking to rationalize the methods and systems and to rely less on intuition.

This was great for the detergent men, and all three factions (P & G, Colgate, and Unilever) fought for the positions. At Christian Dior perfumes, the Procterians seemed to be threatened by the arrival of Patrick Choël from Unilever. But the P & G network took its revenge on the Unilever "gang" at Givenchy, where two of its own, Alain Lorenzo, the chairman, and Gilles Dougoud, Director-France, are now at the helm. On the other hand, Unilever has hoisted its flag at Guerlain, whose president, Christian Lanis, spent all his career inside the manufacturer of Sun, Cif and other boons to the housewife. Only Oréal still resists the attacks of the detergent troops, by training its own marketing geniuses.

In spite of incursions by the competition, the P & G network remains the leader in its category. Unilever and Colgate veterans have imitated their shadowy competitor, and launched clubs. As have the management consultants formerly with Peat Marwick, McKinsey and Arthur Andersen. Similarly, former executives from Rank-Xerox join the Honorix Club. Formed in 1981, this club of 400 leaders in the sector of office automation publishes its own directory and organizes occasional dinner-debates. The decision-makers in food wholesaling, long considered by their former comrades at HEC and elsewhere as vulgar "grocers," have started to organize. When the ENA alumnus Michel Bon was named to head up France Telecom, he remembered his experience as director of Carrefour; and he reckoned that supermarket managers would surely know how to adapt the public company to global competition better than the X-Telecoms who had monopolized the jobs at France Telecom. He therefore named schoolmates from Docks de France and from Carrefour to the top posts for consumer markets and sales management. The alums of the École Polytechnique fear the continuation: the invasion of one their territories by a rival and scorned species. But the Procterians see these attempts as insipid plagiarisms of their initiative. And they may be right.

The Procterian club is so effective that its founder, Mireille Bouisset, has re-tooled herself into a headhunter among the detergent folks. "After creating the club, I worked in a management consulting firm," she says. "I was very often solicited by consultants who asked me whether I knew any Procterians. I often learned afterwards that the aforementioned headhunter had not even had the elegance to mention my name. So I decided to set up my own recruiting firm."

Her clients are not limited to her former colleagues, but those do represent nearly a third of her "market." The others call upon her because of her fabulous network of information on companies. "It is rare that a big company has not, at one time or another, engaged someone from P & G. And that person will always tell me the truth about a company that he knows well; which enables me to give good advice. In twenty years, I have heard so much about what really goes on inside big companies that I sometimes feel like I am managing a confessional."

What creates the strength of this brotherhood is the fidelity to the first professional engagement. When Bouisset goes shopping in a supermarket, she always checks that the shelf displaying the house products has been arranged correctly. If it is not, she puts it into good order. And, of course, she buys only P & G products, except for the dishwasher, because there aren't any. Is she monomaniacal? Not really. Many of them have preserved these astonishing practices twenty years after leaving the multinational. Compared with these phalanxes pro-grammed for life, even the Finance Inspectorate appears to be asleep at the wheel.

Got A Problem? Dial "3615 Krivine"

"You want to get a seat on an overbooked flight, find a bed in top-notch hospital, get your latest book reviewed in a newspaper? Then, dial '3615 Krivine,' and activate the best address book in Paris," jokes the writer Gilles Perrault, old friend and accessory to the head of the Revolutionary Communist League (LCR). Alain Krivine knows every-one. Generations and generations of lawyers, doctors, journalists, ad-vertising executives have passed through the League. But the historical chief of the movement never used his rich contact list for his own ca-reer. He earns $1200 a month and finances his organization and his weekly magazine *Rouge* out of the profits of the printing works estab-lished by SME (the Small and Medium Enterprises agency) in the sub-urbs and directed by the League.

This is a professional trajectory foreign to the usual goals of a fi-nance inspector or a Procterian. The League, however, was an effective and productive school in power, and a seedbed of nomenklaturists par-ticularly at odds with the relations of forces which prevail in the politi-cal sector.

At the time of his militant splendor, Alain Krivine had two associ-ates: Daniel Bensaïd and Henri Weber. The first, a philosophy profes-sor, has remained faithful to the organization. The second has, at the very least, "re-focused" himself. He joined the Socialist party (SP) in 1985, and in 1995 became a Socialist senator. Socialist, that's OK, but senator!?

The increasingly bourgeois nature of the politicians makes them smile, at the League. Some of these comrades have barely recovered from his 50th birthday party, celebrated in 1994 in the studios of AB

Productions. Never would they have believed they might one day drink a glass of champagne at the site where *Hélène et les garçons* and *Premiers baisers* were first shown!

Henri Weber, like many former members of the League who have moved over to the SP, slipped into the wake of Laurent Fabius. These were astonishing conversions, and were at their apogee at the Matignon Hotel between 1984 and 1986. Witness the surprising course of Jean-Paul Besset and Denis Pingaud, two former contributors to the daily newspaper *Rouge* (which had been founded by the League in 1976). In 1984, when he had just joined the SP, Besset received a call from Jean-Gabriel Frédet, director of communications for the new Prime Minister Laurent Fabius. The two men knew each other from *Matin de Paris*. Besset likes a good joke. For him, Fabius was a "Leftist Giscard."[7] Being a realist, he accepted, just like Denis Pingaud and another ex-Trotskyite, Bernard Poulet. Thus in 1985, Besset and Pingaud (alias Ploëch and Séraphin in Trotskyite cover names), found themselves nose to nose with Alain Krivine, who was demonstrating on behalf of New Caledonia in front of the Matignon Hotel.

Socialist recycling does not relate to the LCR alone. While the migration from the extreme left toward the PS has always existed, Lambertists from the Internationalist Communist Party, another Trotskyite dispensary, beat all the records. In 1986, more than 300 former disciples of Pierre Lambert individually decided to join the Socialist party, then directed by Lionel Jospin. Among the defectors were seven leaders of the ICP, including Jean-Christophe Cambadélis, alias "Kostas," Philippe Darriulat, alias "Crimso," Marc Rozenblat, alias "Ibsen," two former presidents of the student union UNEF-ID, Jean Grosset, alias "Saigon," Associate General Secretary of the teachers' union, and the academic Benjamin Stora, alias "Truffaut."

Cambadélis, who holds the highest rank in the Lambertist hierarchy, led the troop and negotiated the "individual" transfers. Shortly after arriving at Solferino, he ran into one of his most intimate old enemies, a long-time affiliate of the rival house, the Revolutionary Communist League. Julien Dray, indeed, had left the RCL, where he directed the student sector under the patronage of Gerard Filoche, and joined the SP in May 1982.

The "Lambertists" and the "Filochards," who already had great militant careers behind them, met in 1973 as students and high-school pupils up in arms against the Debré law. At the time, Jean-Christophe Cambadélis was leading the students of Nanterre. Julien Dray was head of the High School Fight Committees. Belonging to two competing groups, they naturally distrusted each other. So much so that the future deputy from the Essonne would come to suspect the future deputy from the 19th district of Paris of being behind the sabotage of his moped with sugar. A nice atmosphere.

Since then, they have work on the same team, without, however, being able to get along together. In 1980, this not always peaceful coexistence took them to the top of the UNEF-ID, the student union purged of its "Stalinist" elements. The Lambertist became president, the Filochard vice-president. The new organization was formed with financing from *Force ouvrière* (a workers' group), from which the PCI draws the substantial dividends of a cleverly practiced entrism.

The UNEF-ID is a kind of communicating vessel with the young guard of the SP, almost a "school for activists." While Cambadélis took over — successfully — the control of this new apparatus, Dray made one of its auxiliary creations, S.O.S Racism, flourish. Cambadélis joined Jospin, who was drifting until the eve of the 1980's, on the fringes of Pierre Lambert's clique. Dray preferred Fabius, whom Henri Weber already rejoined.

A stroke of luck: only a few months after the Right returned to power, two social earthquakes struck. First came the coed demonstrations against the Devaquet law. The noise began at the University of Villetaneuse, where a certain Isabelle Thomas took note; she was a UNEF-ID and S.O.S Racism militant, and incidentally a protégé of Julien Dray. On this occasion, the comrades polished their art of *agit-prop* more than ever — and successfully. Hundreds of thousands of young people took to the street; the draft law was withdrawn; a minister was forced to quit. Less than two years before the presidential election of 1988, the Socialist opposition was doing well. In the Elysée, General Secretary Jean-Louis Bianco was glad he had some history with the little stars of antiracism.

In thanks, the zealous agitators of the "Mitterrand generation" got their share of "plums" after the re-election of their mentor. Cambadélis was named deputy of the 19th district of Paris, where François Mitterrand had collected nearly 60% of the votes. A golden district, where even a goat (Socialist) had prevailed. Dray just missed out at the State

Secretariat on Youth and Sports, and had to be content with a district in the Essonne (an enviable consolation prize). There he met a recent ally, the young socialist senator Jean-Luc Mélenchon, who came from the rival PCI. Together they founded the "New Socialist School" (NES), intended to bring together those who were "beyond the Trotskyites." One of the first recruits of the NES was not other than Isabelle Thomas. Less fortunate in politics than her friend and mentor Dray, she would be defeated at Seine-Saint-Denis, by Eric Raoult. And so she became an adviser to the Elysée, and got a seat on the Economic and Social Council. In this last body, Harlem Désir, the emblematic president of S.O.S Racism, found a comfortably remunerated ($3,166 a month) sinecure. That is a satisfactory minimum income, but a not very glorious conversion; it caused him to fade from the public memory after a dazzling media apogee. The small band from the winter of 1986 thus dispersed, and crossed the thresholds of the national palaces. And the grandchildren of Leon (Trotsky) thus became, by grace of a presidential election, the spoiled nephews of Mitterrand.

In the Trotskyite galaxy, not everyone had the chance to make his career by belonging to the "Mitterrand generation." Aside from politics, the majority of the former Leftists are massively concentrated in the communications field. "Our basic training consisted, after all, in knowing how to chat people up about anything," explains one veteran who went into journalism. "That is why one finds ex-Trotskyites in the newspapers, television and public relations."

One of the top public opinion institutes, in France as well as in Europe, is managed by a duet of former Leftists. Jean-Marc Lech and Didier Truchot, co-leaders of Ipsos, have retained a libertarian zest in their management style; and activists from Ipsos make up most of their company.

In television, the producer of the *Brûleurs de l'Histoire*" on France 3, Patrick Rotman, as well as the host Michel Field and Hervé Chabalier, the owner of the agency Capa, learned the basics in the Trotskyite movement. Behind them, more anonymous, are many journalists who had the same experience. "I started to do radio thanks to militants who had helped the FLN during the Algerian War. They knew Hervé Bourges, who was at the time chairman of Radio-France International, and he hired me," says a former teacher who is today a journalist at France 2. "Generally, the Trotskyite network follows you all your life. I receive at least one telephone call a month soliciting me for some professional favor. When I can do something, I never hesitate. We don't hold banquets, but our solidarity exceeds the simple circle of people whom one knows. There are all those whom one recognizes, out of respect for a shared past, without ever having met them."

In the newspaper industry also, the Trotskyite concentration is rather high. At *Le Monde*, Georges Marion and Edwy Plenel, who were for a long time the company's sensational investigative reporters, learned their trade at *Rouge*. When Plenel was named editorial director of the daily newspaper, he called in as editor-in-chief Jean-Paul Besset, a friend from *Rouge* with whom he continued to socialize since the time when Besset worked for Fabius. And then there was Olivier Biffaud, political journalist and vice-president of the board, and Laurent Mauduit, leader of the economic service.

At *Libération*, the "Maoist cell" from the early days lost ground, in favor of other clans derived from the Left. The subject seems to be taboo, if one judges by a "right of reply" sent to the newspaper *L'Évènement du Jeudi* in 1989 by Dominique Pouchin and Jean-Michel Helvig, then editor and chief of the political service of *Libé*. He said, "The five and a half lines that are devoted to us make it sound as though the hiring at *Libération* could be related to former service in the Trotskyite movement. This is manifestly false and deeply defamatory."

Defamatory! Such indignation over a form of professional mutual support that is altogether rather innocent.

Such modesty is more understandable on behalf of former members of the extreme Right. Whereas the Leftist sympathies of youth can almost be displayed on a calling card, post-pubescent Fascism is a ball and chain — so much so that the ambitious ones who were too involved in the movement Occident had to take certain secret passages that brought them closer to an honorable political image — with considerable success, for some of them.

The Club of Repentant Bruisers

On January 12, 1967, in front of the university canteen at Mont-Saint-Aignan, in the suburbs of Rouen, Leftist students were distributing leaflets calling for peace in Vietnam. A commando from the extreme Right clique Occident, composed of about 30 people, set off for a punitive expedition. Nothing very exceptional, considering how frequent were the frictions on campus. But this time the young people wore helmets, and hit hard — so hard that some of the leaflet distributors ended up in the hospital.

Among the fourteen Occident militants apprehended were Alain Madelin, Gérard Longuet and Patrick Devedjian. They did not know, then, that they would find themselves a few years later on the benches of the National Assembly, respectable parliamentarians of the most traditional Right.

The ambitious extremists who formed the hard core of Occident in the 1960's had to start by ridding themselves of a bad reputation, which they had acquired by fist and club. The channels that they explored, in seeking to renovate their reputations, are like "career laundering," the way we have "money laundering." They are repentant and respectable in the eyes of their new comrades, but to their former friends who remained faithful to the three "O's", (Ordre, Occident and Oriflammes), they are dreadful renegades.

That violent day in 1967 marked a turning in their career. Is this the same Alain Madelin who, a year later, organized the "Liberal-Thought Weeks"? Financed by business leaders, especially the Parisian branch of the UIMM (Union of Metallurgical and Mining Industries), the program was managed by Claude Harmel, alias Guy Lemonnier. During the Occupation, Harmel had been an associate of George Albertini, himself Marcel Déat's right hand man at the same time.[8] After the war, he continued to support Albertini, who had become a pillar of a network specialized in the anti-Communist fight.

How could one of the leaders of an extravagantly nationalist movement, who suggested (in Occident's bulletin) that "what we have to destroy is cosmopolitanism and liberalism," perform such a dazzling conversion just a few months later? "It is me who initiated Madelin to liberalism," Claude Harmel acknowledges today. He doesn't mind that he was able to detect in the quarrelsome student a promising political future. Another disciple of Albertini, Nicolas Tandler, member of Occident-Université, introduced the two. The students met along the boulevard Saint-Germain, where both the Institute of Social History (created by the anti-Stalinian Boris Souvarine) and the Higher Institute of Labor are located. The latter was Harmel's institute; he would provide activities and emoluments to this impetuous and extremist youth.

Once inside the walls financed by the least progressive business stalwarts, the future minister would remain there until 1978, when he was first elected to the National Assembly. Thus he initiated a true "channel" for his former comrades looking to "go respectable." First was Christian de Bongain, alias Xavier Raufer, journalist, sociologist and specialist in terrorism.

When Harmel launched the Higher Institute of Labor (STI) in 1971, whom did he choose to get things running? De Bongain-Raufer, first General Secretary of the Institute. Independent of the Institute of Social History but housed in the same buildings, STI became the principal employer of the young Madelin and Raufer. The latter took care of management matters, while the former gave courses and conferences for companies on the various Leftist movements, which he knew well, from a certain point of view. The difference between Trotskyites and Maoists, their methods of action, their penetration of the various trade unions and how they infiltrated companies — Madelin became a valued "Leftist-ologist,"and companies from Peugeot to Liquid Air, Péchiney to Aérospatiale, remunerated STI very well for its science on the "class enemies." This adventure lasted until 1978, when Madelin, deputy of Ile-et-Vilaine, resigned from his functions as manager of the bulletin published by the Higher Institute of Labor.

Meanwhile, the future minister was making the school. Since his beginnings in Albertini's orbit, he had been lending a helping hand to another militant of Occident: Hervé Novelli. Married, father of a family, Novelli had a hard time paying the bills every month. To help bridge the gap, he would run the duplicating machine that was used to print the anti-Communists leaflets for Albertini. "Then, through my intermediary he got into the Chamber of the Iron and Steel Industry," remembers Claude Harmel. The young father however left the blast furnaces to make a career under the gilt of the national palaces. In 1986, when Madelin was named Minister of Industry, Novelli became his chief assistant. Whom could you trust more, to keep things under control and to manage the secret funds as well as possible, than a former comrade from the militancy?

Before being elected, in 1993, as UDF deputy of the Indre-et-Loire, Hervé Novelli crossed the desert comfortably. Having hardly packed his ministerial bags, in May 1988, he joined the financial group Drexel-Burnham-Lambert in the capacity of vice-president "Europe." Had the iron and steel industry allowed a virtuoso of the financial markets to escape, an under-appreciated "golden boy"? No; more prosaically, the president of Drexel, Pierre Rochon, was the brother-in-law of Gerard

Longuet. And while Longuet preferred the training given by the ENA over that of the Albertini house, he too had given up a fine career as a rabble-rouser to the right of the far Right.

Gérard Longuet also benefited from the hospitality of his brother-in-law at Drexel between the two cohabitations. Drexel-Burnham-Lambert, the bank that was indicted so many times for insider trading, was thus also a back base of the "Leo's gang."

Alain Madelin was the first of the batch to be hired under the colors of the independent Republicans, where he organized training courses built on his experience gained at the Higher Institute of Labor. He practically never made use of his lawyer's diploma. He pleaded one case before an industrial tribunal, for the GIM (the Paris area Group of Metallurgical Industries), principal backer of Albertini and Co. But he didn't miss the court room atmosphere. He fell in love with the liberal economic theories that he defended within the ALEPS (Association for Economic Freedom and Social Progress), another of Harmel's creations that had a certain appeal for some of the business leaders.

With Madelin's active assistance, this association went beyond innocent conferences on Communist counter-propaganda. Since one cannot spend years in Albertini's entourage without learning some invaluable lessons in the art of manipulation, Madelin set out to try a somewhat specialized niche, that of the scathing attack during elections. At *Est et ouest* (*East and West*), which specializes in anti-Communism, it had been routine since the Fifties to produce broadsides that purported to expose misdeeds and to distribute them to candidates during election campaigns. The young lawyer pushed the limits a few notches further. In April, 1974, while the presidential campaign was in full swing and Valéry Giscard d'Estaing and François Mitterrand were neck and neck, a fake daily newspaper appeared, entitled *France-Matin*. Generously printed in three million copies on the presses of the newspaper *Nice-Matin*, the general idea consisted in frightening the reader as to what would await the country if Mitterrand were elected. Projecting an imaginary vision of January 9, 1975 in a France become socialist, the lead article said, "The President of the Republic, François Mitterrand, has decreed rationing as of Monday. Sugar: 2 kilos per person. Vegetable oil: 1 liter. . ."

What a way to give France the chills. The articles were not signed, but one could suspect who was behind it all. This political fiction was manufactured by a little company that has since disappeared — SERVICE (Society for visual study and research in printing, composition and publishing). The identity of its shareholders and leaders is not an inconsequential matter; they all belong to the extreme Right movement, and the majority of them to "United Front," where Alain Robert and his friends got together after the dissolution of the "New Order" in June 1973.

If Alain Madelin was looking to become respectable, why, one may wonder, would he take the risk of generating such farcical prose in *France-Matin*? Certainly not out of a puerile or prankish impulse. More simply, because it can be highly beneficial to attract the good graces of the leaders at the outset of a political career. Let us not forget that behind *France-Matin* stood ALEPS, which provided its first political financing for young candidates to Madelin; among the generous donors was the chairman of the Parly 2 commercial center.

Still faithful to Madelin in 1993, ALEPS contributed to getting him reinstalled in the sumptuous buildings of Avenue Iéna. This fidelity is reciprocated, since just after he was ousted from the Juppé government, in August 1995, the former Finance Minister would reserve his first public appearance for "Liberal Thought Week," in Avignon.

To the Extreme Right of the Father

"Albertini House," under the wing of Claude Harmel, thus built a very effective network of career re-tooling that gave added life to the UDF. The RPR also assembled a discreet recruitment service managed by Charles Pasqua.

In 1979, at 30 avenue de Messina, not far from the Monceau Park, some old activists from Occident, the New Order and GUD (the Union-Defense Group, created after the dissolution of Occident, at the end of 1968) joined forces. They took a scientific approach to the challenge of preparing Jacques Chirac's candidature for the 1981 presidential election. Pasqua provided Avenue Messina with imaginative and very professional élite troops: two Sciences Po graduates, Jean-Jacques Guillet and William Abitbol, who seemed inseparable since their time at Occident.

That was when they met Pierre Pasqua, Charles' only son, with whom they share the same hard-Right convictions. This friendship from their student days had enabled them to progress within the RPR by the most reliable way there is: the family vector. Once the two ambitious young men were introduced into the house of the father, the doors of the RPR opened wide.

Before becoming, respectively, an opinion polls specialist and the future Interior Minister's designated ghost-writer, Guillet and Abitbol had, in spite of their youth, rendered other services to Gaullist movement. They organized, for example, some powwows for the UDR in 1973. That's proof that of both brains and brawn! But they mastered their trade, communication, from the inventor of political marketing in France, Michel Bongrand.

Dissecting public opinion polls, dreaming up slogans for Chaban's 1974 campaign, Abitbol and Guillet learned a lesson: it's better to be on the winner's side. But winning requires a method. It was most opportune that Guillet founded a public opinion company, Index-Opinion, that put out a never-ending stream of surveys that were favorable to Chirac.

"Boosting" Chirac was alright, but denting Giscard's image was better. The technique of the journalistic counterfeit that had served the "citizen candidate" Giscard so well in 1974 was, this time, used against him. Young communication specialists around Charles Pasqua came up with an anonymous booklet that would be distributed in more than 30,000 copies; it was called *The Kremlin Candidate* — a reminder of Mitterand's irony on "the little telegraphist" from Moscow.

The shock troops gathered around Charles Pasqua also included, at that time, a comrade of his son Pierre, coming from the same background: Joel Gali-Papa. He had known Charles Pasqua since he was 18 years old, and liked to present himself as his "spiritual son." After May, 1981, Joel Gali-Papa helped launch a small Pasquaian group that was savagely anti-Socialist, dubbed "Solidarity and Freedom." The initiative hardly thrilled certain leaders of the RPR, who saw this as the resurgence of a little "SAC," that service of civic action, in whose murky activities Pasqua excelled, officially between 1962 and 1969. Their fears, in truth, were not completely unfounded, for in the wake of "Solidarity and Freedom" one could find old OAS people like the former deputy of Algiers Pierre Lagaillarde, recycled in the SAC, and the former Occident militant Gerard Ecorcheville and his brother-in-law Alain Robert, who looked after its administrative secretariat.

Robert, founder of the GUD, gradually moved toward the center after the disappointing experience of the PFN (Parti des Forces nou-velles, or Party of the New Forces), of which he had been a founder. In 1981, he and some of his comrades threw in their lots with the CNI (Center National des indépendents), an old party of notables who were often somnolent and seldom up to speed on Parisian intrigues.

Quite handy, this CNI — when the established republican Right considers one to be a pestilence. The leaders of this declining party, nostalgic for their great leader Antoine Pinay, had little choice but to accept the input of the new activists. The PFN careerists, worn out with exploiting the relations of forces, knew it well. So they infiltrated, like the Left. The CNI was already the presentable Right. Robert would take a few more years before officially joining his mentor at the RPR.

In 1986, Chirac's appointment in Matignon, and especially Pasqua's at the Interior Ministry, marked the hour of Socialist promo-tions. Named a national deputy at the formation of the RPR in 1986, Robert became cabinet adviser to the Minister for Public Security, Pan-draud, before being propelled to the party central committee in 1987.

But his irresistible rise ran into a serious obstacle: the universal vote, which obstinately refused him a seat at the National Assembly. Since infiltration suits his style so well, Robert quickly moved ahead and in 1989 took the MNEL (Mouvement national des élus locaux, or National Movement of Local Councillors) by storm, for the benefit of Charles Pasqua. Because it covers more than 300,000 elected officials in France, the immense majority of which are apolitical (and the re-mainder clearly on the Right), the MNEL represents an enviable local base for shifting from ideas to action when necessary. For a time, the MNEL leadership even had the added charm of being a family business, since Robert was assisted there by his brother-in-law Gérard Ecorche-ville.

As for Jean-Jacques Guillet, his path never deviated from that of his godfather, whom he followed to the Interior Ministry between 1986 and 1988 before moving to the Senate as Secretary General of the RPR group until 1993. A prudent man, he made an effort to diversify his ac-tivities since 1982; he even headed up (without much enthusiasm) a "temp work" company. Curiously, this one, just like "Index-Opinion," the Pasquaian public opinion institute, had been located at 16, rue Clé-ment-Marot, in the 8th arrondissement of Paris — just Abitbol's profes-sional affiliates (he was working at the same time at communication, publicity and audio-visual production).

And as luck never strikes just once, 14, rue Clément-Marot, next door, had for a long time been the site of an investment firm that was liquidated in 1995 and of which one of the administrators was none other than Pierre Pasqua, son of Charles.

Flanked this small band, Pasqua certainly ran a risk: that of marking himself too openly on the Right. Perhaps it was to clear himself, in turn, of any suspicion that he diversified his own networks. Jean-Claude Barreau, ex-ecclesiastic, former adviser to François Mitterrand in the Elysée, joined him as advisor on immigration questions. Roland Castro, an ex-Maoist, architect and designer of the Mitterandian suburbs, was recruited to humanize the rabbit warrens of the Hauts-de-Seine. As for the dentist Patrick Gaubert, a member of Licra and president of the association DAVID (To Decide, and Act with Vigilance for Israel and the Diaspora), he was responsible within the Interior Minister's cabinet for leading the fight against racism and anti-Semitism.

When it comes to careers, the Pasqua connection does not seem to be quite so gratifying for the old members of Occident as that which passed through the "House of Albertini" and the independent Republicans in the 1970's. For every Patrick Devedjian, who found his political autonomy in the RPR, how many other vassals were condemned to eternal rallying or to repudiation!

Chapter 5

GETTING RICH

It was the enigmatic Groupe Clemenceau, an anonymous gathering of Freemasons, that started things; they denounced the seizure of
property in the early 1990's by "vultures and the envious." "The only
solidarity that exists," they stated in a memo intended for internal use,
"is that of racketeers, whom one finds more and more often." A terrible
assertion, whereas no "case" had yet been made public. Who were the
defendants? Brothers. Was Freemasonry no longer what it once was?

On September 7, 1995, the Japanese tourists who were crossing
the lobby of the hotel Sofitel Saint-Jacob in Paris witnessed a curious
spectacle that their tour operator had not mentioned in the program.
Commedia dell'arte? Street theater? Men of respectable age, in ties and
dark suits, were screaming at each other, gesticulating and even coming
to blows in Saint-Jacob Square, next to the hotel.

The 850 delegates from the Lodges of the Grand Orient were holding their annual convention. These established notables had to elect
the 33 members of the Council of the Order, the executive body, before
the latter could designate the Grand Master. Since the foundation of
this noble institution, in the year of Our Lord 1773, no one had ever seen
such a fight. "Sell-out!" "Scum!" The insults rained down, whistles and
gibes filled the air. The "supervisors," charged with ensuring proper
conduct, were overwhelmed, even the "Terrible Brother" could not in-

tervene.

The dispute seemed to be a dark backroom quarrel. Approved by 80% of the assembly, the report of the outgoing Grand Master, Patrick Kessel, was somewhat removed from the accustomed spirituality of such a coterie: "In this house there are definitely some elements with the manners of hooligans — what a collection of jealousy, hatred, and mediocrity!" This first offensive round was succeeded by a second, equally feverish: Kessel, although he had the backing of the members of the Council of the Order, was blackballed by the 850 deputies who represent to some extent the Parliament of the Grand Orient.

The crisis was profound. "The Grand Orient has become some kind of Spanish tavern, where any opinion is valid, except, of course, ideas from the extreme Right," a former member of the Council of the Order commented. "Since the defense of secularity and the Republic are no longer our common glue, everyone can join our group, including racketeers. Many masons are getting more and more tired of finding their brothers regularly mentioned in the newspapers, under the heading of corruption and fraud."

Indeed, there was the Urba affair, in which several Freemasons played leading roles, from the founder, Guy Marti, to the "manager," Gérard Monate, not to mention the former treasurers of the SP André Laignel and Henri Emmanuelli. But that was nothing compared to the SAGES case. The president-founder of this den, Reyt, was an old Adjunct Grand Master of the Grand Orient as journalists were quick to recall, in evocatively titled articles: "Reyt, Peddler of Influence" (*Libération*[1]), "He Who Brings Scandal" (*L'Evènement du jeudi*[2]), "A Certain Mr. Reyt" (*L'Express*[3]). The death-blow came from François Mitterrand, who scoffed in front of some journalists about "the little clan of Masonic henchmen." To avoid making trouble for his "henchmen," reasonably enough, Reyt resigned from the Grand Orient. But the damage had been done.

Once Reyt was unmasked, certain "brothers" called on the Council to respond. "How can we claim to be working toward the moral improvement of humanity when, if you take some of us for examples, it seems that we demonstrate the opposite through corruption, breach of trust, the trading of favors, all the things that we pride ourselves in fighting?" Thus railed an Grenoble-based architect of the GO in an impassioned letter to his hierarchy.

How could they tell him he was wrong? Since its first steps, Free-masonry had been functioning more or less as a network, but for the better, not for the worst. In the early Middle Ages, the builders of ca-thedrals invented the trade-guild to transmit from generation to gen-eration the secret techniques that make it possible to erect architec-tural wonders. The name "Freemason" came from the English, and des-ignated a mason free to go from one building site to another without any constraint. As for the "lodge," the basic unit of current masonry which must have at least seven members to be recognized, it originally indicated the hut where the companions stored their tools and held their meetings. In the 18th century, this professional masonry disap-peared. It was replaced by associations where the issue is no longer the construction of buildings but the construction of an ideal society ac-cording to the plans of the Great Architect of the Universe.

France counts today nearly 100,000 brothers divided between seven great obediences. Aside from one female lodge and three mixed lodges, three principal obediences compete. The Grand Orient of France (39,000 members), agnostic and rather markedly Leftist, made a name for itself in the defense of republican secularity. The Grand Lodge of France (23,000 members) and the Grand French National Lodge (18,000 members), both resulting from a scission from the Grand Orient and more markedly on the Right, claim a certain spirituality.

A special edition of *Humanisme*[4], the Grand Orient's magazine, de-fines Freemasonry as "primarily a philanthropic, philosophical and pro-gressive institution, that has as a goal the search for truth, the study of morals and the practice of solidarity."

A vast program? For some, it is especially characterized by its third plank. And why not? By tradition, a "hospitaller" works in each lodge — a kind of social assistant at the service of the rest of the group. "He is called that because, in the 18th century," explains an initiate of the GO, "he would visit patients at their bedsides, to help them and to give news from the 'bro's.'" Today, he is the one who manages the "widow's chest," that is, the collection box that is passed around at the end of each meeting and that is used to give a boost to anybody who is in difficulty in the lodge. It is the bond between the Masonic life and the layman's life."

In the same way, the old Masonic orphanage, which covers the schooling expenses of the children of missing masons, has been in ser-vice at the Grand Orient since 1862. To avoid placing this indiscreet wording on the checks that are distributed, the institution has been renamed "Youth Solidarity."

Crisis obliges; the brothers of all obediences have set up a common commission, the "Commission E;" E as in "employment." "We were dismayed to note, a few years ago, that there were as many unemployed among us as elsewhere," says a lodge president. "Since then, on Saturday mornings, unemployed Freemasons started to come in with their résumés. Freemason headhunters and specialists in video training give them advice and try to place them. In the event of success, the recruit must sign a protocol and engage never to reveal that his employer is a Freemason nor to put him in danger because of the Masonic bond."

This employment agency, however, is not so effective as one might hope, since it settles only approximately one third of the cases that are brought to its attention. Therefore, the GLNF bailed out, to found its own "agency," which it claims has been doubly effective. Admittedly, the task is facilitated by the élitist recruitment of this obedience which hunts for chairmen more readily than for office workers.

Territories

"The Grand Orient does not have unlimited resources. Consequently, priorities must be set. Solidarity must initially apply to brothers of the obedience." This internal circular, written by the National Commission of Masonic Solidarity, seriously relativizes the principle of solidarity towards one's neighbor. Masons give, but primarily to masons. That was the case at Vaison-la-Romaine, where the disaster victims who were brothers were helped first by the obediences. The ambiguity of this concept of mutual aid can quickly turn into co-optation, to favoritism and the monopolization of jobs in some sectors where Freemasonry's foundations were "cast in concrete" long ago.

An unexpected chosen terrain, out of view of the general public, is the commercial courts. These jurisdictions are the only ones in French law where voluntary judges sit who were elected by their peers — industrialists and tradesmen. Created in 1563 by Michel de l'Hospital, they are governed by immutable rules and customs, which a written charter brings to the attention of every newcomer. As in masonry, its precepts impose upon the judges a duty of mutual aid, not only in fulfilling their judicial offices, but also beyond the doors, not of the temple, but of the court. As in masonry, the use of "*tu*" (the familiar, not formal, forms of address) is the norm. As in masonry, dress and decorum hold an important place in the communal life. The magistrates are invited in writing not only to wear their official garb during legal ceremonies, but also to wear the gown "with medals" during official dinners. As in masonry, again, the "reunions" held at the "Magistrates Club" are governed by a highly codified ceremony. The handbook of the perfect judge explains at precisely what moment to rise when the president or the vice-president enters the dining room. Moreover, it indicates that the "rump," the last one elected in the last promotion, must illustrate "by remarks that are of good taste" the life of the day's patron saint before starting the meal.

As in masonry, especially, the commercial courts have their "incidents." One official liquidator was sent to jail in Nice, another in Nanterre. Three magistrates from Bobigny, including a chamber president, were put on trial, suspected having supported one their peers during a business liquidation. Associations of victims of the commercial courts are starting to pop up here and there across France, to denounce, rightly or wrongly, agreements that have been made to the detriment of business directors who have fallen on hard times.

In addition to having far more fraternal bonds than average, the commercial courts meet many conditions that encourage occult networks to thrive in their midst. "The elections are organized in a rather Soviet fashion," says a business lawyer. "You don't have a chance, if you have not been 'presented' by the Chamber of Commerce, where the masons are often very active also."

Companies have long understood that it was in their interest to deploy one of their own leaders into this voluntary activity rather than enriching "a judge," explains an agent, "who never really forgets where he comes from. He has a tendency, even involuntary, to interpret the laws in a way that supports his branch of industry."

Banks and insurance companies are thus happy to retain the services of a collaborator whom they continue to remunerate, except if the elected official is retired. And they underwrite the frequent travel expenses when the magistrates organize, as tradition requires, a collective escapade in the company of their wives.

In this atmosphere that encourages conflicts of interest, the Masonic bond adds to the opportunities for negotiation and back-room agreements. In the small world that revolves around the commercial courts, everyone knows it, but nobody or almost nobody will talk about it. "That applies only to a small number of cases, but often the most important ones," this business lawyer continues. "There are what is called the 'hot items,' which are remote-controlled from Day One toward 'good interlocutors.' The instructions are simple. From the start, the head of the enterprise must have in his team an influential Freemason, who contacts the president of the court or one of his assistants. This one 'advises' a lawyer, who can be remunerated outside the usual channels, with part of the difference going who knows where. . . . Thanks to this system, the judge is well chosen, the advisor also, and the receiver even more so."

When his legal and financial situation started to deteriorate significantly, Bernard Tapie applied this prescription to the letter. The former deputy from Gardanne, if he is not a Freemason himself, has always known how to make the best possible use of the facilities offered by fraternal connections. "I was astonished by certain interventions," the UDF deputy of Charente-Maritime Dominique Bussereau (rapporteur of the two commissions charged with examining the possibility of removing Tapie's parliamentary immunity) confided to *Le Point* (3/12/94). "I saw networks being set up. Among the most active in his favor, there were certain Rightist Freemasons and an RPR deputy close to Pasqua." The deputy in question, the former examining magistrate Alain Marsaud, was also a Freemason and he had already intervened in 1992 in the settlement of the dispute between Tapie and the former deputy from the Hauts-de-Seine Georges Tranchant. This latter accused the hyperactive Town Minister of having hidden certain receipts from NAVS, the joint venture which they had created for importing Toshiba products into France. He filed suit and the investigation was conducted by judge Edith Boizette, who indicted Tapie and forced him to resign from the government, revealing that indeed over $5 million paid by Toshiba had been dissimulated by Tapie. The case stopped there. Georges Tranchant withdrew his complaint in return for a compensation of $2.5 million. In the background, two Freemasons conducted the negotiations: Alain Marsaud, close to the RPR of the Hauts-de-Seine, and Francis Szpiner, who was then Tapie's lawyer.

At the end of 1994, in the episode that pitted him against his two principal creditors, Crédit Lyonnais (1.6 billion francs, or $267 million) and the public treasury (400 million FF, $67 million), Tapie again played the Masonic card. He chose as his lawyer Bernard Lagarde, an habitué of the Paris Commercial Court where he had long been an advisor to the administrators of property under litigation. This appears to be a highly profitable activity, since Lagarde was able to buy Thierry Le Luron's very luxurious villa in Saint-Tropez.

Another angle of attack exploited by Bernard Tapie was the President of the Paris Commercial Court, Michel Rouger, who was also allured by the charms of speculative friendships. In May 1992, the two men's first meeting, initiated by Tapie, related to his disagreement with Tranchant, for which he sought a way out via the commercial court. A year and a half later, another interview took place where the deputy informed Rouger of his fears concerning the arrival of Jean Peyrelevade as the head of Crédit Lyonnais: this alumnus of the École Polytechnique did not belong to any of his networks; he was not only liable to cut the feeding tubes that kept the Tapie system going, but also to require accounts. It was Rouger again who received an S.O.S. during the summer of 1994, when the deputy *cum* businessman's furniture collection was seized under conservatory title by Crédit Lyonnais. The two men met informally three more times, sometimes in the presence of Jean Veil, the lawyer of Crédit Lyonnais.

The Paris Commercial Court's first decision, November 30, 1994, was heavily in favor of Tapie. Against the public prosecutor's (district attorney's) demands, which called for the immediate liquidation of most of his companies — a decision which immediately would have involved his disqualification as a deputy — the judges decided for legal rectification and required neither the sale of his private mansion on the rue des Saints-Pères, nor that of the yacht Phocéa. As a consequence, Tapie remained eligible for public office. He could still wangle his way into the town hall of Marseilles and, why not, the presidency of the Republic. Didn't he win 12% in the recent European elections?

This leniency caused much comment. Tapie in the presidential race would split the Left, which would have to find another, more presentable, candidate. *Le Point* even posed this embarrassing question, on its cover for December 3, 1994: "Just Who Is Protecting Tapie?" The weekly magazine reported remarks that suggested the interested party to be President Rouger: "I have the whole government behind me! If you do not believe me, you have only to call Sarkozy!"

Was he bluffing? History, and the protagonists, remain evasive. On the other hand, a few weeks later, the commercial court turned in a second judgment, this time very cruel for Bernard Tapie. His bankruptcy, and that of his wife, were ordained. He would have to exchange politics for cinema, where ineligibility and prohibition do not exist. "This story proves that the networks operate fully when there is a favorable political context, and if no powerful will resists them," comments one who is familiar with the case. "Jean Peyrelevade's determination — he was very bold, and he kept up the media coverage — got the better of Tapies' initiatives, however astute and well-prepared they may have been."

But certain bastions of French society were conquered and defended by the brothers well before Tapie had the first inkling of financial troubles. "From 1923 until the beginning of the 1980's, all the postal directors were Masons," says the journalist-writer Jacques Duquesne. "The president of the Masonic brotherhood of the postal and telecommunications authorities was always consulted on important nominations. After Mitterrand's election, he wrote directly to the Elysée to complain that the new leader was not an initiate. . . ."

Traditionally, the public services represent private preserves of the Masons. And of course education, of which all the ministers were Freemasons until André Marie in 1954; but also the electricity and gas companies, Air France, the police force, social security and some public banks.

Who could believe that at Crédit Foncier, Freemasons took the place of finance inspectors? When the establishment found itself in virtual bankruptcy in spring 1996, it turned out that the Masonic bonds were at least as good as those from the ENA. When Georges Bonin was named governor of the CFF in 1982, he was quick to promote to the strategic post of General Secretary one of his "Masonic superiors," Marcel Gontard. Howls from Laurent Fabius' office in Matignon did not make him yield. Some murmured that Gontard had supported Bonin's nomination in the lodge. Fourteen years later, Crédit Foncier, over which the two men reigned for more than a decade, posted losses of 1.83 billion. With huge investments in hazardous real estate deals, the establishment did not anticipate the crisis nor adapt to deregulation. The Bonin-Gontard duo is certainly not the only one responsible for this rout; their colleagues in the finance inspectorate also share the blame. Nevertheless, they imposed on Crédit Foncier an adventurous management style guided by arbitrary considerations.

More traditional, the sector of mutual benefit insurance companies, generated by the Masonic ideal, remains a powerful bastion that has successfully fought to preserve its prerogatives. In 1982, Michel Baroin, former Grand Master of the Grand Orient and head of the GMF (Guaranteed Mutual Fund of Civil Servants) was concerned that the nationalization of credit would also affect his banking subsidiary, the BCCM. To escape nationalization, Baroin worked his Masonic networks around the brother Jean Garrec, Secretary of State for the public sector, and Pierre Mauroy at Matignon. There, Jean-Michel Rosenfeld, former adviser of the Order to the Grand Orient, was particularly useful. After many adventures, Baroin won his cause. It is true that the BCCM was managing, at that time, accounts that were important to the Socialist party, including those of the design office URBA-GRACCO.

In May, 1981, a serious appetite for power was awakened among many brothers of the Grand Orient whose Leftist labels had hitherto had been an impediment. But these enthusiastic candidates were so outspoken that their Grand Master Roger Leray was constrained to calm them. He was alerted by Guy Penne (a former member of the Council of the Order in charge of African Affairs under Mitterrand), that the Elysée, Matignon and the ministries were collapsing under the deluge of offers of service. On July 16, 1981, he sent a confidential letter to members of the Council of the Order: "It must be understood that such mail is troublesome in more ways than one, if only because it is written in Masonic terms but is received by profane secretaries."

For his part, the brother Charles Hernu, Minister for Defense, an initiate of both to the Grand Lodge of France and the Grand Orient (he is a member of the Locarno Lodge, like Guy Penne), was also irritated by this sudden exposure, sent all his lodges a letter reminding them to retain their reserve.

These warnings were ineffective. Among the most resounding incidents that tainted the Mitterrand years, at least four made a display of Masonic solidarity that did not coincide, needless to say, with their public goal of promoting the general interest.

Family Scenes

Thursday, April 24, 1986: Yves Chalier, the former aristocrat who was chief assistant to the Minister for Cooperation Christian Nucci, was called in to the Elysée by the adviser on African Affairs, Guy Penne.

Upon his arrival, this débonnaire alumnus of the Saint-Cyr military academy could see that the atmosphere was not as friendly as usual. The Secretary was scarcely civil. The adviser was slow to receive him. In the office, a virtual court was waiting, made up of Penne, Jean-Christophe Mitterrand, and Christian Nucci, as well as a notary, Gerard Voitey, Esq.

The Carrefour Development incident was threatening to blow up. Chalier was blamed by his former friends. "I really felt," he would confide later on, "that I was facing a Masonic tribunal where the brothers were reproaching me for conduct, the details of which they had, nevertheless, been following step by step since Day One." Fraudulent invoices, remuneration of inside agents, purchase of weapons for local police forces, the whole paid for under the cover of the African summit in Burundi; the purchase of a château and some apartments that were not really "for the company's use;" the "Carrefour Development Company" financed anything and everything, for the greatest personal benefit of its principal protagonists.

All Freemasons, all brothers, until the hour of reckoning. There was Chalier, who entered into Masonry by family tradition. In the 1970's, he belonged to the Victor-Schoelcher lodge of the Grand Orient, where he met various political figures like André Labarrère and André Rossinot. Chalier integrated himself into this new universe without difficulty and became a venerable leader of the lodge. At the time, his future boss, Christian Nucci, was still profane. He was initiated only in 1984. . . at the Victor-Schoelcher lodge. Does the chief assistant derive from his Masonic precedence some kind of informal and covert authority over his minister? He would always deny it. But, to divert public funds via the "Carrefour Development Company," it was Chalier who acted, while Nucci derived secondary benefits.

Associated with Chalier in this Franco-African intrigue, Marie-Danielle Bahisson was also part of the "family." Former chief assistant to "sister" Yvette Roudy and an initiate, like her, to the Women's Grand Lodge of France, she herself was designated by the association to acquire the château of Ortie, officially intended for the eduation of African executives. The architect paid by Carrefour to restore the famous château was none other than a friend of "brother" Guy Penne. The notary in charge of the transaction, Gerard Voitey (whom one finds in the "Masonic" court of the Elysée), is a member of the Grand Orient of France, associated with Marie-Danielle Bahisson. If "Carrefour" means "crossroads," this was definitely a traffic jam of Freemasons. Jacques Delebois, the police chief who (under the orders of Charles Pasqua) supervised the manufacture of counterfeit passport that allowed Chalier to flee to Brazil was also a member of the club. Moreover, he was a member of the Victor-Schoelcher lodge when, in the early 1980's, the indelicate chief assistant was the venerable leader.

Ironically, Nucci, the most junior Mason, benefited from a convenient amnesty while the ex-venerable Chalier had to serve a prison sentence.

The same fraternal environment presided for many years over the fate of the GMF (Guaranteed Mutual Fund of the Civil Servants) and of its former subsidiary, the FNAC. This small insurance empire thrived under the wing of Michel Baroin, whose entry into Masonry was no small matter. If one believes the *Mémoires* of prefect Jean-Emile Vié, former director of Renseignements généraux (French equivalent of the FBI), this future Grand Master of the Grand Orient was an apprentice working under cover. "The Renseignements généraux also practices infiltration. My greatest success in this field was the surveillance of the Grand Orient of France through Michel Baroin. This young commissioner had been thrown out of the DST (French equivalent of the CIA) . . . I had accepted his assignment within the management of Renseignements généraux and had assigned him the mission of monitoring the Grand Orient . . . Michel Baroin thus belonged to the Grand Orient and, as long as I was a director of the RG, correctly fulfilled the mission that I had entrusted to him. I was thunderstruck by his election in the capacity of Grand Master of the Grand Orient of France in 1977."[2] When Vié's book was published in 1988, Baroin was no longer there to respond. He had died, one year earlier, in an airplane crash.

Meanwhile, he had led a meteoric career in the Masonic galaxy. His rise to the Grand Orient enabled him to take charge of the GMF, the jewel of French insurance companies.

"From his past life as a man of information, Baroin retained some after-effects," says an old lodge-mate. "Alongside the official personnel chart, composed of a traditional management team with some non-Masons as alibis, a parallel hierarchy existed. Its members, who took their orders directly from Baroin, constituted a covert staff that handled all the 'sensitive' investments." The same form of management prevailed at the FNAC. When it was bought, François Pinault's team was astonished by the number of positions occupied by fake executives, but real Freemasons.

Everything seemed to be going on as before when, in 1987, Jean-Louis Pétriat succeeded Baroin. A young engineer in computers and organizational studies at Électricité de France, Pétriat joined the Masons in the early 1960's. He was a member of the trade union of FO, a Masonic bastion, and sympathized with André Bergeron, who asked him in 1975 to audit the information processing system of the UNEDIC (the national unemployment benefits administration). He managed the unemployment program of south-western France, his native land, until his nomination as head of the GMF. Jean-Louis Pétriat was selected. . . because he was the youngest member of the board of directors! In fact, all the various Masonic factions hoped to be able to manipulate this rookie.

"I water my naivety every day like a bonsai," Pétriat pompously claimed in a 1988 portrait in L'Express,[3] which presented him like the prototype of the modern and sympathetic boss. But he over-watered it, apparently. In just a few years, Pétriat committed many strategic blunders. He invested all over the place, in travel, entertainment, foie gras, the exotic hotel trade — deals that would lead to losses of $250 million in 1992 — record in the French insurance world. Pétriat also managed to earn the hatred of most of the company directors. After having liquidated most of Baroin's supporters, he withdrew to his ivory tower.

During that time, some of his opponents became snitches and passed confidential data to the press on their president's catastrophic management. It would take too long to detail his extravagant conduct in this chapter. Let us mention only that he did not resign until 1994, when he was forced to do so, and barely failed to take down the GMF with him. A few weeks later, he was tried for "credit abuse." In trying to save his position, he had signed letters of credit for an amount of $1 million to a rather fishy Belgian intermediary, to be recycled through shaky subsidiaries and converted into fresh flows of cash. In January, 1997, justice would drop the charges against Pétriat for this letters of credit incident. The examining magistrate responsible for the case considered that he was a victim of his own naivety and that his legal responsibility was not at stake. On the other hand, those who made him sign the famous letters would find themselves before the judge.

In retrospect, the longevity of this Attila of businesses at his post as chairman — seven years — is surprising. But at every level, Pétriat's flights of fancy were covered up, stifled by his "brothers" from every side. They were all gathered within a "fraternal order of insurance," a kind of professional association. After all, Jean-Yves Haberer had done even more at Crédit Lyonnais, protected not by the Freemasons but by his peers from the Finance Inspectorate.[4]

Pétriat was believed all the more untouchable since he belonged to the lodge "Tomorrow," founded in 1989 by the former Grand Master Roger Leray. "I will bring together all the best in the Grand Orient," he confided to us at the time. He was brimming with enthusiasm. "I will have Devaquet and Bambuck, Soisson and Stirn, as well as journalists and eminent doctors. . ." In 1993, the 62 current members of the lodge "Tomorrow" also included the former Grand Master of the Grand Orient, Gilbert Abergel (otherwise known as the director of internal communication at the GMF), the radical former minister Jean-Michel Baylet, the former advisor to the Health Minister, Dr. Jean-Martin Cohen-Solal, the Left-leaning Gaullist Philippe Dechartre, the medical professor Jean-Paul Escande, television journalist Jean Lanzi, operetta singer Armand Mestral, the former member of the High Authority and friend of Mitterrand Marc Paillet, not to mention the cofounder of FNAC, implicated in the Pechiney case, Max Théret. . .

Oy! Pétriat was sent to jail on June 27, 1996, but for a different reason. This time he had to explain what happened to the $350 million that were absorbed during the construction of a tourist complex on St. Martin, built on mosquito-infested marshes in an atmosphere that reeks of dirty money and extremely dubious intermediaries. His incarceration enabled his lawyer, Olivier Metzner, to pool his fraternal visits with two of his customers in that summer of 1996: brother Jacques Crozemarie and brother Jean-Louis Pétriat were both at the Santé prison in Paris.

Food Freemasonry

The operation of the GMF is symptomatic of a regrettable distortion of Freemasonry: the multiplication of fraternal orders. These associations by professional, political and geographical affinity thrive at the margin of obediences, especially as they accept members from all three principal lodges. They thus violate the basic rule, that the Masons will only gather in, or in relation to, the lodge.

Some of the fraternal orders, certainly, are relatively inoffensive. The district fraternals, in Paris, Lyon or Marseilles, are properly used to locate tradesmen, doctors or craftsmen who are brothers. And those which bring together golfers, nudists or yachtsmen seldom flirt with influence peddling.

The professional groups, on the other hand, encourage more disconcerting alliances. Admittedly, just because restaurateurs and hoteliers gather within the well-named GITE (translates as "lodging," in English) — the Interprofessional Group on European Tourism) — does not mean that there is a Masonic business conspiracy. These professionals merely publish each year a kind of tourist guide, which is presented in the form of a small untitled notebook. "There's nothing very harmful in it," hedges a user. "This sign of recognition does not entitle you to a free meal. The owner might pat you on the back and offer you an aperitif." But why, then, adopt the attitudes of conspirators? "This directory is a confidential and personal document," reads a preamble to the famous notebook. "Never lend it or give it away, and destroy it every year."

Does the mention of certain culinary superstars, like Georges Blanc in Vonnas or Gérard Nandron in Lyon, justify these excessive precautions? In any case, many glitterati among the brotherhood, like Gaston Lenôtre, Alain Senderens and Joel Robuchon, prefer to do without such publicity.

What the more fastidious initiates contemptuously called "food Masonry," between the two wars, never did stop thriving. The "Palace Dinner," which brings together judges and lawyers, also publishes a directory that can be quite useful in these times that are so troubled by the abuse of public assets.

Another, the "Dinner Association," brings together once a month the brothers who are high-ranking administrators at all the ministries. Topics are discussed that relate to the State, but especially, everyone maneuvers to influence the nominations.

Still, these are nothing compared to the corporatist fraternal order of the HLM (public housing) and that of the BTP (building and public works), where inquests and trials have been increasing over the years. "In certain lodges, the hospitaller must have a lot of work to do, and must spend more time in the visiting room of the prison than at the bedside of patients," jokes one Mason who is fed up.

These "professional" associations are clearly more active than the mythical political fraternal orders, today fallen into relative disuse. The Fraternal Ramadier, for the Socialist members of Parliament, which played a very significant part in the Congress of Epinay, does isn't really up to much and has trouble finding volunteers to lead it. Another club was created in 1982 for Gaullist brothers. The UDF benefits from the feeble competition from the Club on rue de Poitiers, founded by the former minister André Rossi.

But the most picturesque of these associations which never existed except in an informal way is without question the "fraternal order of creditors of Charles Hernu" (sic), which counted twelve members! "During his many hard times," says one of these generous donors, Hernu would hit up his brothers. Never reimbursed, we joined forces in this whimsical fraternal whose goal was mutual comfort! Our friend's chronic impecuniosity had reached incredible levels; he had no peer in his withdrawals from the 'hospitaller's chest,' our Masonic mutual aid fund."

"Brothers" at the Coast

With decentralization, the most active political associations today operate at the local or regional level. The most typical example is surely "Club 50" of Montpellier, uncovered by the journalist Jacques Molénat.[5] To join, you must be both a Freemason and a notable. They meet on the last Thursday of every month in a big Montpellier restaurant. They constitute a selected sample of the local petty *nomenklatura*: a banker, a notary, a commercial lawyer, an insurer, a judge, a police inspector, a former president of the bar, a law professor who is a former Grand Master of the GLF, a former regional director of URBA, an RPR deputy, a buddy of the Socialist mayor George Frêche, the president of the soccer club, the president of the commercial court, the president of the Chamber of Commerce, the director of the regional health insurance fund, etc. They dine, they talk, they swap information and services, all that without paying any heed to partisan labels. The presence of an equivalent number of brothers affiliated with the two local political chiefs neutralizes the relations of power. "On the other hand," explains Jacques Molénat, "it reinforces the ties between Freemasonry and the bosses' world, between the compass and the portfolio."

In Cannes, Michel Mouillot used the same system. Provincial Grand Master of the GLNF, his friendships among the Freemasons doubled as faithful and devoted customers, in particular among the tradesmen and the SME owners. For the local elections of 1995, the RPR decided to run a candidate against this sulfurous character, who was already compromised in the Botton affair. The new candidate Pierre Lellouche, diplomatic counselor to Jacques Chirac, was sent to confront the Mouillot networks. His first rounds along the Cannes boardwalks quickly displayed to him the extent of the phenomenon. When his staff tried to reserve a table in a restaurant, as soon as they identified themselves on the telephone, the establishment would suddenly be fully booked. Maybe by subscribers of the GITE notebook, who continued, come hell or high water, to support their champion however badly bruised he was when he got caught in a dirty corruption scheme in the summer of 1996. A bribe of $500,000 and the municipality gave some English casino owners authorization to install slot machines — indeed, this discovery took some fizz out of his effervescent political rise. And also his Masonic career, already considerably compromised since the Botton incident. In fact, Claude Charbonniaud, the Grand Master of the Grand French National Lodge, told him to take a "rest" after the lawsuit, which had left him threatened with disqualification from public office, and a deferred prison term.

The GLNF was not so vigilant of the Freemasons who surrounded Jacques Médecin office in the City Hall of Nice. Initiated in the United States, Médecin could not be disciplined by a French branch. The members of his entourage who belonged to the Grand Orient of France, on the other hand, received an ultimatum from their headquarters: "You have to choose between the Grand Orient and the Mafia." All except one, it appears, chose not to choose. T-squares and compasses in hand, they went over to the GLNF — a branch that the old Grand Master of the Grand Lodge of France, Jean Verdun, frankly does not carry in his heart. "This Grand Lodge, allegedly national, suffers from an execrable reputation in the lodges of other French branches," he writes, "because it is immured in its pride at being the only Grand Lodge recognized by England and, in consequence, the only one with official relations with the Grand Lodges of the United States. It attracts like lice these racketeers of every stripe who take the dollar for their guiding star."[6]

On the Mediterranean Coast, connections between the Freemasons and Mafioso networks are constantly growing, according to Roger-Louis Bianchini. A journalist from Nice, he is author of *Mafia, argent et politique (Maffia, Money and Politics).*[7] "The manager of the Monaco real estate bank who was driven to suicide, the Cannes real estate agent who was assassinated by the Calabrese of the 'Ndranghetta in a clandestine exchange operation, the industrialist from the Antibes who was "executed" because of commercial competition, various leaders of the "Médecin system," the Mayor Adjunct of Seyne who was victim of two killers on motorbikes, the organizer of the Toulon Fair who escaped from an attack, and most of the protagonists in the Yann Piat episode, agents of justice and judges suspected of corruption in the area of Cannes and Grasse," he enumerates, "— they all belong to Freemasonry. All these connections are impressive; they remind me of that Italian lodge with the sinister reputation, Lodge P 2."

A Flock of Canaries

Eight months after their turpitude was revealed, the Grand Orient resigned itself to suspending three black sheep from Gard in November 1994. A few months later, after two "canaries" of the Grand Orient (that's what they call the brothers who govern the operation of the lodges), noted a Mafia-esque evolution in two lodges in Nîmes, and those were "suspended." The ideals of Freemasonry were sung there with a rare cynicism. The local "godfather," Claude Pradille, Socialist senator-mayor from Sauve, the all-powerful head of the HLM office of Gard, made the sun shine and the rain fall for the lodges baptized "Echo 1" and "Echo 2."

"Echo 1 is reminiscent of Lodge P 2. . . . While I am a member, it has been years since I went there. They are really frightening, they are everywhere." Gilbert Baumet, author of these not very pleasant remarks, is an expert. Another big man in Gard and an unrepentant political weather vane, he is the longtime president of the Gard general council. He was also implicated in all the chicaneries of the local racketeers (his father and his brother were, among others, the happy beneficiaries of favors from the general council), he is eager to denounce his "enemy brother" Claude Pradille, son of a high dignitary of the GO.

Work performed on personal property at the expense of the HLM office, dubious land acquisitions, lax management, fictitious missions covered by the same office for amounts exceeding a million francs for his brother-in-law Max Boulin (a venerable member of lodge "Echo 2"), endemic corruption — Pradille's list of offenses was long enough to fetch him three years in prison — to the chagrin, moreover, of his "brothers" who were senators and who were working very actively to prevent his parliamentary immunity being lifted. Étienne Dailly, a GLNF initiate, was squabbling publicly with his mates over the racket-eering atmosphere yet he called a time-out to stigmatize "the judges' arrogance," and Claude Estier, president of the group PS, was publicly delighted by the senatorial demurrer of the Nîmes judges' first request. "The response was healthy because the judges think they can do any-thing," he commented.

Rumors must have reached Pradille and his brother-in-law Boulin (who by then were sharing even their prison cell in Nîmes), that a new lodge, purely philosophical this time, was being opened where elected officials are not welcome. More and more Freemasons bristle now at the mixture of members from all types of backgrounds, irritated at be-ing constantly under suspicion from laymen. In Montpellier, for exam-ple, some bro's who had had enough of the pretensions of the "venerable" of Lodge Bélisaire 2 (he had made his shop into an élitiste club with "closed meetings" organized in the best hotels, tuxedos *de rigueur* and long gowns for the ladies, at the same time as "open meet-ings") got him closed down for "social excesses." Better yet, six vener-ables from the Montpellier GO, looking for more simplicity and want-ing to make a kind of "Clean Hands" campaign" have even founded a "wild lodge." It has been baptized "JNS" in a spirit of ambiguity: Jésus Notre Seigneur (Jesus Our Lord) for the believers, Je-Ne-Sais (I Don't Know) for the agnostics. The brothers of this lodge of purists meet in sober dress of the humble white apron and with a rare severity win-nows out the new apprentices — for fear of the Mafia, they explain, which has corroded some of the Riviera lodges. "The dream of the lead-ers of JNS," comments Jacques Molénat, "is to add a new symbolic utensil to the Masonic compass and T-square: the broom."[8]

Poor Victor Schoelcher!

The broom! That is exactly what a small corporation took up at the end the 1980's. Several judges decided to take their investigations as far as they would go when a preliminary hearing turned up politi-cally-loaded evidence of fraud. Thierry Jean-Pierre opened fire in Le

Mans, followed by Renaud Van Ruymbeke in Rennes, Jean-Marie Charpier in Versailles, Philippe Courroye in Lyon, Jean-Michel Prêtre in La Réunion, Philippe Assonion in Bourg-en-Bresse, Jean-Louis Lequé in Pau, and Eric Halphen in Créteil.

All these magistrates discovered a nest of intermediaries, half-competitors and half-accomplices, virtuosos of the shell company, fraudulent invoice and suitcases full of cash. And they had another point in common: they were all "brothers"! By order of appearance, since 1976 Gerard Monate had been managing the businesses of URBA, the "official financial pump" of the Socialist party. This old militant had the merit of not growing rich personally through this not very advisable trade and of tirelessly reminding his partners that the objective was not "to make the numbers" but to serve the militant cause. But these creditable warnings did not keep him from knowing the other members of this small, very closed, club.

Jean-Claude Méry, for example. Called "Méry of Paris" (a pun on the "Mayoralty of Paris"), this former member of the RPR Central Committee is the owner and founder of the SEPG, a virtual design office and an intermediary that was nearly impossible to circumvent if you wanted to tap the public capital markets. Tried in September, 1994, by Judge Halphen, this member of the Grand French National Lodge had met the shady banker of the PS on several occasions. "My men knew Méry through Masonic channels," Monate explained to Judge Halphen during a "technical consultation." "I knew that he was doing the same thing as me, only for the RPR. But, unlike me, Méry had the reputation of doing a lot of semi-official financing without any invoices. He worked out of his briefcase, as they say."

It turned out that there were several people working out of their briefcases. Michel Pacary, based in the Center area, was officially responsible for rescheduling the debts of local RPR authorities. In Nantes, "brother" René Trager was politically ambidextrous, from the PS to the PR. In Angoulême, the Socialist former mayor Jean-Michel Boucheron, flushed out by the citizen-taxpayer Marcel Dominici (who was indignant at having his city driven into near-bankruptcy), brought down with him the "consulting engineer" Michel Gabaude, who, in addition to the Masonic precepts, had initiated him into the art of embezzlement. This pygmalion had assembled a whole network to manufacture fraudulent invoices, working for the Socialists in southwestern France and for the Freemasons.

But Hubert, René, Michel and the others remain modest apprentices, in business as in masonry, compared to Reyt. The life of this autodidact could almost be a novel. Before the war, he left public school at the age of 14 to go to the Hotel School of Paris. One year of training, and here he was a waiter at the train station buffet in Montparnasse, supported by his mother — a dull existence, interrupted by the war. Young Reyt made no mistake in choosing sides, and joined the Resistance. He even turned up in Austria, after the war, in the Allied information services. That was the end of his restaurant career. Reyt took up aviation, and became a steward with Air France. He played at being an airman for three years before exploiting his true talent — sales — first in automobile accessories and then as a Renault dealer.

But the enterprising salesman was also a man of the Left, and he joined the Socialist party, supporting Mauroy, in 1963. Another change of employment, in 1969, gave him the opportunity to approach the political galaxy. Reyt was engaged by the SERETE, an engineering company, to solicit the local authorities. If his boss hardly appreciated his Masonic commitments, they would be his great fortune. Reyt decided to create SAGES, an "intermediary for all transactions, except those which are regulated by the law" (sic), according to the amazing definition given by his boss. In a little more than a decade, SAGES succeeded to expand in a spectacular fashion, generating on average $5 million turnover annually. Reyt was making a good living. The company of which he is the majority shareholder made so much money that he increased his the real estate investments; and that enabled him to treat his friends liberally and to hold open table around gourmet meals. There was no shortage of pretty girls at these epicurian evenings that some guests, later, would have preferred to forget. But Reyt has a long memory.

More than his professional route, it is his advance in Freemasonry that explains Reyt's astonishing rise in the high-level trading of favors. Already in 1971 his rank allowed him to welcome François Mitterrand at the door of the Grand Orient of France, on rue Cadet, where an "innocent open house" was being held. But it was in 1979 that he really shifted into high gear.

With some friends, including the businessman Max Théret, Reyt founded the Victor-Schoelcher lodge, in homage to the Freemason who obtained the abolition of slavery in the French colonies in the 19th century. This great man, whose memory is honored in the Pantheon, deserved better than to find himself the sponsor, albeit by posthumous title, of a lodge that embodied the fraternal mixing of business and politics.

The Victor-Schoelcher Lodge meets in Haÿ-les-Roses, in a temple located on rue des Maréchaux. This choice of location betrays only a very scant attraction for the suburbs. "When they created this lodge," says one of its members, "they wanted to keep to themselves, and to avoid the hoi-polloi that surrounds the head office of the GO, on rue Cadet, and which it is difficult to get rid of. Then, Reyt and his friends found quite a practical solution: to open a lodge in Rungis, a town with very few inhabitants. And above all, not to build a temple. So they met in Haÿ-les-Roses, which helped cover their tracks a little more."

As an additional precaution, the 120 members of Victor-Schoelcher meet on Thursday mornings, at a time when the average employee has difficulties getting away without incurring the wrath of his supervisor.

On certain Thursdays mornings, in the early 1980's, rue des Maréchaux would see a procession of big cars. The phoney invoice magnate Hubert Haddad crossed paths with Socialist deputy Alain Vivien. The radical mayor of Nancy, Andre Rossinot, met the chairman of Air Inter Pierre Eelsen. And some of the heroes of the Carrefours Development case like Yves Chalier and Jacques Delebois.

Reyt, who in lay life worked a lot with pro-Poperen currents of the PS neglected by URBA, installed Jean Poperen in person with the Victor-Schoelcher Lodge in 1984. The ceremony of initiation proceeded to Temple No. 1 on rue Cadet (baptized Arthur-Groussier in homage to an old Grand Master and vice-president of the Senate.) "I remember seeing Andre Labarrère there, the mayor of Pau," says a dignitary of the GO who attended the ceremony. "I have to say, the atmosphere was not really that of metaphysical speculation. And my neighbor whispered in my ear: 'Look by the base of the columns, on one side are the mayors, on the other, the salesmen."

Parallel to the expansion of Victor-Schoelcher, Reyt undertook to federate all the fraternal orders — a brilliant idea for a "contact man," the trade he claimed to practice. On rue Constantine, in the buildings of SAGES (which he would later sell to the Republican party), the former air steward made up files for each corporation, then made connections between them.

To assist him in this task, he hired Maurice Pannequier. This

Freemason, who was General Secretary to the Grand Orient for 30 years, is a genuine walking database. With this tool, Reyt could do hundreds of favors. He would renders little services, help the brothers in need, put people in touch with each other. His reputation spread throughout the lodges. "Several years ago, I had to engage in a process of removal against a member in my lodge who had abused the confidence of another brother," says a bank branch manager. "The excluded member immediately ran to Reyt to ask for help."

This activism hardly filled Roger Leray with enthusiasm. As Grand Master between 1984 and 1987, he looked with benevolence on those fraternal orders that behaved themselves, and were not likely to drift into mixing business and politics. But he was afraid that a super-network branching out through all the areas of France and every compartment of the society would lead to the development of a very condemnable Masonry of business. A wise premonition! Simply stated, the measures taken by rue Cadet were not in proportion to the peril. On the one hand, the Victor-Schoelcher Lodge, hardly de-activated by Leray, reconstituted itself at rue Cadet. In addition, the fraternal orders, which escaped any control from their affiliates, continued to thrive.

For the repeated warnings coming from his superiors didn't bother Reyt, who was busy with his bourgeoning business as a "contact man." In 1973, SAGES was founded with a capital of $17,000 francs, including $16,600 that he had brought by himself. In 1987 the company, armed with a turnover of $5 million, was paying him liberally, investing in real estate, and still succeeding in making a profit. That's château living!

SAGES was a big success, particularly due to the "flexibility" that it offered elected officials compared to the rigid rules enacted by URBA. When it brought together, in the context of a public market, a company and an elected official, SAGES would leave half of the commission at the disposal of the latter, and not of the Party treasury.

Because it is directly dependent on the head office of the PS, URBA inevitably supports the majority Socialist faction. Therefore, Reyt prospected first among those who were "excluded" from the URBA system, whom he promised to remunerate autonomously. The head of SAGES, in addition, was hardly checking up to see how the funds that he passed on to the elected officials were used. Political use? Personal use? That was their business; he was satisfied to play cashier.

He kept little cards with each one's credit balance. These "hidden bank accounts" did not finance political activities alone. Did the mayor of Evry, Jacques Guyard, want to offer his little family a trip to the United States, by Concorde? Did Guy Penne, African Affairs advisor to Mitterrand and mayor of Sainte-Cécile-les-Vignes want to remodel his kitchen? Reyt took care of it.

In sum, he had in his portfolio, if we dare say so, the municipalities of Clermont-Ferrand, Nantes, Le Mans, Montpellier, Dunkirk, Conflans-Sainte-Honorine, Strasbourg, Elbeuf, Saint-Brieuc, Lorient, Massy, Evry, plus Angoulême since the time of the comical Jean-Michel Boucheron.

Companies could choose between two formulas: annual subscription or specific missions. The SAGES invoices always followed the same model: "Our commercial activity, assignments, business travel, hospitality," followed by the charge for the aforementioned intervention, estimated at between 0.5 and 1% of the market price, sometimes a little more.

Are these contractors and these politicians with whom Reyt entertained such privileged contact all Freemasons? No, not all. But the Reyt system still functioned very much like a fraternity, with the touch of elegance that a service rendered did not inevitably have an immediate counterpart in terms of the public market. Reyt did not have only a card file. He also had his memory.

In 1985, when his friend and brother Jean-Yves Drian, Socialist mayor of Lorient, asked him to deal with his lodging expenses in Paris, Reyt took care of it without asking for any specified immediate advantage in return. Thus, until 1991 (the date on which Jean-Yves Drian was named State Secretary for Maritime Affairs), SAGES covered his invoices at the Meridian in Montparnasse. A lost investment? Not completely. For Reyt had another friend. And this friend raan the company Transexel, which jointly manages public transport in several French towns including, by fortunate coincidence, Lorient. Transexel thus could hardly refuse Drian, and agreed to reimburse Reyt for the mayor of Lorient's Parisian hotel invoices. To maintain this happy complicity with the agreeable transport company, some time later Reyt involved him in the modernization of the bus services in Le Mans.

This chain of friendship was cruelly broken, on January 14, 1992. That day, Judge Van Ruymbeke searched the headquarters of SAGES on boulevard Saint-Germain. For more than a year, the magistrates who were conducting a preliminary inquiry into the cases of secret financing in Le Mans and in Angoulême had been seeing the name of SAGES crop up. On January 24, Reyt was charged with trading favors and sent to jail in Rennes, a city with which, however, SAGES had not been working! He stayed there for more than six months, and received 1,700 letters of which only one was from a political friend, Jean Poperen.

Thus ended the generous parties he used to offer on Saint-Germain boulevard, to the Socialist bigwigs. Once he got out of prison, Reyt had to liquidate his company and prepare, at the age of 67, for a less golden retirement than he would have wished. Good-bye Paris apartment, country cottage in the mountains, house in Brittany and boat acquired by the SAGES-Naval subsidiary company! As proof that networks do not always withstand fate's little jokes, and that solidarity gives way to individual interests — and fears — Reyt was dropped by his "friends."

"Concrete" Lodges

"Don't tell my mother that I make phoney invoices, she thinks I'm a Freemason." In the spring of 1994, the police officers who were asking question on behalf of Judge Halphen, from the Créteil prosecutor's office, some of the fraud specialists broke down. Whereas secrecy is the rule in all Masonic branches, there are brothers who expose themselves and reveal rites reserved for the initiated. While searching a certain Jacky Chaisaz, a former sales manager of Bouygues who turned up as an intermediary in the public markets, and who was suspected of receiving secret commissions and of "laundering" via taxi companies, the police found a directory of Freemasons from all branches.

The list included members of a curious "fraternal order," and the investigators recognized some superstars of the matter at hand, such as Max Théret, implicated in the Pechiney case, the omnipresent Reyt, some influential executives from the Mutual Guarantee of Civil Servants, and someone they knew, Francis Poullain, a BTP contractor. Faced with this discovery, Chaisaz did not make a mystery of his membership in the Grand Orient, and he even obligingly lingered to describe the symbols and the ritual of his branch.

When they took a closer look at Francis Poullain, in whose possession the tax department had found numerous fraudulent statements, the same scenario was repeated. This initiate of the Grand Lodge of France calmly justified his presence in the famous directory: eager to elevate his spirit, he enjoyed discussing metaphysics with the guys. While the metaphysical quest seems doubtful, Masonic solidarity was not in doubt. In the midst of fraudulent paperwork, the police officers discovered that SAGES and its chairman Reyt had benefited from the services of the SAR! Poullain was not the only one to try to mislead the police officers this way. Others, forewarned, happily eroded their tracks by talking about "philosophical friendships," with investigators who heard "networks of political financing."

In fact, these friendships solidified by the Masonic bonds led to a tight grid of interests where the public markets were negotiated against fraudulent invoices and bags of banknotes. At the center of this politico-racketeer soap opera was Jean-Claude Méry, the briefcase specialist! More familiarly called "the Big Guy," because of his massive and jovial silhouette (after a prison sojourn he weighed 65 lbs less; his friends aptly renamed him "Slim Fast") he was known as one of the principal fundraisers for the RPR. "I have never directly collected money for the party," he defend himself, however. "I encouraged companies to finance it, which is not the same thing;" but it's a sufficiently persuasive incentive in any case so that the CEO's interested in the public markets of the City of Paris would go to his sumptuous offices, at 47, quai des Grands-Augustins. President of the RPR section for real estate professionals, then a member of the central committee of the party under Chirac (until 1989), he solidified his industrial relationships (which were also often Masonic relationships).

The most "profitable" of his debtors was the very spiritualistic Francis Poullain. This generous donor was chairman of SAR, a painting company that was "friendly" to the RPR. A former traffic cop, recycled for a while as a sales representative, this certified militant launched out without too much preparation into a managerial career. He quickly picked up on the system of preferential treatments, kickbacks and other commissions. No need to have made it through HEC to get along with friends like Chaisaz or "Méry of Paris." Poullain doesn't think that Masonic solidarity is a myth. After his sojourn at the Santé prison, where Judge Halphen had sent him to meditate, he made the rounds of some Parisian publishers where he thought he might find support among journalist brothers — a waste of time and effort. One of them, who didn't want his office mates to know about this awkward affiliation, didn't even want to meet with him. He found no more comfort with his friend and brother the sportsman Guy Drut, founder with the GLNF of the lodge "Olympic Spirit."[9] The former gold medallist had, however, been less circumspect in 1982 when Poullain had offered him some stock in his flourishing painting company, and then had participated in a friendly way in the restoration of his residence, in the Nogent-sur-Marne!

Other contractors who were "brothers" relied on the good care of Jean-Claude Méry. They agreed to contribute to this very particular "widow's chest," a necessary step if they wanted access to municipal projects. On the whole, the CEO's who were questioned by Judge Halphen in this affair formed a true "fraternal order" of BTP. Among others, they included a GLF initiate, Christian Curtet, a GLNF mason, Paul Versini, chairman of a painting and joinery company in the Hauts-de-Seine, a mason of longstanding of the Grand Orient, Henri Antona, the chairman of Techni who was active in the Corsican "family,"[2] an associate of the Compagnie Générale des Eaux, who worked at the same time in Paris, in the Hauts-de-Seine and the Essonne — and the list is not exhaustive. No fewer than 45 business paid courtesy invoices to the enterprising "Méry of Paris."

But the Mayoralty of Paris, the real one this time, does not seem to have been the only recipient of this generosity. In the Hauts-de-Seine, Didier Schuller, director of regional HLM and general adviser, seems to have benefited from the leniency of some contractors, via his electoral newspaper, *Clichois*. The advertising pages in this confidential publication cost the obliging advertisers up to $18,000 each! Judge Halphen therefore took a closer interest at this elected official of the Hauts-de-Seine, who was in addition friendly with many protagonists of the Parisian case. Wasn't he one of Méry's best friends, and didn't they rub elbows at the GLNF, and of Poullain who also profited in this department from the juicy markets of the HLM.

Schuller, whose offices of *Clichois* were searched on December 13, 1994 by Judge Halphen, feared other, more thorough, investigations. Then he opportunely remembered that one of his GLNF brothers had called him in two months earlier on the pretext of speaking to him about his mother's health. How small is the fraternal world! Mrs. Schuller's mother had been consulting the psychiatrist Jean-Louis Maréchal since 1988 — a member of the Atlas lodge of the GLNF.

Schuller himself belonged to the "Silence" lodge. Another coincidence: Maréchal was the father-in-law of Judge Eric Halphen. All the elements were in place for a manipulation extravaganza.

Very quickly indeed, Maréchal and Schuller found topics for conversation other than the old lady's health. Which of the two first mentioned the possibility of influencing the judge in his inquiry? Who started who? In any case it was agreed to exchange $175,000, cash, at the airport of Roissy. But Schuller, who wanted to play victim, alerted the police. After this episode, the scandal burst into the open. Mitterrand, not entirely displeased to see the Right embroiled in its turn in nauseating cases of political financing, got involved, and the judge was able to continue his work. Doctor Maréchal, indignant at having been betrayed by a "brother," confided even to the police that he would seek to have Schuller kicked out of the Masons.

For Didier Schuller, the trouble was only just beginning. For an intermediary of one of his friends, Jean-Paul Schimpf, was caught red-handed with a wad of cash, in the parking lot of the Mercure Hotel in Nogent-sur-Marne, at the moment when the manager of a small road-building company was giving him $7500. All this nasty bunch was dispatched to prison, to the great fury of Schuller. For Schimpf was also his underground treasurer. At his residence, the police seized the list of the members of the "Silence" lodge, where he was the venerable before Schuller. This lodge was "speculative," alright, but not in the sense that is usually meant. After their meeting, Monday mornings in Neuilly where the office was located at the time, the brothers of the BTP celebrated still more profanely their meetings at the HLM office. Schuller had entrusted the presidency of a fraternal order named "Gambetta," to Schimpf, definitely an invaluable friend; the order barely had time to function.

The GLNF was, however at the confluence of all the incidents of fraud. As the journalists from *Le Canard Enchaîné* (Alain Guédé and Hervé Liffran) relate in their book, *Péril sur la Chiraquie* (more or less, *Peril Over 'Chiraq'*),[11] which closely documents the blend of business and politics in the Paris area, there was another producer of fake invoices, Henri Montaldo, who appears there. Head of two security companies, Montaldo had to justify to the police $200,000 worth of questionable invoices generated by him and paid by SAR, under Francis Poullain. He preferred to flee the country. "Since then," reveal the two sleuths from

Le Canard Enchâiné, "Montaldo is supposedly being sought by the police. But in what remote hideout is the fugitive hiding, sheltered from the risk of extradition? The answer lies in the 12th arrondissement. . . . It is in the invitation that is sent out twice a month to the members of the lodge 'The Valley of the Quiet Kings,' which is affiliated with the GLNF. In the presence of two of its former venerable Masters, Henri Montaldo and the police chief Alexandre Daurelle, this lodge meets on the first and fourth Wednesdays of the month. And there, in view and in earshot of all the 'brothers,' the two men serenely talk with Chiraquian elected officials and cinder-block vendors."

At the GLNF headquarters, which the old members still call "the Bineau lodge" in reference to its old address in Neuilly, a certain number of brothers do find all the same that the adventures of Schuller & Co. have started to tarnish the image of the branch; especially as this one has been berated by the English Masons, purists who hardly appreciate the mixing of breeds.

"My special relations with the leaders of the United Grand Lodge of England exposed me to their critical observations and their severe judgment on the state of our Order. I think that, unless extreme measures are taken, your honor will be at stake and our order will undergo a serious and major crisis." After having informed verbally some friendly brothers of his concerns, Alexandre of Yugoslavia, Assistant Grand Master, number three of the GLNF (and a renowned member of the Resistance, having been a brilliant officer in the Royal Air Force) decided on October 14, 1995 to write in these terms to his Grand Master, Claude Charbonniaud.

The GLNF had not held up too well under its riotous expansion. A modest branch of 1,500 initiates at the time of the rift of 1913, today it counts 18,000 brothers scattered in 900 lodges. This opulent deist branch, which recruits mostly on the Right, among the notables, set out not long ago to establish a new seat, rather luxurious, on grounds belonging to. . . the City of Paris. "They do so well," comments a dignitary of the GO who was frankly not very sympathetic, "because they recruit massively, with a presentation that cannot be described as ideological."

Invited to lunch by a member of Bineau, one of the largest Parisian real estate developers was invited to join. A positive investigation had been made one him, he was told. Given his polite refusal, the GLNF emissary growled: "That's too bad. In real estate, a lot can go wrong. Some people, and not the smallest, have been saved thanks to us. You might need help someday." What's worse, such laxity would have attracted brothers suspected of political extremism following the example of a prominent leader of the National Front, who was particularly influential within the "pagan" branch, and of Jacques Tauran, an old friend of Le Pen. This former secretary to Pierre Poujade was one of the first members of the National Front. He even became one of its elected officials to the European Parliament while still holding political office. A printer by profession, his printing presses often served the pro-Le Pen publications until his death in 1996.

This proselytism and this ecumenism don't help the reputation of the branch. Shortly after the defection of Alexandre de Yugoslavia, the senator Étienne Dailly, "Deputy Grand Master," had a belated crisis of conscience. "I cannot accept," he wrote on December 28, 1995 to the same Charbonniaud, who was according to the rules of the branch the only one who could impose sanctions, "to preside any longer over a situation that I deplore." In early February, the Grand Master of the GLNF "suspended" the too conspicuous "Silence Lodge," and decided to split up its members to other lodges.

This did not end the GLNF's troubles. The "Friendly Fraternal Order of Sales and Distribution of Trade and Industry" was a cause for concern. Inquiring at the beginning of 1993 into the bribes that Jean-Pierre Destrade (the former Socialist deputy of the Pyrénées-Atlantiques) had received from all the "big guys" in food distribution, the Bordeaux police found an astounding concentration of GLNF brothers among the supermarkets. Could the Masonic bonds have favored Destrade, himself an initiate to the Grand Orient? Of course this was not the subject of their investigations, but the coincidences were disconcerting. However, in this business also, Masonic solidarity has its limits. After eight months of detention, Destrade "cracked" and acknowledged to the judge, in an astonishing confession, that he had acted at the request of "brother" Henri Emmanuelli, then treasurer of the Socialist party. He even claimed to have brought $5.5 million to the SP, delivering the clandestine funds sometimes in cash, sometimes by foreign transfer to Panama and to Luxembourg.

Destrade derived these abundant liquidities from his position on the commercial town planning commission that was charged with deliberating over the establishment of new supermarkets. A favorable opinion, in this kind of authority, is often worth several million francs.

But the other members of this fraternal order found themselves, for a none too festive last reunion, on the benches of the court where they rubbed shoulders with politicians and wholesale food distribution executives, all "brothers."

The Charentais Clan

The embezzling of public funds, the control of municipal contracts, the delivery of stacks of cash and other base acts are hardly recommended by the Masonic ideal; especially since the money thus tapped from the public entities was therefore subtracted from the efforts at solidarity (which the prolonged crisis makes so necessary). With all this embezzlement, how many hospital chests could have been filled!

As regards distorting the fraternal spirit, the ARC affair takes the cake. In complicity with many brothers, Jacques Crozemarie, the former president-founder of the ARC (Association for Research against Cancer) grew rich at the expense of the donors and to the detriment of the patients.

January 18, 1996 was the end, or rather the beginning of the end. Crozemarie, the man who for twenty years was understood to dominate cancer funds in France, announced that he was resigning from his post. He was constrained and forced to do so.

In spite of the report recently given by the Court of Auditors, which had shocked his board of directors, the ARC president still held on. That was his nature. He wanted to use the facilities for a few more days; time, no doubt, to purge his office of some compromising documents. Permission denied. He intended to keep his company car (a comfortable Citroen XM), and the driver. Denied. He asked for a few months' additional use of his company "studio," actually a splendid and spacious apartment at the top of the ARC headquarters, in a nice part of town. Also denied.

So, Crozemarie left the premises. Not without removing the bookshelves and the refrigerator, which were not his. And with good reason: they'd been purchased with fraudulent invoices! Nearly $70,000 had been used to furnish the presidential "penthouse." Paid by the ARC, the invoices read as being related to the installation of research laboratories.

Fake invoices and mythical honorariums, non-existent services. This was the hidden face of the ARC, the biggest fundraiser for the fight against cancer. $100 million in turnover during its best years. The researchers were happy. The donors were happy. Crozemarie was very, very happy.

He could not have been unaware that millions of dollars were diverted every year from their intended use, and that only 15% of the collected money was, in fact, used for the fight against cancer. He could not be unaware of it, since he was one of the first beneficiaries of this scandalous financial imposture. So much so that he was imprisoned, in June 1996, for the extreme gravity of the facts charged against him: he had made himself personally rich on "cancer money." In addition to the pharaonic facilities in his company "studio," Crozemarie was overwhelmed in the mid-1980's with a passion for remodeling. His goal: his two successive residences in the South of France, first in Rians, then in Bandol. In Rians, close to $2 million (extracted from the ARC), were absorbed in renovations and the construction of bathrooms, a swimming pool and other conveniences suitable to the residence of a great man. He managed to finance it all without personally spending a dollar, or a penny, from the massive floral plantings to the construction of a corral intended to assuage a late-blooming passion for horsemanship.

But construction wasn't all. Crozemarie liked to travel. Two stays in Mauritius and a deep sea fishing party in Senegal cost $35,000 paid by International Development (ID), the holding company for the ARC's services firm, which covered the expenses through fake invoices addressed to the association. And then, there were the 82 airplane trips to Provence, financed the same way.

All these advantages did not preclude his having a little pocket money. $650,000 miraculously showed up in Crozemarie's bank accounts in five years! $350,000 came from fictitious fees paid by three American companies managed by friends. But the origin of the remaining $300,000 is still a mystery.

Might there have been, in addition to these embezzlement rings, stacks of cash circulating within the nebula of the ARC? Why not, given all the false invoice books and misadventures of all kinds that swirled through the association for years? The network was more precisely structured than it might appear, and it had at least one common denominator: Freemasonry.

Jacques Crozemarie was immersed as a very young person in this ideal of tolerance, humanism and spiritual quest. It's just that, to the symbolic tools which are the compass and the T-square, he would quickly add chewing gum intended to plunder the chests of public generosity. The Minister (under the 4th Republic) and notorious Freemason André Marie, deputy of Rouen, a friend of his mother, who prevented Crozemarie from settling for the modest status of electrical engineer. As Minister for National Education, Marie assigned his young protégé to CNRS, of which he was the superintendent. Crozemarie quickly climbed the various administrative levels and discovered all the potential that can be derived from the site of Villejuif, where he worked for CNRS.

He established the Association for the Development of Cancer Research at Villejuif (ADRCV, the forerunner of the ARC) in 1960 and in 1966 won recognition of public utility, making it possible to obtain tax advantages on gifts and exemptions from death duties on legacies. The ADRCV became ARC in 1984. At that time, the "Crozemarie network" was already starting to tap the money intended for the ill.

In 1982, Crozemarie brought together the ARC staff in Angoulême. The agenda: to create "regional delegations." Decentralization seemed to be on the agenda for embezzlement, too. The town of Angoulême was not selected by chance — for the capital of Charentes unites, one way or another, many of the protagonists in this corrupt web.

One of the prime members was Charentais by adoption. In 1960, Yvan Ledoux, a specialist in "communication," created FAT (Artistic and Technical Films), a company specialized in the production of institutional films, then BERES (an office ostensibly for economic and social research). The two companies were known in the Socialist movement. But Ledoux wore another hat, too: until 1988, he was General Secretary of ARC, and therefore principal assistant to Crozemarie. Ledoux was thus his own supplier since FAT and BERES worked for ARC. At best, an extravagant conflict of interests. At worst, the starting point for diversions of funds that would continue to grow until Crozemarie was rendered harmless, in early 1996.

All the tributaries converge toward that city rendered sadly famous (in the annals of such "affairs,") by its former mayor Jean-Michel Boucheron, another Masonic idealist. Ledoux had always sailed in the murkiest waters that sometimes surround the Socialist party. He worked particularly closely with brother Hubert Haddad, the head of OFRES. This organization, officially specialized in selling advertising space in the municipal newspapers, had in fact acquired advanced skills in the fraud industry, under the terms of a cocktail mixed in simple proportions: when a company places an ad in a local paper, half of the money is allocated to the local councilor, the other half to OFRES. Good money! However, it was learned that Haddad worked actively for *Vivre ensemble*, the monthly of the town of Angoulême, as head of publicity and printing works. It was those funds that were diverted jointly by OFRES and Jean-Michel Boucheron that led Marcel Dominici, a modest manager from Angoulême and the man who brought down the indelicate mayor, to file his first complaint, which blew the lid off the "Boucheron affair" in 1987.

"In 1996, when Crozemarie found himself kicked out of the ARC, my friend Dominici announced his latest discovery to me," wrote Jean Montaldo in *Le Gang du cancer*.[12] "'When the ARC scandal broke,' he says, 'I was on my feet in a heartbeat. I dashed to the basement of my villa, to the armored cellar where my files are stored. Consulting the old issues of *Vivre ensemble*, I found a whole series of advertising inserts paid for by the ARC, via OFRES.'" In fact, every issue of *Vivre ensemble* between 1984 and 1987 had ads for the ARC, purchased at top price. Introduced to ARC by Yvan Ledoux, Haddad produced for behalf of the association, starting in 1983, the magazine *Plus*, whose editor-in-chief was... Jacques Crozemarie.

Haddad started his career in the advertising department of the Socialist magazine *l'Unité*, whose director, Claude Estier, also a Freemason, had been a longtime member of the ARC board of directors.

Among the small political glories born from the alternating of parties in power, Haddad also knew brother George Fillioud, Minister of Transport between 1981 and 1986. Fillioud counts among his advisers one Jean-Claude Remaury. Like Yvan Ledoux, of whom he was a friend, this young manager was active in both the creation of companies and in politics. A one-time aide to Pierre Maille at Brest City Hall, he created two communication companies, Im'Media and Paris Marketing — a painful memory since he was nailed, on that occasion, for swindling a charity (with regard to the CFCF, the French Committee for the World Campaign Against Hunger). He also worked for ARC, whose communications in the province he managed. What could be more natural between brothers, since one finds among his shareholders... BERES and Yvan Ledoux!

If it were not a matter of stealing money from cancer research, the mishaps of these nickel-plated professors of the fraudulent invoice would merely be grist for burlesque comedy writers. These sinister figures were, in fact, involved in all kinds of trafficking. Jean-Claude Remaury and Jean-Michel Boucheron had a common friend, Marc Proux-Delruyre, who had the brilliant idea of creating "Bolster." This French organization for Panamanian Rights was devoted to an interesting activity: producing artificial champagne in Cuba, under the denomination of "Moët et Chandon brut imperial." For this inventiveness, Remaury was condemned to 18 months in prison (with deferment), a fine of $17 million and $1 million in damages to Moët et Chandon. During this time, Crozemarie and his friends bought 1,700 bottles of champagne, the real stuff, at the expense of the association. And who was in charge of communications at Bolster? The inevitable Yvan Ledoux.

Better, these "Charentais" were associated in various businesses, with Michel Simon, a character who shares with Crozemarie the leading role in the sorry saga of ARC. Simon is not a Socialist, he would even be rather on the Right. But he was born in Angoulême. And he came into contact with Ledoux through business. One of the companies where he was a director, Publicadvise, a designated supplier to ARC for the installation of laboratories and the design of promotional events (often fictitious), frequently dealt with FAT and BERES with friend Ledoux.

When, in the late 1970's, Ledoux's two roles at ARC (both leader and supplier, by means of his two companies) began to become too conspicuous, Simon took over. He founded International Development in 1979. This modest corporation, capitalized at $16,000, became the flagship of ARC's subcontractors. With the subsidiary companies that it created to suit every need, it invoiced up to $34 million per annum to the association, for services that were hypothetical more often than not.

Ledoux, Remaury and Simon became so close, so "accessory," one might say, that they pooled all their economic interests in the GECA (Associated Consortium of Communication) in 1984, which included their respective companies, all service firms — and especially sources of fraudulent invoices — for the ARC. The "cancer gang" was complete.

Simon was its best godfather. In five years he got close to $3 million in wages from the International Development group and its subsidiaries. His bank accounts were credited, between 1990 and 1995, with some $5.6 million. Add to that the sums used to finance, via the fake invoices paid by ARC, for a hunt in the Sologne for more than $1.5

million.

The château life seemed eternal in those days. The Charentais clan did not imagine, early in 1996, that the rout had already begun. Thus, at the very time when Jacques Crozemarie was being removed from his post, and all this embezzlement was the object of a legal investigation, the gang believed it could continue its lucrative games. When FAT, one of Ledoux's companies, was declared bankrupt, who proposed to take it over? Michel Simon and International Development. This solution was finally rejected by the commercial court. Luck had turned, definitively. The protection that Crozemarie enjoyed due to the interweavings of several networks (the Masons, the lists of peole who owed him favors — including eminent researchers who had profited from ARC subsidies, political networks like the irresponsible Bernard Pons who helped ARC avoid public controls — all these chains suddenly broke down.

This evolution would wind up disturbing even the most forgiving brothers. In every branch there was a spring cleaning, a relentless tracking of the racketeers who disdained the common ideal. But how to proceed in organizations based on secrecy and compartmentalized information?

The Grand Orient of France was the most prompt to react at the highest level. Patrick Kessel, to attract his brothers votes in the race for Grand Master, in 1995, had taken on the label of "Mr. Clean." Not without ulterior electoral motives; none of the principal groups in the branch (republican, esoteric, political) could claim a majority.

But he acted, as he learned at his own expense, on a strategy that is risky in an institution whose transparency is not of the first quality. One of his closest collaborators was indeed found guilty, in the midst of the Masonic election campaign, of incredible indelicacy by making out to himself a check for over $10,000. That corresponded to the annual contribution of the Montesquieu lodge. Once the swindle was discovered, Kessel let go his collaborator, but with an allowance, so that he might refund the product of his misdeeds. Such an attitude was accommodating at the very least, and counter to expectations of a self-proclaimed enemy of embezzlement.

This mishap did not contribute to relaxing an already crackling atmosphere. Any Mason, or almost any, ended up suspecting the others of political or financial ulterior motives. What was true at the Grand Orient was more still at the Grand French National Lodge, whose other branches denounce today openly kindness with regard to the racketeers than it tolerates in its midst. "Just imagine that something terrible should happen here or there, some horrible business like what happened at Lodge P.2 in Italy where false Masons were hiding behind real ones. What court room will believe that in more than twenty cities we were unaware of this branch?" The former Grand Master Jean Verdun worried about the GLF, then prophesied: "A major change is undoubtedly coming for the French Masonic situation, and soon;" and necessary, in any case.

Chapter 6

MONOPOLIES

Alexandre Lazard wasn't cut out for work. At the beginning of the 19th century, this son of a Lorraine vegetable farmer, of a frail constitution, did not seem destined to shine in rural labor. He become a hawker, for want of anything better; but Lazard heard talk about "the Americas," a mythical place of all the possibilities.

The "Americas"! He already had a cousin settled there, in the amusingly named "New-Orleans." Alexandre emigrated and set up a hardware shop; he soon became so prosperous that he had his brothers, Simon and Lazare, come join him. Thus was born, in News-Orleans, in the year 1840, the commercial firm "Lazard Frères." The sons of the Phalsbourg farmer Elie Lazard hoped to make a fortune. They worked without a break. One day destiny smiled on them, as it does on everyone who is ambitious. In the spring of 1848 two fires, one after the other, devastated most of the city, but not the Lazard warehouses! They were thus on hand to re-equip the unfortunate souls who had to rebuild everything.

But the three brothers did not tarry. Pumped up by the unexpected windfall, they left for a village with hardly a thousand inhabitants, located at the edge of the Pacific Ocean: San Francisco, seized by gold fever. Who needs hardware more than a gold prospector?

The Lazard brothers' fortune, soon joined in California by their cousin Alexandre Weill, was made. For them, but especially for their name and for their descendants who continued to make the family heritage bear fruit. After the demise of his father Pierre David-Weill, in 1975, Michel David-Weill (the great-grandson of Alexandre) would reign over the "House of Lazard," an extraordinary and indefinable entity. Is it a commercial bank? Yes. Established in Paris, London and New York, Lazard incontestably belongs to this category. But such an appellation is quite limiting for an institution that has its finger in everything, in major corporations as well as governments. The 18 associate-managers who make up Lazard Frères-Paris cultivate their relationships with all the care of horticulturists. To the point that they all represent one of the most powerful networks of France.

With a few rare exceptions, all the great captains of industry chose Lazard as their commercial banker, and as. . . their confessor, so they can share their secrets with discreet and imaginative people. "Without resorting to the term 'network of influence,' I would rather evoke the expression 'network of friendship and services rendered.' And the fact that a Michel David-Weill or a Jean Guyot can call a minister or a top leader at the drop of a hat is a fundamental element of the power of Lazard,"[1] explains Jacques Calvet, president of the Peugeot board of directors.

The Rake Technique

"Network of influence": the expression is pronounced by one of the most emblematic bosses in France. The list of the chairmen who have entrusted their business, and the destiny of their company, to Lazard covers just about everyone who counts in France: Antoine Riboud, of Danone (ex-BSN); Bernard Arnault, the petulant captain of LVMH, a group that was built thanks to Lazard; Jean Gandois, ex-CEO of Rhône-Poulenc, Cockerill-Sambre and Pechiney, today president of the CNPF, and his vice-president Ernest-Antoine Seillère, chairman of the CGIP which manages the interests of his family, the Wendels. And also Vincent Bolloré, Didier Pineau-Valencienne, Schneider, Serge Kampf (owner of Cape Gemini-Sogeti). And also Jean-Louis Beffa (Saint-Gobain), Jerome Monod (Lyonnaise des Eaux), Jerome Seydoux, CEO of Chargeurs Réunis and owner of the daily newspaper *Libération*. These last three have paid for an annual service that entitles them to unlimited discussions and advice at any time, lavished by their designated officer at Lazard.

Some networks follow the structure of a star; this one looks more like a rake. Since the heroic times of the American conquest, Lazard has preserved the same legal form: a society of people in a simple mixed liability company, where each associate-manager is responsible for his own assets. Each one thus plays with the money of all — a particularly motivating device, which makes it possible to use the rake far and wide.

What Lazard offers to its prestigious clients is its grey matter and the ability to handle people, which enable it to conclude marriages between companies, to organize acquisitions and to invent defense strategies against possible financial attackers. Ideas and influence: that is the minimum necessary if you want one day to penetrate the magic circle of the associate-managers.

In the inter-war period, the house recruited among the higher government officials. One was Georges Wormser, alumnus of the École Normale Supérieure and a distinguished scholar, formerly in the cabinet of Georges Clemenceau, son and brother of collaborators at Lazard. And then there was Jean-Frederic Bloch-Lainé, a finance inspector whose son François, likewise an inspector and an octogenarian today, would embody the image of the exemplary high-ranking civil servant of the post-war period.

But the man who made Lazard's destiny does not appear on any parchment. André Meyer was exceptionally gifted on the Stock exchange. Engaged in the Thirties by the Paris branch, he crossed the Atlantic at the very start of the war to escape anti-Semitic persecution. During the hostilities, he reformed the New York office, then at its apogee. He and Pierre David-Weill, the house's heir, shared the feeling that Lazard must become a cobweb that could collect all the profitable "deals."

One of Pierre David-Weill's and André Meyer's contacts was named Jean Monnet. This father of unified Europe, an influential man respected by both the high administration and the politicians, introduced to them one of his protégés, the young State Counselor Christian Valensi, who was working under his orders in the Free French Army. A one-time financial adviser with the French embassy in Washington, Valensi navigated easily through the subtleties of the Marshall Plan. He became, in 1949, an associate-manager and conducted his first "big coup" by restructuring "Le Printemps."

Also in Jean Monnet's orbit was a finance inspector, just thirty years old. Jean Guyot did not balk at the task since he was at the same time an assistant-manager that the Treasury and responsible for financial questions to the High European Authority. A high-ranking civil servant with such a resume cannot help being of interest to Lazard. Having become an associate-manager, Guyot managed to have his bank designated to raise a loan in dollars for the ECSC (European Coal and Steel Community), created and chaired by. . . Jean Monnet.

Thus the network is woven. Among the "misfits" was Antoine Bernheim, who did not come in via the "Monnet channels." When he came to Lazard in 1967, he already sat on a comfortable fortune consolidated by his father, the lawyer and businessman Leonce Bernheim. His financial creativity, his money management skills, his incredible obstinacy allured André Meyer. Bernheim brought a share of his fortune to the capital of Lazard, and launched a new activity. From now on the bank would hold stakes in various stock investments, so complex that only Bernheim could find his way through the tangle.

Vincent Bolloré owes to him the multi-stage financial arrangements thanks to which the heir to the Breton SME could attain multinational status. Aggravated at always being called his protégé, Bolloré curtly claimed recently that Bernheim would not spend more than 3% of his time on his case! Which is already not so bad.

Bernard Arnault, chairman of LVMH, would not have become the emperor of luxury in France without him, either. He first met Bernheim back in 1984. Arnault, then chairman of a modest family real estate company, Férinel, wanted to buy the textile group Boussac, which had been ailing for years. An impertinent young heir? Bernheim, on the contrary, was astonished by Arnault's determination, who had done all his homework. But, within the administration that chooses the buyer, Bernard Arnault was a complete unknown. Lazard agreed to put its reputation and its money into the balance, bringing as much money as Férinel to the transaction. A winning association, which won out over the other candidate, the Bidermann group. Bernheim bet right: Lazard's investment appreciated wonderfully, and helped open a bright future in large transactions.

A few years later, the two men launched an even more daring operation that would earn them many reproaches later on. Whereas Laz-

ard (under the wing of Bruno Roger, another baron of the house who
became associate-manager in 1978), was celebrating the marriage of
Louis Vuitton (property of the touchy Henri Racamier) with Moët-
Hennessy (directed by the dashing Alain Chevalier), the Arnault-
Bernheim tandem was trying, *sub rosa*, to withdraw the new group,
LVMH, from the authority of its president, Alain Chevalier. The hidden
stake? A shell company located in Luxembourg, and that Chevalier
thought he controlled — whereas it was already in the hands of the enemy! The situation was delicate at the very least: at the same level,
within the same institution, Bruno Roger was trying to save Chevalier
while his associate Antoine Bernheim was working to cut him down.
Not good! "But how can it be otherwise," an associate-manager can-
didly defended himself. "Lazard knows everyone, and is therefore involved in almost all the big financial deals!"

The Young Man with the Address Book

In 1982, a young finance inspector joined the technocrats club poetically entitled "The Association for the Study of Foreign Experi-
ments." Under this aegis, he went to Great Britain to observe the methods used by Thatcher to trim down the State. This was a fortuitous
initiative that enabled him, upon his return to the Inspectorate, to get
some further guidance from Jacques Friedmann. This childhood friend
of Jacques Chirac, who became a close adviser of Edouard Balladur in
1986, called upon him to orchestrate the program of privatizations, for
the cabinet of the Finance Minister. And that was a strategic post during this first governmental cohabitation.

Mitterrand's re-election in 1988 was small potatoes, for him. The
summer was hardly over when Jean-Marie Messier became an associate-manager at Lazard. His move made tongues wag. Wasn't Lazard
among the banks and advisors selected by the government to carry out
certain privatizations, in particular that of Saint-Gobain? Wasn't this
precocious *pantouflage* a conspicuous violation of the penal code (article
175), which forbids a civil servant from joining a company with which
he had dealings, until five years had passed? Jovial, pleasant, incredibly
hard-working, as his often fascinated portraitists describe him, Messier
lost none of his cool demeanor in answering, "I set myself a deontologi-
cal rule: to refuse offers from companies that I had taken private, or

from members of the hard core. If I had wanted to take a safe, cushy job in the private sector, I had that choice. My decision was to take a risk-ier route."[2]

"Risky" may be going a little too far. But lucrative, surely. Under the second cohabitation, Edouard Balladur, Prime Minister, continued his program of privatization. And it was to Lazard that the most pres-tigious fell, that of BNP. But the social universe of Jean-Marie Messier exceeds by far the Club of the Friends of Balladur. They still tell sto-ries, dazzled by the party he threw for his tenth wedding anniversary in 1993, in a private mansion on place Saint-Georges, where the greatest stars of the political and financial worlds mingles. Both the Nicolases, Bazire (whom he introduced to Balladur) and Sarkozy, but also Jean-Louis Beffa and Didier Pineau-Valencienne. A concentration of power, in 150 people.

And what were the activities of this new godfather with such a youthful appeal? They were countless. He was, for example, president of the Orchestra Club of Paris, an association intended to finance the dissemination of music in the capital city. A stroke of luck: this volun-teer activity allowed him, during a concert, to meet Didier Pineau-Valencienne, chairman of Schneider. After the arpeggios, a little busi-ness. Shortly afterwards, they managed together Schneider's acquisi-tion of Square D, the largest acquisition of an American company car-ried out to date by a French company.

At Lazard, Messier's many ties with the upper crust quickly made him a very visible associate-manager. In spite of his successes, the young wonder boy preferred to join Générale des Eaux. His former bosses then set out to secure the collaboration of someone familiar with the corridors of power. A high-level official of the same generation as Messier was brought in as associate-manager. A great first: they chose a woman. And what is more, someone from Mitterand's camp. Anne Lauvergeon, from the École Normale Supérieure and a mining engineer, was "sherpa" for the former President during the international summits before becoming associate General Secretary of the Elysée. "The first contacts took place while I was still in the Elysée," she says. "Then, my new associates were incredibly efficient. They continued to court me. I had no trouble accepting. Intellectually, it was the most exciting thing I could do." Not sufficiently exciting, however, to put up with the in-trigues woven by Edouard Stern, the boss's son-in-law, madly enam-

ored with power. So in the end she preferred to join the Alcatel group.
A Strategy: "Buy at the Bottom"

To consolidate their networks, Lazard does not only hang around
with the people in power. "They have the particular knack of buying at
the bottom," says one former minister. "When you have just been
transferred, and your telephone does not ring any more, and your appointment book remains hopelessly empty, they call you and invite you
to lunch. They did this with me and many others. It is a very effective
method, for the interested parties remember it, once they have returned
to center stage." Those at Lazard remember it, too, and they invoice
their services at a very high price, far more expensive than most of their
competitors. To take offense would be to commit an error of taste, especially after being hosted at "In the Breeze," Michel David-Weill's
southernmost sumptuous residence. General opinion has it that he
knows how to treat his guests like princes. "Fundamentally, it is a little
like in psychoanalysis," a former associate from New York comments
with some irony. "For something to be really good, it has to be expensive. Obviously, for that to work, everybody has to be fully convinced:
both the therapist and the patient."

This near-monopoly goes beyond the framework of the company,
where Lazard starts to find competition from the Rothschilds and the
American banks that have set up shop in France. But Lazard's antennas
are spread as far as the ministries, at the fringes of political activity. "To
negotiate with the Treasury, for example, I always recommend Lazard
to my customers," tells a business lawyer. "Nobody is better placed
than they to knock on the right doors."

This complicity with all the governments, whatever their political
color, did not start yesterday. Lazard saved the franc already in 1924,
or, at least, strongly contributed to its salvation. While the pound sterling was climbing dangerously, the Poincaré government acknowledged
its impotence. The bank proposed a risky but original solution to him:
to stake France's gold reserves and negotiate a loan in dollars; buy
francs, and thus stop the speculation. Thanks to their relations in all
the important money markets, Lazard was able to buy up the franc the
moment when, with the pound losing ground, the speculators got
scared and abandoned their positions.

The bank mobilized itself again, in the lead-up to 1981, to escape
the wave of nationalization of credit. It was a question of survival!

Since 1978, Michel David-Weill had been probing the heart of certain Socialists. Contacts were cemented, in particular with Jacques Attali (who had done his business internship for his ENA degree at BSN, where he met Antoine Bernheim and Michel David-Weill). Lazard made the point that they were a bank only in name, or practically so; that they were a company of people not producing anything other than grey matter. And could there be anything more impalpable, more priceless, in a word less susceptible to nationalization than human creativity?

The tension went up all the same, in 1982, on the eve of the Council of Ministers' deliberation on the law of nationalization, when it was rumored that the threshold of deposits would be set not at a billion francs as envisaged, but at 500 million. In this case Lazard, which had taken every precaution not to exceed the billion, would be liable to nationalization. Finally, the threshold was fixed at a billion francs. "They chose a strategy diametrically opposed to that of Pierre Moussa who, at the head of Paribas, wanted to be more uncooperative and protect part of his empire from nationalization, according to a Leftist banker. "They developed dossiers of explanations, organized luncheons so they could understand what the Socialists had in mind. They also made them understand, admittedly, that the power would have need of them to borrow in dollars on the capital markets. An argument which, I believe, may have carried some weight."

Impossible to circumvent, Lazard makes some people jealous. To place in perspective the dispute over LVMH by the Arnault-Bernheim duo, a close relation of the bank asserts that between a quarter and a third of the cases pose problems because the opposing party is already a customer of the house. An associate-manager nevertheless maintains that the deontology is respected perfectly. "On the one hand," he says, "our meetings on Thursday mornings keep us apprised as to which deals the others are working on. In addition, we have engaged a lawyer, formerly with the COB (Commission of Stock Exchange Transactions), who examines all our contracts. We cannot commit ourselves without his agreement." That's all well and good. Nevertheless, British and American bankers are astonished by this, shall we say "informal," means of handling the conflicts of interests. "In the American and British banks, there is a guy whose sole responsibility is to ensure compliance with the ethical rules," explains one of them. "Over here, a deal like that of Bernard Arnault and LVMH, where the bank emits with one hand (that of Bruno Roger), a paper which it buys with the other hand (that of Antoine Bernheim), would be mind-boggling. *Idem* the acquisition of Bénédictine by Martini Rossi where two associate-managers, François de Combret and Antoine Bernheim, belonged to the opposite camps. It is said that the matter went all the way up to Michel David-Weill for arbitration."

This rather singular vision of the conflict of interests is explained by the relatively restricted size of the business world in France, and by the absolutely remarkable position that Lazard occupies. Far from being a simple service firm, this bank pursues its own goals: prosperity and expansion. Because its network is exhaustive and multifaceted, it chooses its allies of the moment according to its interests. But it happens that the members of the network put it in danger through their internal competitions. Like the Trotskyite organizations, Lazard can be the object of factional fighting, even of "scissions" between associate-managers. At the Internationalist Communist Party (PCI), at least, the intrigues form part of the folklore!

Bosses in Adversity

"Messrs, with the AFEP, I want to recreate the Establishment, which was damaged by the nationalizations . . . . I wish to give strength back to capitalism and to the market economy, for you know that I will always defend capitalism. I want to reconstitute an Establishment with solidarity between its members, solidarity that will be expressed every time one of its members is in difficulty."[3] These remarks by Ambroise Roux, the former chairman of the electricity company CGE[4] in 1982, may be read as a clear-cut definition of what a network of interests should be.

At that time, the Left had been in power for a year and a half. Many business leaders, heads of the famous Establishment, had been out of power for ten months — since the law of nationalization had relieved nearly all of them of their functions. Among them, Roux was the only one who had, calmly but firmly, indicated that he would not direct a nationalized CGE. On December 15, 1982, hehehe entered into the resistance, a courteous but determined resistance.

Until May 10, 1981, and a little bit earlier for the most intuitive, the "business circles" had been going their merry way. There were two banking poles, on one side Suez, on the other, Paribas. There were transitory alliances, matrimonial bonds as much as patrimonial. There were burning hatreds, therefore. And still the crisis was brewing. . . But then again, to allay this new concern, there was the permanent co-habitation with the State. This one, princely, entrusted to the great companies its best elements, ex-administration officials, *pantoufleurs* who were not repelled by the color of money. In the event of any problem, the Republic flew to the aid of a group in difficulty, with all forms of support and subsidies. That was "capitalism *à la Française*."

Even before this lovely month of May 1981, the CNPF was already but a shadow of itself. A façade, a place to organize press conferences; but nothing that resembles a network of influence. Thus in 1969 was born the AGREF (Association of Large French Companies Calling for Investment), under the initiative of Roger Martin, X-Mines and then chairman of Saint-Gobain. Seven years later, Roux assumed the chairmanship, to replace Jacques Ferry, president of the Chamber of Unions of the Iron and Steel Industry, the heir of the Committee of Forging Mills. In AGREF one could find all that was done best in industry and finance. With the nationalizations, this small group lost its *raison d'être*.

"The more a company's goals stray from the corporative mission that its very nature assigns to it, the less the solidarity of its members can be preserved," explains the historian Jean-Noël Jeanneney in his book *L'Argent caché* (Hidden Money).[5] "Except under one circumstance, however: when a serious threat seems to weigh on the political and social system. Then, and only then, people close ranks and the elementary collective reflexes take over." It could not be better said. And thus, Roux's initiative on December 15, 1982, was crowned with success, because a threat was there, but also because it was a question of restoring the Establishment.

He called them together, that morning, at the Hotel Crillon, to exhort them to have heart. There was the elegant Antoine Dupont-Fauville, a finance inspector, thanked with the presidency of the Crédit du Nord for its nationalization. And Jean-Marc Vernes, former owner and director of the bank that bears his name, a man of mighty political connections and mighty political battles, who was compensated (liberally) and ejected.

Among the score of business leaders who answered Roux's invitation, some had escaped nationalization and were still at the helm. And first and foremost was his friend Guy Dejouany, chairman of Générale des Eaux, which after the nationalizations became one of the leading French private companies. Roux and Dejouany had known each other since their days at the École Polytechnique, in 1940. Since then, they were always shoulder-to-shoulder, so much so that in 1995, Roux helped manage his friend's succession to the presidency of Générale des Eaux. It was he who engaged in talks with Jean-Marie Messier, and who convinced the young buck, the great hope of the Establishment, to forego part of his income in this prestigious transfer.

Another figure crowding into the Crillon on that rainy December morning was Alain Chevalier, owner of Moët-Hennessy and potential opponent to Roux within the CNPF, Marc Fournier, of Navigation-Mixte, Gilberte Beaux, the very legal-minded general director of Générale Occidentale, Jerome Monod, chairman of Lyonnaise des Eaux, François Dalle, chairman of L'Oréal, René Granier de Lilliac, of the Compagnie française des pétroles (CFP), Gerard Pélisson and Paul Dubrule, who so boldly built the Accor group, and several others.

All accepted Roux's proposition: to create the AFEP, the French Association of Private Companies, an avant-garde of a militant capitalism. Obviously, all the members had to belong to the private sector. Obviously, they must display unambiguous convictions. Obviously, new members, like those of the Jockey Club, would be voted in only unanimously.

Over the months, Roux personally approached the possible candidates. In the beginning, some of his closer allies, such as Edouard de Ribes of the Rivaud bank, were slow to join the AFEP. One can never be too careful. Others, on the contrary, enthusiastically accepted a proposal that they regarded as an honor.

François Pinault was one who accepted promptly. In 1983, he was as yet only an unknown self-educated contractor outside of the wood industry. But this Breton was already rich, thanks to his exceptional intuition. In 1963, at the age of 26, he had created a small wood trading company in the suburbs of Rennes, and sold it ten years later for $5 million. Two years later, he bought it back for 1 million! Meanwhile, he had rounded out his portfolio by several million dollars through speculation in sugar. And he was also making friends, among others Jacques Chirac, whom he met in 1976. Always ready to render service, he agreed to buy a bankrupt sawmill in Meymac, the future President's home district.

In spite of these rather promising feats of arms, Roux was rather daring to recruit Pinault into the AFEP in 1983. And the industrialist was incredulous when the godfather of the large-scale employers invited him to have a cup of tea in his lair on rue Margueritte, in the 17th arrondissement. He easily convinced Pinault. Was it an old patriarch's whim? The existing members were amused. But Roux would remain always faithful to "thunderbolt" of identity that he claims to have felt for Pinault. He would support him in all his undertakings. A Breton complicity, perhaps. . .

One year later, it was David de Rothschild who received a call from the president of the AFEP. His father, the baron Guy, had chosen to emigrate after the Left came into power, not accepting the loss of his bank. The son tried to set up a new finance company, but in 1984 the name of Rothschild was not the best passport to accelerate administrative procedures. David de Rothschild was thus satisfied to open a modest establishment, Paris-Orléans Gestion, where the only sign of ostentation was the ancestral portraits lining the walls.

A Rothschild in the AFEP, that was Roux's secret dream; and once again, he would never regret his choice. A decade later, Paris-Orléans Gestion had undergone several mutations and become Rothchild Co. Banks, and it was ranked second behind Lazard for mergers and acquisitions in France.

With the passing years, the AFEP grew. The 69 presidents of the largest French companies surrounded Roux, and met at least once a month for lunch or dinner around a noteworthy host. The menu was unanimously considered to be gastronomically insig-nificant, but the speakers were interesting. On the Right, the first were Chirac, Barre, Giscard. But very quickly, the opposing camp also began to be invited: Ministers like Jacques Delors, Laurent Fabius, then Pierre Bérégovoy; advisers to the prince, like Jacques Attali and Jean-Louis Bianco. Pierre Mauroy was the only one banned: nationalization, that was him!

These good relations were quickly nourished with the power that had disrupted everything, as Roux had wished. Each member paid an annual contribution of $38,000. This was spent neither on expensive meetings nor exotic travel, but to finance studies. The AFEP functioned as a provider of ideas, a clandestine factory of draft legislation that would be discreetly deposited on the desk of such and such minister, slipping him a suggestion that suited everyone: "Of course, we have nothing to do with it."

This original formula of legislative subcontracting was a great success during the Mitterrand years. Roux, who shared a great complicity with Pompidou, never got close with Giscard. With François Mitterrand, it was another thing. The two men met for the second time at Robert Mitterrand's early in 1981. Roux, far-sighted as ever, had hired this "somebody's brother" in 1975 thinking that he might, one never knows, be useful one day. Well done! Once Mitterrand was elected President, Roux was received (and listened to) on several occasions in the Elysée.

Subtle and crafty, he did not directly oppose, for example, the wealth tax; he only suggested higher thresholds or cases for exemption. He also proposed the law on "stock options" that allows companies to grant a second form of income, taxed at a lower rate, as well as reducing the tax rate on company benefits.

This discreet collaboration by no means prevented Roux and his buddies from preparing for the change of parties in power. Even before the creation of the AFEP, in the summer of 1981, when nothing had been committed to as yet regarding the extent and the methods of nationalization, the leaders of the AGREF contacted the business lawyer Jean Loyrette, who headed one of the biggest legal offices in Paris, to "see what could be done." "In the beginning, we held weekly meetings, and that stopped in September," Loyrette says to Stéphane Denis in Le Roman de l'argente.[6] "All that was semi-official. Seated around the table we had a series of representatives of the big companies, and lawyers." Jean Dromer, a protégé of Roux, finance inspector and president of the BIAO, chaired a secret committee of the "torture victims," as the heads of Suez, Rhône-Poulenc and Thomson called themselves. Out of these meetings would come a bulky report, argued very closely, that would address every detail of the question. For the record, the text in three volumes was conveyed to François Mitterrand by one of Loyrette's collaborators, the lawyer Jean-Marie Burguburu (whose wife, Danièle, the future president of the Higher Council of the Magistrature, was a close friend of the President).

Years Go By, Ambroise Roux Remains

It's one thing to limit the damage done by the prevailing power. It's another to prepare the restoration. Jean Dromer wasted no time.

Since 1983 he had participated in a working group intended to prepare privatizations. The group was headed by the finance inspector Jacques Friedmann. Roux, obviously, was not very far away. Since the autumn of 1984, he was concocting (with Balladur) the famous "hard cores," intended to lock up the capital of the companies returned to the private sector.

These hard cores became so many networks that were interwoven in friendship. One was that of Société Générale. The AGF and CGE (which was renamed Alcatel-Alsthom after its privatization) appeared among the largest shareholders of Générale. However, who exactly was the biggest is precisely the first shareholder of CGE? Paribas. After privatization, those who sat on the board of CGE were Bébéar (Axa), Jean Gandois (Pechiney), Jean Dromer and. . . Ambroise Roux.

In 1993, once Balladur was installed in Matignon, privatizations could pick up their interrupted course. Now, no one was talking about "hard" cores, but of "stable" cores. A simple nuance of vocabulary. For one might notice that the two large companies privatized during the second cohabitation, BNP and the UAP, actually form a pair: the first held 20% of the second, which held 15% of the first. Always these irresistible delights of dealing with one's own, enhanced by considerable fees for participating. Namely, an average of $16,000 per annum for sitting on a company's board of directors. The ones who were most active were the chairman of the Crédit Lyonnais Jean Peyrelevade (on 14 boards), that of BNP Michel Pébereau (13), Ambroise Roux (11), Guy Dejouany (10), and Michel François-Poncet (Paribas, 9), followed by Jacques Calvet, Marc Viénot, Jacques Friedmann, Jean-Louis Beffa (Saint-Gobain), Bébéar (Axa). In short, all these corporate bigwigs know how to combine business with pleasure: to cultivate a prestigious network of relations while deriving some palpable benefit from this exercise.

Since December 15, 1982 and the meeting of the "torture victims" at the Hotel Crillon, French capitalism has been restructured but still practices the sacrificial rite of having the leaders swap among themselves, in a vast display of solidarity, the positions of power in the great companies. As proof, Roux, fifteen years after his forced retirement, continues to play the "godfather."

Still president of the AFEP, he got to work again in 1995 and convinced Jacques Chirac to boost consumption with a tax bonus for well-to-do households. At 74 years, Roux almost feels young again. Has he given any thought to a successor, a man of influence on his scale, equipped with a network comparable to his? Roux says that he has proposed this impressive heritage to Claude Bébéar, but says it was turned down. The chairman of Axa says he is too busy to assume this heavy burden. His elder understands, benevolent and. . . a little condescending.

The Bébéar Gang

"The company heads and the undersigned wish to express very clearly their feelings upon learning of the measures taken against Didier Pineau-Valencienne, president of the Schneider Group, whose rigorous morals, deontology and competence are unanimously recognized." This "advertising" message, if one dares call it such, inserted in *Le Monde* and other newspapers at the end of May 1994, followed upon the incarceration in Belgium of the chairman of Schneider, who was charged with having injured the minority shareholders of two Belgian subsidiary companies, following certain transactions. Among the signatories were thirteen of Schneider's board members. 26 other signatures followed, nominally signaling their support on a personal basis. The most notable was that of Edith Cresson, whom Pineau-Valencienne had recruited into the group. And in addition, one could see just about every name of the new French capitalism.

Most of the petitioners belong to the "Bébéar Gang." In addition to the chairman of Axa, there was Bernard Arnault (LVMH), Jean-Louis Beffa (Saint-Gobain), Jean-René Fourtou (Rhône-Poulenc), Michel François-Poncet and André Lévy-Lang (Paribas), Bertrand Collomb (Lafarge-Coppée), Vincent Bolloré, Pierre Dauzier (Havas), Pierre Faurre (Sagem), Claude Heurteux (Auguste Thouard), Serge Kampf (Cap Gemini), Henri Lachmann (Strafor), Michel Pébereau (BNP), François Pinault, and Philippe Villin (then at *Le Figaro*).

Pineau-Valencienne, obviously, belonged to this distinguished club. "Company and City" was a club for promising leaders, created in 1983 at the periphery of the Republican party. Its members, numbering 28, have been the same since it was created. There have been no new members, and only one departure. The pleasure of dining together once a month wins out over any other consideration. There is much talk about great vintages, a passion that Bébéar shares with some of his peers, and a little about the economy. They all call each other "*tu*" and sometimes they regress to adolescence in this delicious closed-door session for the powerful. The semi-monthly breakfasts centered around a personality, a sort of intellectual alibi, definitely get fewer votes!

From its beginnings, this group was structured around the "X" Bébéar. He came out with rather a low rank from the École Polytechnique, having enjoyed life too much during school, but he kept excellent contacts with his classmate Bernard Dumon, chairman of the sugar group Saint-Louis, who perished in a tragic air crash in 1994. Jean-René Fourtou, graduated from the great school a few years later; but Bébéar met him in the orbit of the UDF. What is more, the two had much in common: they are alums of the École Polytechnique, certainly, but also they are Gascon, sons of teachers and lovers of good food. Fourtou, for his part, maintained good relations with two former classmates: Bertrand Collomb and Jean-Louis Beffa, both of whom graduated in the first ranks, and consequently became engineers of the Mining Corps. Serge Kampf, the very discrete founder of Cap Gemini, a great rugby fan like Bébéar and Pierre Dauzier, met Fourtou in the 1970's. At the time, he almost confiscated the majority of Bossard's capital from its consultant-shareholders, of whom Fourtou was the boss. He finally stopped at 49%, and the two men learned to do well by each other.

And it was Jean-René Fourtou again who contacted a chairman he'd met in meetings of the Republican party — Claude Heurteux of the Auguste Thouard company — to bring his talents as a lawyer and his invaluable good humor to the group. With Gérard Brémond, the chairman of Pierre et Vacances, he represented the real estate sector. Igor Landau was part of the board of Rhône-Poulenc, chaired by Fourtou. The latter was a pivotal member of the ensemble, and had known Pineau-Valencienne since he was a consultant. Bossard, of which he had been chairman, had audited Creusot-Loire, a property of the Schneider group which DPV had had to shed with sorrow, gaining a reputation as a company grave-digger.

Pineau-Valencienne is not X, but HEC (Haute école commerciale, a top business and management school). That's not as impressive, but the Establishment could stand to be opened up a little! During business school, he had met the Alsatian Henri Lachmann, with whom he got on well, and who evolved to become the chairman of the co-opted Strafor. Bébéar also called Vincent Bolloré to join the ranks — the eternal young star of French business, whom he had met when Bolloré Technologies first got listed on the stock exchange in 1982, and with whom he created a foundation for humanitarian aid. David de Rothschild, in 1983, was not yet impossible to circumvent in putting together a successful round table, even if it had been only gastronomical. But Bébéar, even before Roux, took the happy initiative to invite him to join the club.

The bonds woven between all and sundry are thus multiple and sometimes go back many years. But what good is "Company and City" to them? That Claude Heurteux and Igor Landau go arm in arm to Edinburgh to watch the France-Scotland match, that Bébéar and Fourtou adore finding themselves impromptu, on a Sunday evening, tasting an array of pâtés washed down with a fine white wine, that Pineau-Valencienne and Lachmann ski together on the snow-covered slopes of Val d'Isère, that's all very nice. But would these so-busy men have created a network from scratch, just so they could enjoy their too rare moments of leisure together?

Obviously, a band of great buddies which account for, all told, almost $100 billion turnover (that is approximately one the third of the French national budget)[7], also has concerns that are more down to earth. They might, for example, talk about the boards of directors where they sit together. Bébéar is an administrator of Paribas and of Schneider; those two companies are represented on the boards of directors of Axa by Michel François-Poncet and Pineau-Valencienne. Out of respect for symmetry, Poncet also sits on the council of Schneider, and Pineau-Valencienne on that of Paribas. This is a means of guarding oneself against inopportune intrusions in the capital and the management of these companies.

In December 1995, for example, Andre Lévy-Lang, another "X," who joined Paribas long ago on the recommendation of Jean Riboud (his former boss at Schlumberger), was questioned by Judge Eva Joly. His legal troubles stemmed from the Ciments français affair (a subsidiary of Paribas): it seemed that the company's accounts had been made up. Lévy-Lang, according to the evidence, had nothing to do with it. But this kind of legal mishap plays rather poorly in the temple of old-style capitalism. On the Paribas board of directors, Bébéar made it clear that any initiative to destabilize Lévy-Lang would be unwelcome. Of course, that is a matter of solidarity, as is well understood.

The AFEP, a brotherhood of the heads of top private companies, and "Company and City," a generation-specific network, do not, even so, cover all the powerful men in the French economy. Witness Jacques Calvet. At the moment when the AFEP was being created, it would have been diplomatically delicate to choose between one of the two leaders of Peugeot, Jacques Calvet or Jean-Paul Parayre. It was even more unthinkable for the automobile group to not be represented at all, in the incipient clique of capitalists who had entered into resistance. Not to make either one jealous, Roux took a different route. GEFCO, one of the group's companies, was chaired by a member of the Peugeot family, and it was he who joined the AFEP. Finally, "nobody really complains about Calvet's absence," explains an eminent member of the association. "He is unmanageable, often lets loose with theories that cannot be applied, and does not show a great propensity toward solidarity."

Certain leaders are straightforwardly banned. Since the creation of the AFEP, Roux has managed a "red list" of chairmen to be avoided. A half-dozen of names, at the head of which is that of Jean-Luc Lagardère. Why? The godfather of the Establishment, when he is questioned on this subject, almost loses his legendary urbanity, without openly giving the reason for such hostility. "Ambroise" holds onto this chart of dishonor, which enables him to pronounce severe and final judgments of value on those whom he will never accept in his network.

"Godsons" of the Third Generation

Already, behind Company and City, ambitious young people hardly 40 years old are pushing. It would be too much to say that Roux sponsors them. But he manages with care, if not affection, the career of the most brilliant, Jean-Marie Messier. The forty ambitious young forty-somethings of the "Club 40" revolve around him. Every month, they meet for lunch on the sixth floor of the Hotel Raphaël, which proves that the taste for luxury does not always wait for advanced age. To be like the big guys, they invite one or two personalities from the political, scientific or intellectual world. The guests are requested to state their "ten commandments;" a kind of Proustian questionnaire in the careerist mode.

Initially, a young headhunter, Eric Besson, had the idea to assemble a club of "baby-managers." He took as a starting point a list of young managers with great potential (as they say), that he had established during an employment search. These are the ones who are found regularly at the Hotel Raphaël: François Auque, of the Court of Auditors, financial director of Aérospatiale, Patricia Barbizet, the "financial person" of the Pinault group, Jerome Contaminates, an X and an ENA, financial director of Elf Aquitaine, Patrick Kron, rising star of Pechiney, Veronique Morali, finance inspector and right arm of Marc de La Charrière, Cyrille du Peloux, X-Bridges and head of Lyonnaise-Communication, Guillaume Pépy, member of the Council of State, former chief assistant of Martine Aubry who also turned up under Marc Ladreit de La Charrière, Jean-Marc Forneri, ENA alumnus and a banker at Worms and Co., Lionel Zinzou, alumnus of the École Normale Supérieure, veteran of the Fabius cabinet and general manager of Danone.

Our Literary Friends

The friends of Roux and Bébéar do not have any greater monopoly on anything than do the Masters of the political intellocracy. Examples are rife; but one of the most emblematic godfathers of the "media mouthpieces," as the journalist Jean-François Kahn calls them, is without question the philosopher-editor-chronicler-playwright-screen writer Bernard-Henri Lévy.

The career of this flamboyant ENS alumnus started early and to great fanfare. Since his arrival at the publisher Grasset in 1973 (when he was 25 years old) as director of a collection, BHL remembered some friends from the ENS prep school and he astutely requested their manuscripts. And so is fed a writer's reputation and. . . the media machine. In 1977, Lévy and his friends proclaim themselves the "new philosophers." "In 1966, Guérin, Jambet, Lardreau, Lévy, Némo and some others were in the prep classes of Louis-le-Grand. . . Is it any surprise that they are all published by the same house, in collections directed by Bernard-Henri Lévy?"[8] Roger-Pol Droit prudently asks. A prudence that probably has to do with the fact that he too belongs to the prep school clan that publishes at Grasset. Moreover, when Lévy published *La Barbarie à visage humain* (*Cruelty with a Human Face*), the small troop, including the same Roger-Pol Droit, went out of their way to talk it up.

But these favors between editor and chronicler, between chronicler and editor, such routine transactions in the logistical life of letters, were only the first steps of the BHL network, which extends far beyond the literary perimeter alone. "Today, the same ones have reviews, write books, produce newspapers, are supported by the Ministry of Culture and direct Yves St. Laurent," the philosopher Alain Finkielkraut spat out one day.[8] Who was the target of this perfidy? Lévy, of course.

To recapitulate: the periodical is *La Règle du jeu*,* with refined esthetics, and one of its key contributors is Jean-Paul Enthoven, who defected from *Le Nouvel observateur* to *Le Point*, and who might be regarded as Lévy's best friend. Books, Finkielkraut would have bad grace to reproach BHL for writing. As for newspapers, one may suspect an allusion to Globe, the defunct pro-Mitterrand weekly that was financed by Pierre Bergé, and to which BHL lent his talent and his name (since he was a shareholder). He also brought there some of his trustworthy friends like Laurent Dispot, another alum from ENS, and Vincent Léry and Gilles Hertzog, two former collaborators at *L'Imprévu*, the daily newspaper that he had created in 1975 and which lasted for ten numbers. Hertzog, homologue and rival of Enthoven in the heart of the master, is a specialist in organizing and accompanying trips to ex-Yugoslavia. At the Ministry of Culture, the same BHL chaired the commission of advances on cinema receipts, a nice high-level position where they distribute subsidies to eternally grateful film producers. As for "directing Saint Laurent," BHL was content, in fact, merely to sit on the board of directors of the couture house. (A sinecure that is, in itself, already enviable.)

Besides, he met there another of his friends among the "media-mouthpieces," the commentator-finance inspector Alain Minc, who advises ten big company chiefs including François Pinault. This great friend of Jacques Chirac also appears in the first BHL Club. Lévy's father, André, made his fortune in the timber industry, and was associated with Pinault. Eclectic, the great helmsman of "PPR" (Pinault-Printemps-Redoute) today performs works of patronage by co-financing the cinematographic works produced by the son of his former associate and friend, such as *Le Jour et la nuit* (*Day and Night*), distributed in February 1997. Definitely spoiled by his friends, BHL had already benefited in 1990 from the staggering assistance of Pierre Bergé, Yves St. Laurent and the Cérus Society, whose chairman at the time was Alain

(*The Rules of the Game.* The 1998 edition of this collective work is available in English from Algora Publishing.)

Minc, for his televised saga on the history of the intellectuals.

Minc is a finance inspector who is never put off by the hint of a monopoly; he combines his activities in the business world (where he continues to shine in spite of the bankruptcy of his own company) and in the intelligentsia. Examples: he meets Jean-Jacques Delort, the former president of Printemps, at the Saint-Simon Foundation, a chic club of reflection that brings together business leaders, high-ranking administration officials, intellectuals and journalists. He gets him into the board of directors of Yves St. Laurent, where Bernard-Henri Lévy also sits, the friend of François Pinault. Then Minc plays intermediary between Delort and Pinault. Some time later, he introduces Pinault to the shareholders of *Le Monde*, of which he chairs the board of trustees. In summer 1996, he supports his friend Pierre Bergé, president of Yves St. Laurent, in buying the *Nouvel Economiste*. It would be hard to "weave" a better network, or to do more to satisfy, one after the other, all its influential members!

"I don't have a network, I only have friends," claimed Lévy in 1981, forgetting that friends form one' network as voyages form one's youth. But, it is true, BHL has friends. That is even how certain of his peers explain his extraordinary media success. "He has an authentic kindness and true fidelity," an observer of the intellocracy claims. "Two qualities that enabled him to gain the recognition of a second circle that includes celebrities like Philippe Sollers, Christian Delacampagne, Luc Ferry, Dominique Grisoni and Michel Onfray. In exchange, he requires perfect loyalty." That is how he was able to gather support amongst all of the Parisian intelligentsia when he was preparing a petition on behalf of Alain Carignon, that he insisted on defending in spite of the overwhelming evidence of his dishonesty, at the end of 1994. Certain friends, being solicited for support but anxious to preserve their reputations, did refuse to stand up for the prisoner. But they trembled some, wondering what media retribution this treachery would earn them!

For an intellectual like BHL, the great causes are an occasion to redistribute the cards in the complicity of the high intelligentsia. At the beginning of the conflict in the Balkans, the most active media figure was a competitor, Alain Finkielkraut. Finkielkraut was an unconditional defender of the Croats and a zealous supporter of the "small nations," with the writer Milan Kundera. Over the months, the spotlights moved from Zagreb toward Sarajevo. Finkielkraut was obsolete: his theory did not apply much to the multi-religious and multi-cultural situation of Bosnia. Lévy waited for the right moment. The values that he defended through Bosnia — multiculturalism, tolerance — these are simple concepts, easily sold, that would quickly dethrone the Croatian equation in popular opinion. Then the pro-Bosnian lobby was born, that would succeed better in the newspapers and television than in the political sector, and the so-called "Sarajevo list" maintained by Leon Schwartzenberg was torn up.

Powerful in all these feats of arms (from publishing to international politics, from perfumery to cinema), Lévy is the only intellectual who has succeeded in creating his own network. No need for him to appear in such or such men's club to prove his existence and make an impression. BHL is a network unto himself.

The "Salon des Refusés" against the "Club of the Established"

The competition, even the antipathy, burst into the open on the eve of the 1995 presidential campaign. The "established," a scant hundred success stories, found themselves within the Saint-Simon Foundation. The "refused," a smaller number, promised to make resistance within the club "Phares et balises" (Lighthouses and Beacons). These two clans would spar until summer 1996. The "Lighthouses and Beacons" then decided to abandon ship, considering they were no longer making a useful contribution to the intellectual debate.

The first of these two clubs was baptized in 1982 by historian Emmanuel Le Roy Ladurie, otherwise known as the brother-in-law of Roger Fauroux (then chairman of Saint-Gobain). Saint-Simon was destined to become a club of élites drawn from the reformist Left and the enlightened Right, to promote a "realistic" form of national government. Pierre Rosanvallon, an expert on social movements, became its General Secretary. The central core included Alain Minc and the historian François Furet. Meeting on rue du Cherche-Midi, they would make appointments for a working breakfast or a simple lunch around a topical speaker. They worked, they published notes in the form of an austere green booklet. In short, they reflected.

That is the official story. According to Rosanvallon, it would be risky, even inaccurate, to see this concentration of élites *à la Française* anything more than an idea factory. "Analyzing facts through the lens of networks is tantamount to a perversion of totalitarian thought," he retorts when this sensitive ground is approached. "Seeing everything in terms of networks is anti-sociology, it simply means equating every form of loyalty with a secret organization."

Seeing everything in terms of networks? Yes, that would be going too far! At the same time, Rosanvallon does not scorn secrecy. If the club is so open, why refuse to provide a list of members? "A quarter are from the company world, a quarter from the universities, a quarter from high public office, and the remainder from civil society," he comments soberly.

On the business side, there is in fact a powerful "sub-network," Saint-Gobain, represented by the former and current leaders of that large company: Jean-Louis Beffa, the chairman, Roger Fauroux, the ex-CEO, Philippe Crouzet, International Director, and also veterans like José Bidegain, who was an assistant general manager of the company between 1982 and 1989, Xavier de Villepin, ex-CEO of Saint-Gobain Glazing, today a senator, Francis Mer, an X-Mines who then became interested in the iron and steel industry as the head of Usinor-Sacilor, Pierre Blayau, who was head of Pont-à-Mousson. And let us not over-look, of course, Alain Minc, who began his career at Saint-Gobain.

At their sides, a few mascots of French industry labor away, such as the former chairman of AGF Michel Albert, the head of France Tele-com Michel Bon, the number one of Publicis Maurice Lévy, and Jerome Monod (Lyonnaise des Eaux), Jean Peyrelevade (Crédit Lyonnais), Pi-erre Richard (Crédit local de France), Gerard Worms, the ex-CEO of Suez who became an associate-manager at Rothschild, and so on.

The university provides some of its most attractive representa-tives. In addition to François Furet and Emmanuel Le Roy Ladurie, the philosopher Luc Ferry, the medical professor Philippe Meyer, and the sociologists Edgar Morin and Alain Touraine also counts among the regulars at Cherche-Midi. The political scientist Olivier Duhamel, who met his wife Evelyne Pisier in this coterie (she is an academic and a for-mer Book Director for the Ministry of Culture); Duhamel created a sub-network Saint-Simonian. Functioning the same way as the working meetings and the public talks by leading figures, this branch specializes in neo-Rocardism.

The "civil society" section, if one excludes a few big lawyers like Jean-Denis Bredin and Georges Kiejman, brings together mostly journalists, including Jean-Pierre Elkabbach, Philippe Labro, Christine Ockrent, Anne Sinclair for audio-visual, Serge July (not a very assiduous attendee), his successor at the head of the editorial board of *Libération* Laurent Joffrin, Jacques Julliard of *Le Nouvel observateur*, and Jean-Marie Colombani from *Le Monde*.

Here thus banded together we find the "Master-Mouthpieces," who embody the legitimacy of the word and the power to diffuse it. How do they use this privilege? By hammering out consensual theses. So consensual, in the eyes of their detractors among the intelligentsia, that those "who do not think right" are excluded.

Then, the "deviants" built their own network, which became fashionable after being ignored for a long time. This is a place where the art of trans-party consensus that excels within the Saint-Simon Foundation is scorned. In 1991, Jean-Claude Guillebaud, journalist, writer and editor, and Régis Debray, philosopher and "mediologist," created the club "Lighthouses and Beacons," with some close friends of Jean-Pierre Chevènement, affirming their opposition to the Gulf War. This cause, at the time, was not too popular and the Parisian Nomenklatura did not fight their way into the monthly meetings.

"Lighthouses and Beacons" was named by General Buis (not your typical soldier), a talented polemologue and contributor to various publications. When he was in Egypt, during the war, those who represented free France would meet clandestinely in a warehouse of the Suez Canal company, on which was written, "Lighthouses and Beacons." "That name was enthusiastically adopted, since our idea was to be London against Vichy," a fan of the club comments. "Lighthouses" first started attracting reinforcements when the debate on Maastricht was heating up. Saint-Simon defended the treaty vigorously. Not Debray's and Guillebaud's club, where one had the exciting feeling of serving in the resistance. Very quickly "Lighthouses and Beacons" became the salon des refusés," the historian Alexandre Adler humorously explains. He was one of the pillars of the club.

It turned out to be a rather productive salon, even outside of meeting hours. "I invented the term "La pensée unique," [*Trans. note*: "the only way," a particular slant on "politically correct" thinking] while splashing around in a swimming pool with Régis Debray," continues Adler. "I had just finished reading all the weekly magazines and I declared to Régis that I had had the impression of reading the same newspaper over and over again, their contents were so identical." Thus was born an expression that would achieve immense media success.

While they popularized some concepts, "Lighthouses" remained voluntarily obscure for a long time. The first Tuesday of every month, they would meet in the district of Odéon and host a public figure, often someone from the political world, for a talk over a simple meal. "The ambiance," summarizes a faithful attendee, "was resolutely opposed to the plush and cushy rue du Cherche-Midi. We did it more like a country- style buffet. It wasn't "Viva Socialisma," but it was sort of like that."

"Long live Socialism," maybe, but not just any kind of Socialism. Out of forty people, certainly there was a proof reader and an unknown poet, but also the president of Arte, Jerome Clément, the fashionable economist Jean-Paul Fitoussi (also a member of the Saint-Simon Foundation), the philosopher Blandine Kriegel, Mrs. Adler, the literary columnist Bertrand Poirot-Delpech, the academics Pierre-André Taguieff and Emmanuel Todd, the pro-Chirac writer Denis Tillinac and the journalists Serge Halimi, Denis Jeambar, and Laurent Joffrin.

The "Torcello Diners"

"Lighthouses and Beacons," to tell the truth, perhaps would have remained a nice group of buddies, curious and cultivated, if the evening of October 4, 1994 had gone differently. That day, the club's guest was "Jacques," a sympathetic presidential candidate. The mutual detestation between him and "Edouard" was out in the open. The Prime Minister was gaining ground in public opinion polls, the Mayor of Paris was receding into the background.

So on October 4, Chirac was not in a very good mood. He was tense, he "hated" to take on a fashionable image. The evening was rather dull until the moment when, introduced by Guillebaud, the sociologist Emmanuel Todd showed an electoral analysis based on the results of the European elections that he had just conducted for the Saint-Simon Foundation, of all people. In substance, Todd explained to Chirac why he had every chance of being elected he could detect and promise to reduce the "social fracture." Chirac was not familiar with this intellectual, but he pricked up his ears when Todd claimed that he should go after the electorate of the workingmen and the employees, who detested Balladur.

Meanwhile, the opposing camp got busy. Methodically. Saint-Simon, or at least some of its members, deployed their skills and persuasiveness to "launch" politicians. In the mid-1980's, they saw Michel Delebarre as a promising protégé. Alain Minc then carried out the operation in the name of the foundation. "The members," the journalists François Bazin and Joseph Macé-Scaron say cruelly in *Politocrates*,[10] "saw him as the modern prototype of the social democrat from the north of Europe, whereas he was only an heir to the aging SFIO from the Nord-Pas-de-Calais."

The abandonment of Delebarre in favor of Fabius for the conquest of the SP, then his failure for the presidency of the Nord-Pas-de-Calais area ended up discouraging the most convinced. Attention then gravitated toward Michel Rocard, without a consensus being really established, and next on the very promising Martine Aubry. But already, the 1995 presidential pre-campaign was beginning. And with it, more subtle combinations.

"To the Torcello diners": that is the enigmatic dedication Alain Duhamel used in one of his books, *De Gaulle—Mitterrand, La Marque et la trace*.[11] There were really only three "diners": the author himself, the public opinion poll specialist Jerome Jaffré, and the director of *Le Monde*, Jean-Marie Colombani. The name of "Torcello" comes from their shared passion for the island of Torcello, close to Venice.

But Duhamel's allusion goes beyond the simple Italian gastronomical reference. Some two months after Chirac visited "Lighthouses and Beacons," Jacques Delors, the Left's candidate, had lunch with the "diners." That day, the three political analysts dissuaded Delors from presenting himself. In the event he was elected, they told him, he would not have the parliamentary majority necessary to govern.

Did these discouraging predictions influence Delors' decision? The pro-Balladurians, in any case, saw it as a way of consolidating the presidential future of their own candidate, by setting aside his most credible adversary. However, not far from the "diners" there were members of the Saint-Simon Foundation who were not stinting their efforts for Balladur.

Early in March 1995, Chirac was invited to the Saint-Simon Foundation. His position in the opinion polls had started to worry the Prime Minister's fans. The Mayor of Paris transformed this incursion into enemy territory into a personal revenge. First, he explained that he did not believe the representatives of the "civil society" in the government. Gasping in the audience, especially from Bernard Kouchner. Then came, as if by providence, a question from Minc about how Chirac intended to finance his expensive promises and make up the resulting deficits. With eager effrontery the candidate retorted, before this captive audience, "Mister Minc, do you know what happens when the head of a household can't pay her rent anymore? No, you do not know, Mister Minc? These are things that you do not know. Me, I've met people who could not pay their rent any more. And do you know what happens to them? They are thrown out. And their children are handed over to the Health Department. And do you know how much it costs when a child is placed with the Health Department, Mister Minc?"[12] And so on. A lesson that his audience did not relish.

The Real Chic of Risoul

Once the presidential election was over, the Saint-Simonians, being pragmatists, realized that having the pro-Chirac head of Lyonnaise des Eaux Jerome Monod was no longer enough; although the absence of presidential support was nothing new for them: Mitterrand, already, had been leery of what he regarded as a den of the "second Left." His faithful pals were hardly represented there, except in the persons of Robert Badinter and Georges Kiejman.

As a sign of pluralism, the Saint-Simonian network welcomed with open arms the superstar economist from "the other side," Jean-Paul Fitoussi, with whom Pierre Rosanvallon had written a research paper in 1996, *L'Age des inégalités* (*The Age of Inequalities*).[13] But the war was already being waged on a different battlefield.

At the end of 1995, while France is was paralyzed by strikes, two other clans clashed: the "Touraine" group against the followers of Bourdieu. The first supported Juppé's plan, the second revisited the concept of class struggle.

In fact, for the intelligentsia, it was the review *Esprit* directed by Olivier Mongin that first expressed enthusiasm for the rescue of Social Security. It took advantage of support from the Saint-Simon Foundation (via Rosanvallon) to launch a call in favor of the governmental plan.

Opposing that was a group of young academics, forty-somethings, from the extreme Left, who took the initiative of drafting a petition in support of the strikers in general, and of public services in particular. As fine experts, at least theoretical, of the mechanisms of power, they knew that some form of media engine would be required to sell their ideas. Along came the sociologist Pierre Bourdieu, and the philosophers Jacques Derrida and Étienne Balibar, respected sexagenarians whose signatures give weight and power to any text.

Once the strikes were over, this very young network endured via the Club Merleau-Ponty, resolutely on the Left. A month after the end of the strikes, four of its members signed (in *Le Monde*)[14] a tribune that indicated the adversary clearly. "The sudden outburst of petitioners that accompanied the recent social movements seem to be a symptom of the transformations of the conditions of intellectual activity. How were certain 'Leftist experts' able to use their media interventions, the valets for the 'privileged,' and make a trade-union leader hostile to the strike pass for a 'courageous woman'? Certainly we cannot prejudge the various intentions of the call launched by *Esprit* and the Saint-Simon Foundation. However, when its initiators chose to publish a text supporting a governmental plan already fought by a broad social protest, maybe it is the entire Enlightenment that is going out." Oh, is that all?

Philippe Corcuff, master of conferences at the IEP of Lyon, Bastien Francois, professor at the university of Rennes, Delphine Gardey, research director at the City of Sciences and Industry, Sophie Wahnich, head of research at the CNRS, denounced this text for its "soft violence of (self) censure" that "restricted the margins of what is thinkable and say-able in the intellectual and media space." "The Saint-Simon Foundation," they claimed, "is also a product and an agent of this process." Golly!

If they attacked the famous foundation tooth and nail, it was not only for ideological reasons, for behind the great jousts there are less glorious battles that are played out in the back corridors. The French university would no longer be what it is without these tactical confrontations, alliances, and calculated treasons that govern the least attribution of status in a faculty and where intellectual micro-networks, completely invisible to the public, work in the background to destabilize some and to promote others.

The competition for positions is all the more complex and strategic when admission to the coteries of higher education requires one to be elected twice by his peers. First, one of the 80 local advisory commissions proposes names. Then, a national commission does so as well, in each discipline. It's best, obviously, to have solid support at both stages. Thus, in sociology, you can't get anywhere without the sponsorship of one of the two enemies, Pierre Bourdieu and Alain Touraine. To further complicate things, two minor gurus disturbed the game for several years by imitating the strategy of the small parties. The academics Raymond Boudon and Michel Crozier thus joined forces, according to their interests and those of their protégés, with one or the other of the two leaders.

This brief detour through the university world makes it possible to clarify under a harsher light the quarrels between the factions of the intellocracy. The media, publishing, and higher education are three pillars under which more or less stable, more or less circumstantial networks are built, working together or at cross purposes according to the occasion.

Old alliances dedicated to nostalgia and emotional commemoration, are sometimes pressed into service again. A sign of the times? Trotskyism is back in style. It is good to be one of them. But not just any Trotskyism. Not the cult version, not the Workers' Struggle, or the conspirators after the style of Lambert. It is the convivial version of the Revolutionary Communist League that appeals these days to a fringe of intellectuals who are repelled by la pensée unique.

A small club thus federates some old thinking heads from the "powder-keg years." SPRAT, the "Society for Resisting the 'Air du Temps'" for example, meets once a month in the national buildings of the LCR, on rue de Charonne in Paris, close to the Nation. Created in 1992 by two "fellow travelers," the writers Gilles Perrault and Didier Daeninckx, SPRAT brings together old men and woman generally recycled into journalism or teaching, but also doctors, advertising executives. . . They talk about Vietnam, humanitarian aid, unified Europe or ex-Yugoslavia. Then, they drink a glass or dine in one of the nearby restaurants.

Alain Krivine, the tireless leader of the movement, is careful not to attend SPRAT meetings that have long been led by Daniel Bensaïd, his "second," a professor of philosophy. He is too afraid, says he, that his presence would "Trotsky-ize" the club's image. Nonetheless, politics is always on the prowl. "We got bludgeoned together, some of us lost teeth there," he says. "When I joined, there were 172 members. So there remains the complicity of a past in the minority. Given the rise of Le Pen, many decided to get over their torpor. The majority of veterans are 'dormant,' ready to be used again in the event of a real attack." These are among the networks that partly feed the increasing number of demonstrations that take place all over France to counter the extremists of the National Front. They are the same ones that are the life blood of associations and collectives of all kinds that were born these last few years to claim the "right to housing" or the naturalization of "undocumented" aliens. Compared to the traditional parties that are stuck in their power struggles, these networks monopolize, after their own fashion, a whole landscape of social and every-day questions that was left unclaimed.

Proof of this growing success: every summer, the League's summer school in Risoul, in the southern Alps, attracts a little bigger (and higher class) audience. With four seminars per day during a week, attendance claims something more than conviviality. One finds there the writer Gilles Perrault, the actor Philippe Caubère, the documentary film-maker Paul Carpita and even. . . Régis Debray.

Well-placed in the intellocratic landscape, the media specialist (who was also cofounder of "Lighthouses and Beacons") knows very well how complex and fluid is this milieu, much more fluid than that of business. "There is the diplomatic corps, and the medical profession. Teachers, and the principal trades, are clearly visible," he analyzed already in 1977 in *Pouvoir intellectuel*.[15] "Is there an intellectual corps, and what would be its framework? How would you encapsulate it, and in what terms could you define it? The higher realms of the private and public sector are nearly all listed in *Bottin Mondain* (a French *Social Register*), are members of well-defined circles or Clubs (the Jockey-Club, the Automobile Club, Rotary, Saint-Cloud Golfe, etc.). Where do the intellectual and moral higher realms of the country come together? We still lack a *Who's Who of the Intelligentsia*." If we still lack that, it's because the networks that exist have nothing to gain from transparency. Reporting on the behavior that prevails in the artistic, literary and journalistic milieux in his *Mémoires*,[16] Jean-François Revel gives a caustic recipe for success. "Don't resist the pressures of the networks of influence of the intellectuals. Or, at least, don't open hostilities against any of them, unless you are sure of being squarely supported by others, on whom you can rely in defense as well as in the attack . . . To live in peace, you must, if not approve of everything, which would annoy, at least be installed as a designated defender of a trend or a clan, including everything they do, the worst as well as the best." In the absence of a *Whos's Who*, here at least is a definition that is precise and to the point!

Chapter 7

CONSPIRACIES

A club of "30," "40," or "100," a secret society of "13," there is no threshold that constitutes a mutual aid or mutual assistance network. On the other hand, there is a magic figure that for decades has fascinated all sorts of conspirators on the fringes of the extreme Right. Before the war, that figure featured in the dreams of those who were eager to reverse the Republic, and today it still makes its mark on extremist networks that are apparently less vindictive, but quite as underground.

A paradox: these fanatics from another age drew their inspiration from a psychological précis of action whose author was not exactly one of their familiars. Indeed, the *Technique of the Coup d'État* by the Italian Curzio Malaparte, first published in 1931, reveals, *inter alia*, the tactics employed by Trotsky to carry out the Bolshevik revolution. His basic theorem: the masses don't matter; just a small group of technicians drawn from the élite, deeply committed and well organized, can change the course of history. In fact, underlines Malaparte, "a thousand" men are enough, attack troops and technicians combined, to overturn everything.

"A thousand." The figure set two attentive readers dreaming, in the 1930's, an engineer and a doctor.

The first, even his worst enemies agreed, was no ordinary character. His bowler hat, his 3-piece suits were not enough to disguise the exaltation that consumed his bulbous, vaguely worrying eyes. Graduating in the first ranks from the École Polytechnique in 1912, Eugène Deloncle chose naval construction. A valiant soldier during the War of 1914, he was just 20 years old when he was decorated with the Legion of Honor.

Like all the successful alums from X, he did not wait long to "*pantoufler.*" He joined the Construction Sites of Saint-Nazaire and Penhoët. Very highly regarded, the engineer became an expert counsel to the courts and sat on ten boards of directors.

Deloncle, however, was an original. How else can we explain why this competent, well-to-do, happily married man would launch out in the most extremist conspiracies?

Indeed, he was only in the upper classes on a part-time basis. In the 1920's, when his career was taking off, he would sit on the boards of directors during the day in order to be better prepared to throw a punch in the evening. This man with the gruff air, who seems born to command, became a disciplined militant as soon as he joined the 17th team of the Camelots du Roy, based in the 16th arrondissement of Paris. The group was proud of its reputation for violence and its chief knew how to get respect.

This chief, whom Deloncle, like all the others, obeyed without hesitation, was called Jean Filliol. Sharp, and small of stature, he was popular with the royalist young ladies. To make them shiver, he would tell them horrible stories of assassination, not all of which, unfortunately, lacked a grain of truth. Originally from Périgourd, Filliol did not tarry too long over his education, and took up provisional employment at Hachette transport, which left him sufficient leisure to lead his men as he intended. Had he already become a killer when he met Deloncle, the militant? Perhaps not. But he was undoubtedly charged up, even inflamed. Later, when he became the executor of Deloncle's high and low deeds, Filliol, eternally devout, never failed to kneel after every crime of blood and ask: "Lord, must we cut all their throats?"[1]

Commander of a committed clique, Filliol also had under his orders a young decorator, Jacques Corrèze. Born in 1912 in Auxerre, in Yonne, this former pupil of the Boulle and the Beaux Arts schools had known Deloncle back home. His father, himself a decorator in Auxerre and comfortably established as president of the Society of Fabrics and Carpets, was one of the engineer's suppliers, as he had a property in the area. Is this a gauge of the effectiveness of Deloncle's proselytism? Jacques Corrèze, in any case, went up to Paris, joined the 17th team of Filliol and, in 1934, got himself hired by the store "Au Bûcheron." He gradually became Deloncle's right-hand man.

The boss, the killer, the right-hand man: the distribution of roles, the construction of a secret society, takes shape. A few more characters were missing before "La Cagoule" (The Hood) took on its final shape. First, a small man, Jean Bouvyer, son of a good family, devoted to a mother who was savagely monarchist, friend of the Mitterrand family with whom he would spend his summers in Charente. Glorified in his street battles, with the young people of French Action, February 6, 1934, when he was only 17 years old, Bouvyer too began to fight under the orders of Filliol. Then a smart young man, Gabriel Jeantet, joined this fine team. Born in 1906, coming from a royalist family as well, Jeantet was less of a firebrand, and more malignant than Bouvyer. For La Cagoule, he became responsible for weapons purchases, a delicate task if ever there was one. He also took care of the great majority of their financial questions. He was not badly positioned for that, since his brother-in-law was none other than the owner of Byrrh aperitifs, a supporter of the cause. From French Action to National Front, via the Vichy government where he sponsored Mitterrand in August 1942, this sinuous man does not go unnoticed.

In January 1936, Deloncle and seven of his comrades were kicked out of French Action. On February 4, they created the National Revolutionary and Socialist Party, with Jean Filliol, Jean Bouvyer, Jacques Corrèze and the industrialist Jacques Lemaigre-Dubreuil, owner of Lesieur oils, the primary fundraiser for La Cagoule.

A few days later, Deloncle dined downtown. His table mate was a retired soldier, General Lavigne-Delville, and he described to him his overall plans. This latter was interested. He kept company with a strange doctor, Doctor Martin, with whom he used to amuse himself by collecting information on Communists and keeping files on them. The Doctor, too, had read Malaparte's manifesto, and was attracted by the theory of the "thousand." A monomaniacal plotter, he conspired throughout his life against the "Bolsheviks" of the Front Popular, against Laval, against Synarchy, against the "boches," de Gaulle, and even against the Coal and Steel Community — his last crusade.

These two obsessed conspirators were made for each other. "The enemy" had just won the elections in June 1936 when all these high society plotters took to the shadows to create the mysterious "Higher Council" of the CSAR (Secret Committee of Revolutionary Action, the true name of La Cagoule).

On paper, a federation of district committees was created to fight by every means against the Marxist danger and to generate propaganda. "Every new Cagoulard must stay in his original party or movement, create a privileged position there, and be able to involve, on D-day, sympathetic militants who will be Cagoulards without knowing it," reports Henry Charbonneau, who would later be Jacques Corrèze's assistant in the MSR, the collaborationist party Deloncle created during the German Occupation.[2]

Another character appeared in the first Club of La Cagoule: a former active officer and artillery captain in the reserves, François Méténier had the reputation of liking pretty women and a lavish lifestyle. Having converted, without conviction, into industry at Chamalières, he was the kingpin of a regional group innocently dubbed "Children of Auvergne," a funny, folksy association, made up of visceral anti-Communists, more or less consciously waiting for "D-day."

Méténier, on occasion, also put himself to good use abroad. He concluded an agreement with the Italian fascists: guns, in exchange for "lending a hand" here and there. Two Italian pacifists, the Roselli brothers, were thus executed on June 10, 1937 at the request of Count Ciano, son-in-law and Minister for Foreign Affairs to Mussolini.

Then would come the assassination of Dimitri Navachine, a Soviet economist who was too great an Anglophile and too "cosmopolitan," in their eyes, and the elimination of two gun dealers, Leon Jean-Baptiste and Maurice Juif, who would have eternity to think over what it costs to betray La Cagoule. And then anti-employers' attacks, considered by their instigators to be the last word in subversive provocation. The business leaders' headquarters blew up on September 11, 1937, killing two police officers responsible for protecting the building. Orchestrated by Méténier, this event was intended to discredit the Communists. In the weeks that followed, the Cagoulards' objective seemed to have been attained, since the police arrested an anarchist considered to be a suspect.

But La Cagoule was already under close surveillance. With each assassination, they had left behind signs. The police managed to place some informers within the Cagoulard movement, and they completed the work. A few days after the double attack against the business leaders, two Cagoulards were stopped for traffic in weapons, as well as a certain Aristide Corre, the movement's archivist. It was quite a catch: the imprudent Corre was caught with his list of the organization's members, and the police quickly deciphered the code he had used. Corre, afraid of reprisals from Filliol, did not dare to admit to his companions that the police were in possession of the file.

Did they sense that the vice was tightening? That fall, 1937, La Cagoule decided to go all out. They set the night of November 15 for the famous, long-awaited anti-Communist blast. The network tried to poison the army and make them believe that the Communists were on the verge of seizing power, in order to cause a "putsch" in reaction.

But the soldiers did not march. The conspirators' scenario was a lamentable failure and most of them ended up in La Santé prison. Eight days later, Leon Blum's Interior Minister Marx Dormoy (whom the Cagoulards would assassinate during the Occupation) distributed a press release stating that "a plot against the Republican institutions has been discovered."

After the war, nearly fifty of them, including Jeantet, Corrèze, and Méténier, found themselves on trial. This was a strange trial covering a whole parade of former collaborators and former resistance fighters, the Cagoulards being divided into two camps. Eugène Deloncle was not involved; he'd been cut down in 1944 by the Gestapo which suspected him, rightly, of being a turncoat. Not all his friends, having been sentenced, lost their taste for underground activities. With the Cold War, some of these unrepentant conspirators would even get back into the game.

An Odd Duck

The theory of the "thousand" that had so appealed to Deloncle and Martin still enticed people into conspiracies after the war. Jean Ousset was one of them. If he had had to write an autobiography, Ousset probably would have called himself "an odd duck."

"An odd duck," originally from the provinces, who had time to evolve his action plan during the Occupation. In his prison camp, he questioned a Communist fellow captive — in order to better encircle the enemy and to understand the way he thinks and acts. Once released, this young Catholic admirer of Maurras (whom he met in 1934 in Bordeaux) saw the national revolution of Vichy as the practical application of his convictions. He became "chief of the planning office" of the "Youth Legion," that was attached to the French Legion of combat-ants. And there he shared a Secretary with a certain François Mitter-rand.

He devoted his time to education of recruits, via training courses, as well as to penning a small bulletin, where the broad topics of Pétain-ist anti-capitalism are outlined. Thus, the October 15, 1943 issue con-tains praise of the "corporation" which, contrary to the enterprise, "protects without imprisoning" (sic). Until September 1, 1944, Ousset occupied himself with glorifying the family, according to all the Pétain-ists models. The end of the war was obviously less glamorous: with purges imminent, he had to cross the Lozère by bicycle, armed with a cleverly adulterated identity card.

But, very quickly, things picked up again. In the company of his friend the printer Jean Masson, he created a "Center for Critical Studies and Synthesis," the embryo of what would become "Catholic City," an underground network that he founded three years later.

The movement's periodical, *Verbe*, took as its epigraph a quotation from Jean Ousset, "Nothing that really made a difference was ever ac-complished without the preliminary training of 'a few': tireless crusad-ers for the truth, apostles, men of fire who, wherever they are, wherever they go, with whatever movement they belong to, leave everywhere a trail of light and truth." The "thousand" knights, again! To bring them together, Catholic City copied, in a more modest and more secretive fashion, the pyramidal system of the Communist organizations. Every week the future "knights" met within a "cell" to study the texts of the master, Ousset. In the mid-1950's, all the big schools, including the Polytechnic, Central, the Mines, HEC and Sciences Po were sheltering, unbeknownst to themselves, a cell of Catholic City.

Like La Cagoule before the war, Ousset's organization was founded on a core drawn from the élites, the only ones who could save a society on the brink of perdition. At the very top of this pyramid built by Ousset were five leaders, including a "head of networks," who over-saw seventeen "regional networks."

During their heyday, in the mid-1960's, the organization employed 26 permanent workers, enjoyed subsidies from the most anti-Communist businesses, and found in French Algeria a cause that was made to order. For Catholic City, from the first sparks of the Algerian conflict, made a great breakthrough in the military staff. Officers stationed in Algeria made up their own clandestine cells that came to in-corporate a thousand members (finally, the thousand!), all with offers' commissions. During this time Ousset, at his best with future seditious leaders like Colonel Gardes and General Zeller, was solicited by the Fifth Office to write a psychological guide to action. In *Pour qu'il règne*, a book that did not become a bestseller even with the soldiers as its cap-tive customers, Ousset provides adherents of counter-subversion with a theological and moral justification for two practices that were re-jected by French military tradition: torture and activism. An entire doctrine of "national security" was expounded (and successfully ex-ported to Latin America, in particular). But this patient labor of con-viction, at the top, and in the core, and at the intermediate levels, was questioned by Ousset's former school-fellow at the college of Mon-tauban. Henri Fesquet, the religious columnist of *Le Monde*, wondered in a two-page spread, "Is it OK for a Republican army to consist princi-pally of a hotbed of fundamentalists?"

Rifles, No More "Social Psychology"!

A "hotbed?" There were plenty of them at the time. Georges Sauge, who knew Communism well (having been in the Communist Party before the war), would also head up one of the most active funda-mentalist networks.

As a Resister, he was active since the Liberation against purifica-tion, in the name of necessary forgiveness. In 1949, the former under-ground operative, employed by Crédit Lyonnais, created the "Center For Advanced Studies of Social Psychology." Even while he remained friendly with Communists like Jacques Duclos and Pierre Hervé, it was with Rome that he now maintained privileged relations. He especially hooked up with the Pope's new nuncio in Paris, a certain Roncalli, who had been the obscure representative of the Holy See in Turkey but who would become Pope Jean XXIII.

The modest movement, well-received by the clergy, corrupted pri-marily the army and the employers. Recruits would undergo a three-phase training, from analysis of Communism to psychological action, and then the Christian doctrines.

Many officers, who regarded the Algerian War as a crusade, were trained by Sauge. At the invitation of the Fifth Office, he developed a series of conferences in all the military academies, starting with X and Saint-Cyr. The speaker was welcomed all the more warmly since he was manifestly anti-Communist. A goldsmith of activism, he and seven friends succeeded in overturning a Congress for the Peace Movement. "We distributed ourselves throughout the four colleges of the Congress," he says today. "Since the resolutions had to be passed unanimously, seven people were enough to sow disorder among 15,000." In 1956, Sauge played the same tactic in an even more spectacular way. The Soviet tanks had just entered Budapest. Sauge took advantage of the general indignation to divert three demonstrations planned for that day, including one led by the former president of the Council Georges Bidault. In spite of themselves, the demonstrators found themselves caught up in a rush for la place Kossuth to set fire to the seat of the Communist Party!

Sauge's pro-French-Algeria activism attracted not only the opprobrium of Pierre Messmer, the Armies Minister who dissolved these "clandestine Fifth Offices," but also the attention of justice. He spent a few days in prison in early 1960 for "attacking State security and plotting."

While he lost his principal "market," the officers of the French army, escape his reach, still during the Algerian War he had made an interesting acquaintance with a man who was inherently very distant from his convictions: Charles Hernu. Against any expectation, the Catholic traditionalist and the freemason fraternized around a common passion: everything military. This friendship was not immediately cemented even though, since 1965, Sauge had been calling for people to vote for Mitterrand. A member of the office of "The New Army," a "military fan club" created by Hernu at the fringes of the SP to ponder military questions, he was now dispensing his wisdom to militant Socialists!

But Sauge remained the only pioneer of such an extreme political transformation. Other conspirators took the exact opposite route and were exiled to Portugal and Spain. Those two countries, then headed by extreme Right dictatorships, were home to a couple of very odd cliques. One of them, established in Lisbon, was called Aginter Presse. Formed in 1965, it was more than a simple press agency; according to the Portuguese investigation conducted in 1974 after the Carnation Revolution, it was a center of international fascistic subversion financed by the Salazar government and the French, Belgian, South-African and South American extreme right movements.

The idea for this multinational of subversion initially germinated in the mind of Yves Guillou, alias Yves Herlou, alias Ralph Guérin-Sérac. This French army officer served in Korea and Indochina with a courage that earned him very precociously several citations as well as the Legion of Honor. In 1959, Guillou was assigned to the "11th shock," an élite parachute unit. After three years, he deserted to rejoin the OAS, where he directed a commando in Oranais.

For him as for many others, the race began with the declaration of independence in Algeria. Spain initially, then Portugal.

In Spain, he created the embryo of a network with veterans of the OAS. He came into contact with Colonel Pierre Chateau-Jobert, a companion from the Libération and an OAS commandant in Constantinois. Chateau-Jobert, who had meditated considerably on the blind terrorist actions of his comrades in arms, then underwent a return to religion under the influence (the world is so small!) of Jean Ousset and Catholic City's publications. With Guillou and some other "refugees" from Algiers, he founded the Army of Christ-King, a fundamentalist movement to fight against Communism.

Guérin-Sérac had already gone to Portugal where he sought to make contact with the "first generation" of emigrés, composed primarily of former Nazi collaborators. Among them was Jacques Ploncard, known as Ploncard d'Assac. This specialist in the anti-Masonic struggle, a disciple of Drumont, made a name for himself during the German Occupation as the librarian responsible for examining the files of the Grand Orient of France. Decorated with the *francisque* symbol by Vichy for his scrupulous study of the Portuguese secret service, he quite naturally took refuge in Lisbon, where he became nothing less than the personal and hagiographical adviser to President Salazar.

How was *Aginter* used? To recruit a network of European agents, whose cover was the bulletin. "The majority of these correspondents, who were of course sympathetic to the cause, began modestly while they were being tested on their ability to collect confidential information," explains an old-timer. "Then, little by little, they were asked for more specific information, for example on members of the Portuguese opposition that had taken refuge in their country."

In France, one of the Aginter Presse "correspondents" was none other than Jean-Pierre Stirbois. He was not yet National Front mayor-adjunct of Dreux but he was already director of a movement on the far Right, Group-Action-Youth.

"Even in Lisbon, most of the staff came from Algeria, like the former head of the *Echo d'Algiers*, Jean Brune," says one of them today. "There were former parachutists, vets from the '11th shock' who were disoriented and converted into mercenaries;" and also former collaborators like Ploncard d'Assac and Robert Leroy, who trained with La Cagoule before joining the Spanish Phalanx and then the Waffen SS. Condemned to twenty years of forced labor after the Liberation, Leroy served less than half of his sentence before he began working for the secret services of various Western powers.

As both an expert in plots and an organizer of intensive training for apprentice-terrorists, Aginter Presse was no adventure for romantic and scatterbrained fighters. The damage that it caused was not so limited as its lack of notoriety would incline one to think. Its "provision of services," especially in Latin America, contributed significantly to the repression in banana republics like Guatemala, Bolivia and Chile.

The epilogue? Not very heartening. Benefiting from Mitterand's amnesty, Guérin-Sérac retired as a colonel! His assistant, Jean-Denis Ringeard de Blétière, a Breton aristocrat, he converted himself into a humanitarian aid worker in Africa. That's (comforting) proof that destinies sometimes take unexpected turns. The one who bore the rather transparent code name of "Jean Denis" during the Aginter era thinks that there is no solidarity any more among the old gang. "All those people do not really want to remember their past," he explains. "And then, the extreme Right was divided into many cliques and there was no strong ideological thread to bind them together. That does not help to create bonds. These networks died out by themselves. Except for those who made a career elsewhere."

The Fan Strategy

The networks of Catholic City, on the other hand, survived, but at the cost of two successive mutations. In 1964, the City became "the International Office of Works of Civic Education and Cultural Action According to Christian Natural Law," (sic). An intentionally unpronounceable name, apparently in order to further obscure their tracks.

In 1981 came a new shift under the crook of Jacques Trémolet de Villers, who had become president of the organization renamed ICTUS. This lawyer, who made himself famous as an impassioned defender of Paul Touvier, met Jean Ousset's son in a far Right organization in the early 1960's. But it was with the father that he discovered an immense intellectual complicity. "ICTUS," says Trémolet de Villers, "was born when François Mitterrand came to power. The leaders of the old majority, its back to the wall, then asked us to develop a training scheme for their cadres. We worked all summer there. But in the autumn, those who had urged us on so insistently did not feel they needed our help any more. The fever of electoral hope had gripped them again."

ICTUS (Cultural and Technical Institute of Social Utility, but also Iseos Christos Theos Uios Sotem, or Jesus Christ, God, Son and Savior) manages some twenty "subsidiaries." Family and School Action, directed by Arnaud de Lassus, had no cultural justification but found its customers among most radical members of the parents' associations of the free school. The Center for Study of Enterprises (the EEC), developed with the encouragement of the industrialist François Michelin (who gave several speeches there), proposed to track "subversive ideology" (in other words, budding Marxism) in the arcane details of management. It found a niche in the edification of studious young hearts in the great business and engineering schools. This "supplementary training" lasted two years, during which the students would meet once a week under the sponsorship of some company like Michelin and Lafarge-Coppée, whose assistant general manager, Jean-Marie Schmitz, was a vice-president of ICTUS, and the brother of one of Jacques Trémolet de Villers' associates, Thierry Schmitz, Esq..

Still attached to this movement but somewhat more original, because it drew its inspiration rather directly from the countryside, the "Secretariat of Information of the Local and Regional Authorities" (SICLER), proposed "to save both the villages and the families, by installing the families of the unemployed in villages where it has proven difficult to renew the ranks of the craftsmen and rural workers." The organization's intentionally neutral acronym is part of the traditional obfuscation. It seems to be an effective strategy, since the former minister Jean François-Poncet lent his enthusiastic support to the initiatives of SICLER a few years ago.

To broaden a restricted audience, lecturers were exchanged with some "brother-organizations" like the Charlier Center, created in 1979 by Bernard Antony *alias* Romain Marie, who was already militating for French Algeria at the age when most people are first borrowing their parents' car. Today he leads the movement "Nationale-Catholique" within the National Front, while working for the pharmaceutical group Pierre Fabre. Among the close relations of the Charlier Center are dom Gerard Calvet, son of a family of Bordeaux wine merchants and the father-abbot of Barroux, a Vauclusien monastery that welcomes everyone in France that might be considered a fundamentalist. This priest, who sided with Rome after the schism caused by Mgr Lefebvre, has given rise to rumors that he may be a leader of anti-abortion commandos.[3]

These traditionalist "institutes" try to expand beyond their clientele on the far Right. Thus the Christendom-Solidarity Committees, a political offshoot of the Charlier Center, were active within the Association for Free Russia (ARL). Bernard Antony served on the association's sponsorship committee alongside of François Léotard and Jacques Godfrain, Minister for Cooperation under Alain Juppé. And the ARL was chaired for awhile by Karine Loverger, a press attaché for the Republican party.

For ICTUS was always looking for more respectable connections besides the young members of the National Front. Certainly not in order to make a better impression on those two stalwarts, Colonel Argoud, organizer of the Generals' putsch, or the widow of Jean-Marie Bastien-Thiry (the ex-École Polytechnique who originated the attack on Petit-Clamart and was condemned to death). But the group also cultivated close relations with the academic Gerard Léonard, RPR deputy and joint author of a noteworthy 1996 parliamentary report on fraud, the former mayor of Versailles André Damien and the lawyer Jean-Marc Varaut, all three of them members of the Paris social circuit. And Varaut also shared the same law firm as the Socialist Roland Dumas.

From this point of view, the most effective sympathizer of ICTUS was without question Fr Jerome Lejeune, the talented doctor and researcher who discovered the trisomy 21 gene. An unwavering adversary of abortion and proponent of "Let them live," Lejeune was also president of the Pontifical Academy of Sciences in Rome. He was often cited as a close friend, even as a member of Opus Dei, which Jean-Paul II raised to the ranks of a "personal prelature." Another of his daughters,

Anne-Marie Meyer, and her husband Jean-Marie, philosophy professor, had been chosen (along with some twenty other couples) by the Pope to represent French Catholic homes within a Family Board in Rome. An honorary doctor of the University of Pamplona, which was created and managed by Opus Dei, Lejeune was an invaluable "fellow traveler" for this order founded in 1928 by the father Jose Maria Escriva de Balaguer (beatified by Jean-Paul II). The goal of the organization? To make reign a very Christian order reign on earth.

To achieve that end, Opus Dei was based on the theory that was so dear to Malaparte: that a few "crusaders" recruited among the élite can shift the tides of history. The order thus intended to infiltrate society from the top, in order to have greater leverage. In France, according to historian Emile Poulat, Opus Dei had no more than 1,300 to 1,400 followers, but it is supposed to have had more than 80,000 throughout the world. The *modus operandi* was, at the very least, intriguing. Members of Opus Dei include a small number of lay persons who have given vows of chastity, obedience and poverty, and who live in community and are called "numeraries." These semi-monks, who continue to pursue their original occupations, especially if they are prestigious, represent less than 2% of the troops but are the true bosses of the Work, since they can be found in all the shell companies that it controls. The "supernumeraries," who do not declare any vows, conduct an ordinary family life, and are especially appreciated for their financial contributions and the influence which they can exert on the life of the city. For they are enrolled, often while very young, in the promising élite. "This élitiste principle adds an element of intrigue," says the Catholic review *Golias*.[4] They talk about a "way of working that enables us to spread ourselves like a fan."

A mysterious and intriguing "fan." The secret "constitution" of The Work, written in 1950 but only published in 1986 thanks to some renegade former members, states in article 191: "The numerary and supernumerary members know that they must always observe a prudent silence as to the names of the others who are associated, and that they must never reveal to anyone whatsoever that they belong to Opus Dei."

That is a rule that recalls something of Freemasonry, and that adds a certain zest to all the betting as to the *Who's Who* of this secret organization. The first to have launched out in this type of census was, by amusing coincidence, the Grand Orient of France. In 1962, the bulletin published by its documentation center gave the names of Robert Schuman, a builder of Europe pending beatification, Raymond Tribou-let, former minister for General de Gaulle, and Antoine Pinay. It could have added the names of sympathizers like the Gaullist Maurice Schu-mann, Edmond Giscard d'Estaing (father of VGE), and the former Min-ister of Justice Jean Foyer.

Today, only about thirty people in France are claimed openly by Opus Dei. In the political world, nobody wants to assume publicly the heritage of José Maria de Balaguer. Hervé Gaymard, Juppé's Minister for Health and son-in-law of Pr Lejeune, even made a point of publicly denying his membership in The Work, on the air waves of Europe 1.

More daring, since 1978 Raymond Barre was willing to lend his credit as Prime Minister to support the beatification of José Maria Es-criva de Balaguer. "His writings are already very widespread, and the growing audience of his doctrines, so clear and sure, the action of the members of Opus Dei lead me to think that Mgr Escriva de Balaguer is a person who is marked by signs of holiness," he wrote at that time to The Holy See. That is a declaration that was in line with the general thrust of history, since the "father" of Opus Dei was beatified in 1992, just seventeen years after his death. Among the 300 VIP's invited to Rome for the ceremony was the mayor of Marseilles Jean-Claude Gaudin, who was later publicly thanked for the assistance that he had given.

For his part, Jacques de Chateauvieux, Chairman of the Bourbon companies in La Réunion (which realize some $750 million in turnover and control the local television channel Antenne-Réunion, as well as several supermarkets, fishing vessels, and sugar plantations), readily acknowledges his membership in The Work, where he recently went from the status of "supernumerary" to that of "numerary." His family's links with Opus are old. When The Work decided to conquer France, in the Fifties, it was based on two industrial dynasties: Chateauvieux and Bardinet, manufacturers of Negrita rum.

On trial for corruption in a supermarket scandal in La Réunion, he freely declared: "I did not take part in corruption until after having consulted my spiritual adviser." The court would surely take that into consideration.

At all times, Opus Dei showed a particular interest in the large owners. Moreover, its official representative in France, François

Gondrand, handled communications at CNPF for a long time before assembling his own consultancy.

The "Garnelles Center," one of the real jewels of The Work, located in the VIIth arrondissement of Paris, at the corner of rue Jean-Nicot, likes to host prestigious lecturers from the business world. Among them have been Bébéar, chairman of Axa, the former president of the CNPF Yvon Gattaz, and Michel Albert, finance inspector and habitué of high positions. This last, in addition, chairs the International Christian Union of Enterprise Managers, a network of bosses who all sympathize with The Work.

Opus Dei, is it a network with conspiratorial tendencies? In Spain, the Matesa case, in Italy the Ambrosiano Bank scandal, in France the assassination of Jean de Broglie (considered a close friend, in convictions and in business, of The Work), cast some doubt on its unique spiritual dimension.

In truth, Opus Dei proceeds by infiltration. In the secrecy of their belief, bankers, academics and managers, otherwise seemingly indistinguishable, kiss the ground each morning, attend at least one religious office per day, and regularly wear the hair-shirt for mortification; thus they conform to their profile as civilian monks.

Like all networks of this type, Opus Dei relies on a pyramidal system, composed at the bottom of "cells" that work at the task that is assigned to them without knowing anything of the whole structure to which they owe obedience. With its opaque, international, very hierarchical style, and with the deterrent force that its infiltration brings even to the heart of the Holy See, The Work carries on the eternal battle against modernism that was started well before its birth.

As for "Models"

From Doctor Martin to Jean Ousset, La Cagoule to the OAS, the reference to Trotsky remains an unexpected pivot point around which a strange ballet of fascination-repulsion is choreographed. But what have the heirs to the former commander-in-chief of the Red Army become?

Once there were the networks of the Egyptian Communist Henri Curiel, who played a major role in supporting FLN (the National Liberation Front in Algeria), especially after some of the teams put together by the Sartrian Francis Jeanson were dismantled. But two "families" mobilized alongside the Algerian nationalists: the Catholics of the Left, and the Trotskyites. The first, out of conscience, could not support the existence of second-class citizens on other side of the Mediterranean; not to mention the torture. The second plunged themselves into the breach opened by the instability, under the 4th Republic and then under de Gaulle.

The end of the Algerian War, was by no means taken by the extreme Left as the death knell for revolutionary hopes. In any case, those who were close to giving way to violence at that time were not part of the Trotskyites but the Maoists. After 1968, the "proletarian Left" (which enlisted among its leaders Alain Geismar, the charismatic leader of the May Movement, and Serge July), created a clandestine structure baptized the New Popular Resistance. This group counted on its list of wins the aborted kidnapping of a Gaullist deputy Michel de Grailly, the highly publicized detention of Robert Nogrette (an executive at Renault) after the assassination of the militant Pierre Overney by the employers' militia. The "clandestine operatives" also wanted to seize de Touvier and another of his colleagues in the militia, and narrowly gave up abducting Henri de Wendel. But always, these dramatic events were carried out using guns that weren't loaded, in order to be sure they would not have to shoot.

Alain Krivine, indomitable guardian of the competing Trotskyite clique, gave his parish this sermon. "If terrorism did not develop in France as it did in Germany and Italy, it is thanks to the presence of an strong extreme Left in the post-May period, in particular within the League, that gave prospects to people who would otherwise have sunk into despair."

Trotskyism, indeed, kept the militants busy. First, due to the conspiratorial folklore that accompanied the least meeting, the least action. The ABC's consisted of a second baptism. Getting into a Trotskyite organization requires adopting a pseudonym. "It was a question of being able to go clandestine at any moment," says a former member. "Not after some plot or *coup d'état*, that wasn't our kind of thing. But in case of possible police repression, if the 'masses' should finally decide to make a revolution." The pseudonyms lasted longer than the active militancy. Years after the end of their engagement, the ex-Trotskyites sometimes remember their former comrades' pseudonyms more easily than their true identities.

So they had *noms de guerre*, but no weapons. "What good would plots like La Cagoule's or the OAS's have done? We would then have infringed our own logic," a old hand says. "We worked to have the people rise up themselves, not to make a putsch." Nonetheless, the organization sometimes asked a militant to give in his identity papers. Why? The principal was generally ignorant of the reason, although it was not very difficult for him to imagine that they were to be used for a comrade who had encountered problems crossing the borders. After a few weeks, he would be told that he could claim the loss at the police station.

Between clandestine activity and institutionalization, movements like the Revolutionary Communist League (official representative of the 4th Internationale in France) and the dissenting house, the Internationalist Communist Party (PCI) of Pierre Boussel-Lambert, always floated in ambiguity. Thus for a long time there were meetings of both the "heads" and the "tails." Clandestine meetings were reserved for hard core apparatchiks, who discussed the real objectives of the movement. The other meetings, which took place officially, were intended to build loyalty among the sympathizers and thus offered the spectacle of a "Trotskyism with a human face." Almost a vote-catching maneuver!

This structure it impossible to raise significant legions of militants. At the best of its form, the League never reached 4,000 members. Only the exquisite intoxication of crisis periods swept tens of thousands of demonstrators into the streets of Paris. Now abandoned by these groups, the strategy of secrecy continues to prevail in Worker's Struggle (Lutte ouvrière, or "LO").

Created under the Occupation by active militants who shared the convictions of the 4th Internationale, this group owes its notoriety to the presidential candidate "Arlette." Did anyone ever question Arlette Laguiller on her private life, on the lack of husband and child? She always eluded such bourgeois anecdotal questions. However, private life was such an obsession of the cadres of "LO" that they were abjured to have neither a partner nor a child, in order not to dissolve the revolutionary fiber in the family chemistry. Structured concentrically around a core of unknown leaders, whose indomitable "guru" bore the pseudonym of "Hardy," Worker's Struggle was only the visible face of a "flip side" structure that was entirely clandestine, the "Communist Union."

The only element identified as being from this organization, Arlette Laguiller was not its leader. A puppet, she tirelessly defended a political line decided by others.

The Cuckoo Method

This taste for secrecy, compartmentalization, and anonymity certainly correspond to the decorum essential to prepare for the Great Event, if it ever comes. Above all, it corresponds to a requirement that is almost consubstantial with the inherent nature of Trotskyism: infiltration. As old as the 4th Internationale, the principle consists in infiltrating in a neutral, even hostile, organization with the aim of dividing it, of weakening it, of controlling it or, in certain cases, of taking it over.

Michel Rocard noticed this, at his own expense, shortly after his arrival in Matignon. In autumn 1988, the nurses were in the streets. Very quickly, a "coordinator" took the lead in the dispute, thus shuffling the cards in the usual game of negotiations between trade unions and government. On Wednesday, October 19, Rocard's buddies met in the office of his chief assistant, Jean-Paul Huchon. This "impromptu crisis cell" suspected the deputy from the Essonne, Julien Dray, of a plot against the Prime Minister — although he had solemnly voted his confidence in him a few months before.

The Matignon advisers were perhaps unaware that at the very moment when they were vituperating against the conspirator, the nurses who were clamoring at gate of Matignon for an interview with Michel Rocard were being carefully managed by an official from the Revolutionary Communist League (to which Julien Dray belonged). Within the League, it was Serge Roux, member of the polit buro and union liaison for CFDT at Sainte-Anne hospital, who ensured the cohesion of the nurses' protest. In regular contact with him, Dray had no trouble finding an area of agreement which the government had hopelessly sought for days, during fruitless all-night negotiations.

The outcome is simple as a Trotskyite operation: while Claude Evin, the very pro-Rocard Minister for Social Affairs, was vainly discussing with the trade unions, Julien Dray was schmoozing with the national coordinators and delivered the result of his interesting talks to the Elysée entourage, where no one was dying of love for the Prime Minister. One way of harming Rocard was as good as another, and this one was carried out single-handedly by a close contact of Laurent

Fabius, Dray. And that is how Trotskyism is occasionally put to the service of underhand battles of various factions at the top of the State.

But the League was also endeavoring to infiltrate the trade unions, especially the CFDT, and they were already showing results in the sectors of Education, Finance, the health trades and the SNCF (the railroads). Thus the great railwaymen's strike of winter 1986, which was started from two depots: Paris-North and Rouen-Sotteville. Indeed, the October meeting during which this event was prepared was held at the head office of the LCR. In its October 2, 1986 issue, the organization's weekly magazine *Rouge* was open about its objectives. "The mode of organization to be promoted is that of autonomous figures. When they are strong in their given sector, they really speak in the name of this sector and are thus impossible to circumvent in negotiations." A clever means of destabilization, in these times when trade unionism represents only itself... The same approach would be used for the December 1995 transport strike.

But good coordination, and conviction on the part of the agitator, these are nothing without the logistical support of a trade-union apparatus. The battles between the partisans of Alain Krivine in the LCR and those of Pierre Lambert (real name Pierre Boussel) at PCI are sometimes fought establishment by establishment, profession by profession. The LCR, during the nurses' strikes of 1988, controlled Pitié-Salpêtrière and Sainte-Anne, in Paris, as well as most of the psychiatric hospitals in the suburbs. The PCI had the Lariboisière hospital, in Paris, and was preeminent in the radiology sector.

Rearguard actions? There was one noteworthy exception. The PCI survived for years thanks to the sinecures granted by Working Force (Force ouvrière, FO). The infiltration began under André Bergeron, Secretary General of the trade union; he knew just how to play on the various tendencies that inspired this traditionally anti-Communist organization.

Osmosis with FO was all the easier given that PCI militants are often Freemasons, following the example of their chief Pierre Lambert. Some lodges, like the Eugène Varlin workshop in Villeurbanne, were thus won over to the Lambertist cause. This meddling in the Masonic universe made the head of the Grand Orient of France grind his teeth; it annoyed him so much that certain dignitaries suspected former Grand Master Patrick Kessel of belonging to the PCI movement. A one-time activist with the LCR, in the 1970's Kessel took part in a scission, the majority of whose authors took up with the Lambertists. Therefore, Kessel's opponents within the hierarchy of the Grand Orient claimed that he was one of the 500 "dormant agents" of the PCI, whose identity were known only to Pierre Boussel-Lambert and, possibly, to his lieutenants — an affiliation that the principal interested party savagely denied.

These intrigues could not displease the leader of Working Force, where the reference to "Great Architect of the Universe" is rather well received. However, an alliance with the leadership of the trade union was vital to the PCI for many years. It is less so now, since FO lost the right to manage health insurance cases in 1996.

When André Bergeron was General Secretary of FO, his right-hand man, responsible for organization, was Roger Sandry — a personal friend of Lambert. And the Trotskyites used the moment of succession to great advantage. Bergeron's candidate Claude Pitous was defeated beaten by Marc Blondel. The PCI had dropped Bergeron. By way of thanks, immediately upon being installed, Blondel named the Trotskyite Claude Jenet as confederal Secretary with the organization. Especially, he allowed the PCI to collect the tailings from the gold mine that the health insurance process represents: infrastructure, trade-union staffers, employees who had been "trimmed" from payrolls. Jacques Mairé, Blondel's adversary for his re-election in 1996, had focused part of his campaign on a denunciation of the Trotskyite influence, exaggerated compared to the number of its members. But Blondel won... precisely due to the flawless support of the Trotskyites.

Alas! 1996 would be registered, however, in the annals of FO as a disastrous year. In a few months, the trade-union lost the right to manage the CNAM (Conservatoire national des arts et métiers), and then lost the elections in two thirds of the social security offices dealing with health insurance.

The "trade unionists" of the PCI long considered the CNAM as their own laboratory for testing in a natural environment their ability to cause trouble. Misters Rochette and Poulet, respectively representing the FO federation of employees and that of the Social Security executives, thus set out (not without a certain talent) to overturn a plan for modernizing the classification of personnel, in the early 1990's. Who was the promoter of this reform? Gilles Johannet, then director of the CNAM. A dangerous reactionary? An ultra-liberal? Not exactly: this magistrate at the Court of Auditors was Pierre Mauroy's adviser at

Matignon between 1981 and 1984. But in the eyes of the Lambertists, he was perhaps worse. In the name of this "revolutionary strategy," in any case, these two "internationalists" obtained the return of promotion by seniority. Everyone to the barricades!

"The Lambertists always act under cover," says an expert. "They use the notoriety of so and so, then drop him without notice. That is what happed to the lawyer Denis Langlois, whom they used in all the protests against the Gulf War. Moreover, when their methods are reproached, they do not hesitate to practice intimidation: "But you know, we have your home address." This kind of method allowed the Lambertists gradually to extend their influence and to infiltrate, for example, the free-thinkers, and to dismiss their president without a second thought.

The Reds and the Browns: A Marriage of the Extremes

These indefatigable conspirators are convinced: it's always the next plot that will succeed where others have failed. How else can we explain this century's eternal renewal of networks based on destabilization? Even if the causes of yesteryear seem to have lost their steam, the networks of conspiracy against the Republic still have not entirely disappeared. There is a strange objective alliance between the most Stalinist of the Communists and a fringe of the anti-Semitic extreme Right and a sympathy for negationism on the part of the far Left which give rise to a new network, sufficiently structured to conduct active campaigns by insinuating their message into some of the media, but sufficiently fluid to allow plausible denials of its existence.

Thus there was a certain clique that grew up around a journalist, unknown to the general public. Marc Cohen was an active contributor to Karl Zéro's *Vrai journal* ("*True newspaper*") on TV Channel Plus. A member of the French Communist Party, and former director of the UEC (Union of Communist Students), he began his journalistic career on the airwaves of TSF, the Communist radio station financed by the General Council of Seine-Saint-Denis; in fact, he supervised its political coverage. But it is was as co-editor-in-chief of the *International Idiot*, Jean-Edern Hallier's iconoclastic, ragingly violent newspaper, that he gave, if one dares to say so, the best of himself.

The credit "agitator of ideas" who can plead this glorious CV was also instrumental in the "Communist Collective of Media Workers." That was an institution that was as unknown as he was himself, but which represented, with the defunct *International Idiot*, one of the meeting places of the "red-brown" networks.

"Red-brown"? Red as in Communist, brown as in fascist. The hyphenated form relates to a limited number of people, of course. However, such a network is not trivial, for it works to make racist and negationist speech acceptable. This strange movement was uncovered in the late 1980's by the writer Didier Daeninckx. With his balding crown, long, straight hair, and moustache underscored by a small triangle of beard, this famous author of detective novels one day slipped into the skin of one of the investigators to whom he gives life in his novels.

During a demonstration in support of the "Billancourt Ten" (trade-union militants fired by the management of Renault, in 1989), the *International Idiot* was broadly distributed under the high protection of the service of order of the CGT (Confédération générale du travail, a major French trade union, affiliated with the Communist party). Flipping through the November 8, issue, Daeninckx discovered a violently anti-Semitic article entitled "The Chosen People's Chosen Candidates Are Still In Place," and subtitled as follows: "The Jews of the SP — Eaten Away A Little More, from the Inside, by the Cronies of Mitterrand's Reign." Was the anticonformist newspaper, led by the provocative writer, sheltering a hate group?

Another article made a scandal in the columns of the *Idiot* in May, 1993. "Toward a National Front," as explicit as a title can be, suggested bridging the Left-Right divide in favor of an "authoritarian policy to set the country straight" based on "the alliance of the Communists and the Catholic, national, military and Maurrassian Right. . . " in order to restore "the grandeur of the nations against the balkanization of the world under the orders of Wall Street, of international Zionism, the Frankfurt Stock Exchange and the dwarves of Tokyo."

This prose was signed by Jean-Paul Cruse. A hard and fast militant of the National Front? Wrong. This CGT trade unionist was, at the time, a journalist with *Libération* and a member of the daily's board of trustees. Admittedly, he had hardly written in recent years, following an estrangement with Serge July (with whom he had crossed paths way back in the political office of the very proletarian Maoist Left).

Shortly after this article was published, the "Communist Collective of the Media Workers" mentioned its satisfaction with the "legitimate anger" that was expressed there. In addition, its leader, Marc Cohen, was a friend of Jean-Paul Cruse. A happy coincidence. All these jolly fellows would meet at 120 rue Lafayette, the seat of the Parisian Federation of the PCF, which gave it access to offices, telephones and a fax. Among the participants in these symposiums were Thierry Séchan, brother of the singer Renaud and in *chargé de mission* to the Communist General Council of Seine-Saint-Denis, contributor to the *International Idiot* and an extreme Right magazine *Le Choc du mois* (*The Shock of the Month*), Alain Sanders, editor of the pro-Le Pen daily newspaper *Le Présent*, and Bruno Tellenne (alias Basile de Koch), editor-in-chief of the anticonformist review *Jalons* (*Reference Points*).

At the *International Idiot*, Marc Cohen found another of his "comrades." Edouard Limonov, a Franco-Russian writer, was a punk dissident before becoming one of the standard-bearers of the sinister Zhirinovski, who sought to awaken in Russia a nationalist-Bolshevik, xenophobic and anti-Semitic faction. In Moscow, Limonov was active for his cause. In Sarajevo, along side the Serb militia, he condoned ethnic purification. In Paris, he would indifferently tell about his wars in the Communist magazine *Révolution* or the *Le Choc du mois*.

Jean-Edern Hallier's newspaper was thus the nexus where the "red-browns" crossed. Several journalists of *Révolution*, the weekly magazine of the CP, were contributors, as was Patrick Besson, a long time writer at *Humanité*. Were these freelance journalists unaware of the antecedents of their neighboring columnists? Ignorant of Alain Sanders, from *Le Présent*? And of Marc-Edouard Nabe, who calls himself a writer and specialist in "the literary insult," if possible with racist overtones? Alain de Benoist himself, the guru of the "New — and nevertheless extreme — Right" in the 1970's, had an honored place at the *Idiot*. Cohen also invited him on several occasions to speak on the radio, and he invited Cohen, in return, to discuss "the shifting of the French intellectual landscape" under the aegis of the review *Eléments*, the newspaper of GRECE, hard core of the New Right.

In spring 1992, Alain de Benoist was received with great pomp by the very orthodox *Institute of Marxist Research* (IRM) during a debate with Arnaud Spire, the lead-writer of *Humanité*, on "awakening the critical spirit." In the room where the event was taking place were Antoine Casanova, member of the Party Central Committee and responsible for relations with the intellectuals, and Francette Lazard, member of the political office and president of the IRM (among others). Were they in the wrong room? In any case, this excellent audience listened to the speaker explain that the LeftRight divide, in his eyes obsolete, had been succeeded by a "center" and a "periphery." "The first is the dominant ideology; the second covers all those who do not accept this ideology," he continued, before concluding by a extending a hand: "there is room for everyone in this debate at the periphery."

More extravagant still, the leadership of the Communist Party supported Hallier and his *International Idiot. . .* financially and in the media. On December 28, 1991, Hallier published the entirety of a speech by Alain de Benoist at the closing of the XXVth congress of GRECE. François Hilsum, a member of the PCF Central Committee, was indignant. Over the remarks that were made? No, over the fines that the newspaper was obliged to pay for slander, and which endangered its survival.

At that time, Hilsum was also the CEO of Messidor Publishing, a "subsidiary" of the Communist Party. In 1990, he signed a contract that was highly advantageous to Hallier. He agreed to create a collection of bulletins entitled *"The International Idiot"* and to publish JeanEdern's lead articles. And as a pledge of friendship, JeanEdern received, in the weeks that followed, nearly $100,000 as an advance. The only concrete result of this expensive collaboration was the publication by Messidor, at the end of 1990, of *Conversation au clair de lune* (*A Conversation by the Light of the Moon*), a book of flattering interviews by "JeanEdern" with "Fidel" (Castro). And when, in 1991, the *Idiot* experienced increasingly serious financial problems, Hilsum proposed to make some of its offices available to the newspaper. Only the reaction of the employees constrained the publisher to forego that notion.

Once this publishing house disappeared, its literary director, Francis Combes, created a new imprint, *Le Temps des cerises* (*The Time of Cherries*). Among the works published was the collection of Patrick Besson's columns in the *International Idiot* and, especially, a book by Roger Garaudy. Certainly, that was before the former Communist launched out in a revisionist campaign intended for the general public. But could its editor have been unaware of the fact that he had collabo rated, since 1991, with the extreme Right review, *Nationalisme et Répub-lique*, led by "revisionists" who deny the reality of the genocide of the Jews, like the Lyonnais academic Bernard Notin?

A Nasty "Old Crone"

In a remarkable study published by the review *Esprit* on the nega-tionist networks and their strategies,[5] the philosopher Pierre-André Taguieff recalls a very awkward "French exception": "the contempo-rary anti-Zionist negationism is above of all, especially in France, a mis-adventure of the Left and the far Left." This faction would only later meet up with the most extreme Right, which readily claims a share of the Nazi heritage.

Historically, two figures who were *a priori* dissimilar "invented" revisionism. In 1948 Maurice Bardèche, brother-in-law of Robert Bra-sillach, published *Nuremberg ou la terre promise* (*Nuremberg or the Promised Land*), which expressed doubts on the existence of the death camps and suggested that the Allies had used them to mask their own crimes and that the Jews had used them to obtain their own territory. Paul Rassinier, a former Communist, a pacifist in the SFIO of the pre-war period who was deported for resistance activities, offered a more suit-able profile. Except that in 1950, he published in the same vein *Le Men-songe d'Ulysse* (*Ulysses' Lie*), an openly negationist work that Bardèche would seize upon with enthusiasm.

Bardèche attracted the extreme Right, Rassinier the extreme Left. And the two cliques ended up coming together. In 1967, after the Six-Day War, an issue of *Défense de l'occident* (*Defending the West*) appeared, with the signatures of Maurice Bardèche (who ran a monthly magazine with a confidential distribution list), Paul Rassinier and François Duprat, his second-in-command who joined the National Front in 1974 and became one Le Pen's closest colleagues. But Duprat disappeared in a curious accident in 1978: his car blew up.

Too bad, the combat continued under the aegis of a few extremist militants of the far Left, who readily made common cause with the "browns." In 1979, the Old Crone reappeared. Behind this strange com-pany name hid a publisher that distributed the works of the humanities professor Robert Faurisson, another Lyonais and spiritual heir to Rassinier. When it was created, in 1967, the Old Crone (La Vieille taupe) was a bookshop in the Latin Quarter dedicated to the literature of the ultra Left. But its organizer, Pierre Guillaume, formerly of the group "Socialism or Barbarity," had a change of heart in the 1970's, and published an openly negationist bulletin, *The Social War*. In April, 1980, a hitherto supposedly antiracist researcher at CNRS, Serge Thion, sign under the patronage of the Old Crone a book reiterating the bulk of Faurisson's theses.

Several groups fell into the same breach. The "Bordiguists," disciples of Amadeo Bordiga (who was excluded from the Italian Communist Party in the 1920's) joined this faction by publishing a "great classic," *Auschwitz or the Great Alibi*, which would be re-printed by the Old Crone. Their leitmotiv? That Nazism is only a excrescence of capitalism, the camps were used only to over-exploit a source of labor that it was thus not "profitable" to exterminate, and we were reminded of the horror of the Shoah only to better mask the monstrosity of the liberal system.

The last spectacular illustration of this complicity of the extremes: the "Garaudy-Abbé Pierre" incident, that had nothing to do with the simple hazards of media amplification. When the Old Crone published Garaudy's revisionist pamphlet *The Founding Myths of Israeli Politics*, at the end of 1995, Guillaume had already prepared his battle plan. He knew that Garaudy's image among the general public was that of a man of the Left. Wasn't he one of the leading intellectuals of the CP for twenty years?

On December 15, Guillaume thus wrote to "the friends of the Old Crone," announcing to them the imminent publication of Garaudy's book, but still concealing the author's name according to a traditional advertising technique: "This viewpoint will undoubtedly be a decisive turning point, because it is likely to release the word of many revisionists who have been "dormant."

The book was initially distributed in a controlled milieu, making it known to certain journalists. The operation's instigators waited patiently until indignation was mounting. On April 18, 1996, Jacques Vergès, Esq., visited Roger Garaudy for a press conference where he made public the letter of support from Abbé Pierre. The shock was guaranteed. On the following day, Robert Faurisson published (from the town of Vichy!) a victorious press statement. "I am happy because I see people who are in the spotlight taking up on their account what I got tired of repeating for nearly a quarter of a century. . ."

Negationism, as Pierre-Andre Taguieff notes it, thus escaped the boundaries of the cult where it hitherto had been confined. Red-browns and Leftists gone astray together in revisionism are still trying, like their ancestors of La Cagoule, to drop bombs. They are intended to explode in the media first, then to make their way into the public mind. That is another way of conspiring.

CHAPTER 8

PROTECTING EACH OTHER

All his discretion had been in vain; at the back of the church on that cold morning of February 1994, most of the faithful recognized him and went to greet him. That was hardly prudent on their part, but they were among their own. Paul Touvier, disguised behind thick dark glasses and enjoying his last moments of freedom before his trial, undoubtedly thought that the person who was being buried that day well deserved that he should come out of his den to pay a last homage to him. For, to those who were nostalgic for the old order, the deceased, 68 years old, had been for nearly fifty years the unfailing pillar of a system of assistance and solidarity for those who had been purged.

Jean-Pierre Lefevre, whom Touvier and his friends mourned that day in the Church of Saint-Mandé, was known in the penitentiary crowd as a devoted visitor to the Melun penitentiary. But this veteran of the Charlemagne division of the SS (he was 19 years old in 1944) was also interested in the former political prisoners who had known the rigors of the jails after the Liberation.

While the Resistance provided models of networks that persisted after the war, the solidarity among former collaborators is a model of another sort. Robert Paxton, the American historian of *La France de Vichy*[1] practically states outright that the bonds created, for example, between all the senior civil servants under Vichy were even tighter than the friendships woven in the underground. "The resisters expected to govern," he writes. "However, the 'Republic of silence,' to use Sartre's expression, breaks down as soon as it becomes an apparatus of administrative management . . . The 'black sheep' returned to power after 1953 . . . part of the élite came out intact after five years of vicissitudes. Seeing who survived, who sank, and especially knowing why, is very revealing in itself."

Secret connections, hidden allegiances, services rendered in other times, can explain why such different personalities and so unambiguously compromised as Eugène Schueller, founder of L'Oréal and financier of La Cagoule, René Bousquet, the high-ranking administrative official of Vichy, and Georges Albertini, the organizer of the RNP, could at the same time protect themselves from the purges and protect in their turn other less favored companions.

It is difficult to imagine, but more than fifty years after the first trials of the Collaboration, the brotherhood of the purged (most of them condemned for "intelligence for the enemy" and condemned to infamous sentences, forced labor and national indignities), is still active.

The Plot of the Cassocks

A Catholic fundamentalist like the majority of these untouchables, Jean-Pierre Lefevre very quickly understood that he and his peers could rely on that chain of discreet and benevolent allegiance formed by ecclesiastics who took the initiative to protect more than one collaborator in France, Switzerland and Italy.

The head of the Militia, Joseph Darnand, was thus sheltered by the monks of the Servants of Mary at Notre-Dame de Tirano, in northern Italy, before being arrested by the English. His wife and her son Philippe were admitted to the convent of the Sisters of Mercy in Rome. And to cover their living expenses, Philippe Darnand even became an announcer for Radio-Vatican!

Marcel Déat, the chief of the National Popular Gathering (RNP), was taken in hand with his partner Hélène by the pontifical commission at the Italian border. They were arriving from Sigmaringen, where they had taken refuge after fleeing Paris in August, 1944. Their protector? The cardinal Eugène Tisserant, who nevertheless had been at loggerheads with very the Germanophile Pius XII throughout the Occupation.

Did Déat's conversion to Catholicism upon his arrival in Italy and his church wedding with his partner impress the cardinal? Mgr Tisserant, the Vatican's special envoyé to Paris immediately after the Liberation, bitterly negotiated with de Gaulle the many lawsuits of the French bishops who were "compromised" with Vichy, and he was somewhat prematurely frightened by the rumors that were circulating as to a "wild and arbitrary purification" that was going to affect hundreds of thousands of Frenchman! Suddenly, he came to consider with relative indulgence this "charming couple who had been persecuted by the French police."

Like many other Monsignores, he felt that the anti-Communist fight had become the number one priority. An irony of history: while he was sheltering Déat in Italy, he forged a strong friendship in France with the No. 2 of the RNP, Georges Albertini, who had turned up as an anti-Soviet expert. They became so close that Tisserant even became an occasional contributor to Albertini's magazine, *East and West*, until his death in 1972.

In his refuge near Turin, Marcel Déat, who was called Joseph the Red, passed his days peacefully with his wife, renamed Hélène Buridant. He died there in 1955, while his wife would survive to him by more than forty years. Ill and growing old, she ended up returning to France, to the vicinity of Marseilles, then went to her niece's in Châtenay-Malabry, where she died on June 24, 1995.

Many other collaborators used what the RG and the DST of the era call "the way of the convents," or less pleasantly, "the rat route." Georges Dumoulin, former Secretary General of the CGT, recycled into the RNP with Déat, hid in a convent until 1951. He ended up converting. Raphaël Alibert, Minister of Justice under Pétain and author of anti-Jewish laws, spent a few months among the Cistercians. Marc Augier, in Minister Jean Zay's official representative under the Popular Front, engaged on the eastern front during the war and a journalist with the *Combattant européen*, the LVF's weekly magazine, and with *Devenir*, the French SS magazine, hid out in Argentina with the Benedictines. Previously, he managed a whole tour thanks to charitable complicities, staying with the Salésien fathers in Turin, then the Benedictines on rue de la Source, in Paris.

What a peaceful and comfortable building was that convent: it enjoys a double entry, including a very discreet one for those who want to duck out without calling attention to themselves. And Georges Soulès, one of the heads of the MSR, a collaborationist party, warmly praised the hospitality of this safe harbor in his second novel, *Les Yeux d'Ezechiel sont ouverts* (*Ezekiel's Eyes are Open*), which came out in 1949 under a new identity, Raymond Abellio.

But the police of the DST came to disturb the quietude of the grounds in 1947. During one search they discovered a stockpile of false identity papers. Only Zap! there was no other trace of the "rats" who opportunely had been informed of the visit. The groundskeeper, Dom Olph Strong, resisted police curiosity. However, from that point forward the "refugees" were constrained to be even more discreet.

The threads were not, however, dissolved. The gendarmes who launched out in May 1989 in search of Paul Touvier discovered something that was based on more than random meetings and the pity that the former militiaman inspired. There was is a militant network, that shared Touvier's hatred of the Freemasons, the Jews and all the democrats. The "Fraternity of Our Lady of Mercy," of which the very devoted Lefevre was then the General Secretary, was acting out of "political" conscience.

This was a quite curious association, and the godfather, far in the background, was a Lyonnais abbot, Stéphane Vautherin, who was the self-proclaimed chaplain of the Militia during the war. This abbot of shock had also founded an "anti-Bolshevik" youth movement, the "Chevaliers of Notre-Dame." With the Liberation, while he was meditating in prison, his association was taken over by one of his young disciples, Gerard Lafond (whose father, owner of the *Journal de Rouen*, compromised himself in the Collaboration). On August 6, 1945, Gerard Lafond, who had just pronounced his vows at the abbey of Saint-Wandrille, renamed the famous Chevaliers with a Latin name, the "Militia Sanctiae Mariae." And he created an affiliate, the "Fraternity of Our Lady of Mercy," specialized in assistance to prisoners — those of 1945, of course, but also a few years later the OAS soldiers who had gone astray!

The Chevaliers of Notre-Dame, who still today have an outpost on a street close to the basilica of Montmartre and a château close to Chartres, are still active. They are active in the organization of holy processions, with Lefevre at the head (what a curious alliance between the Vichy battle axe and the fount of holy water!) and their networks were still omnipresent when the anniversary of Clovis's baptism was celebrated in September, 1996. The manufacture of the 253 embroidered banners that welcomed Jean-Paul II in Rheims was coordinated by a chevalier, Pinson. And another chevalier, Edmond Fricoteaux, a notary and president of the Fraternity of Our Lady of France, organized a great pilgrimage in September 1996, sending thousands of the faithful to visit the statue of the Virgin which he had had set up in Baillet-en-France, in the Val de l'Oise, Rheims.

Lefevre, a member of the Chevaliers and the famous Fraternity of Our-Lady of Mercy, never dropped Touvier. Every month, he gave him money ($500 at the time of Touvier's arrest) in a Paris bank account, where a friend, Geneviève Penou, would pick it up. A volunteer with Catholic Aid, she is the cousin of Abbot Duben, a friend of the Touvier couple who clandestinely celebrated their marriage in 1947. The old lady would send the money in an envelope to Versailles to a retired soldier. He would send it on to the fundamentalist monastery of Saint-Michel-en-Brenne, in the good care of the prior, Abbot Buron, who was charged with giving the envelope to a certain Paul Lacroix, one of Touvier's many pseudonyms.

When, in May 1989, the gendarmes poked their heads into this monastery, they discovered some luggage belonging to the former militiaman. Abbot Buron ended up cracking and gave away his refuge: the Saint-François priory in Nice, whose leader is called Dom Edouard Guillou. An old acquaintance! The latter was a "renegade" from the Abbey de la Source, where he was in 1947 at the time of the police raid. Since then, he had refused the *ordo missae* of Paul VI, was expelled from the order of Saint-Benoît and was ordained a priest at Ecône by Mgr Lefebvre.

With the end of hunt for Touvier and the death of Lefevre (from whom the gendarmes had seized many pounds of files in 1989), a network died out. But a certain state of mind survives. The burial mass for Touvier, celebrated on July 25, 1996 at St. Nicholas du Chardonnet, brought out all kinds of nostalgic people, with every generation represented. "Celebrities" like Pierre Sidos, the founder of Oeuvre française, and Pierre Bernard, the mayor of Montfermeil, a temporary deputy of the minister Eric Raoult and editor of a municipal newspaper with a sinister and evocative name, *La Gerbe* ("*Fireworks*"), and anonymous figures, accomplices or not of his time spent in hiding.

The Perfume Clan

"For us, it is clear: L'Oréal was able to diversify internationally thanks in part to former collaborationists and their families." When Jean and David Frydman, two businessmen having some difficulties with the cosmetics multinational, discovered in December, 1990, that L'Oréal had taken on some of the purged men, they set to work spreading the word about these inadmissible connections.

Who remembered that Eugène Schueller, L'Oréal's founder, was more than a "genius chemical engineer"? Admittedly, the success of this son of an Alsatian pastry chef born in 1881, constrained to sell fabric in the markets to pay for his chemistry studies, is an edifying "success-story." A simple student at the Central Pharmacy School of France, he hastened to get himself launched. He developed a new process for hair coloring, baptized L'Oréal, and got some publicity in a small cosmetics review, *La Coiffure de Paris*. Then, after the war of 1914, a happy association with the baron Henri de Rothschild enabled him to launch Monsavon. It was the beginning of a stunning success.

From the first months of the Occupation, the businessman who in the 1930's lent an attentive ear to the founder of La Cagoule, Eugène Deloncle, was listed in the organizational chart of the Revolutionary Social Movement (MSR) as "President and Leader of Technical Commissions and Research Commissions." The professions of faith in the MSR, published in 1940, were quite direct: "Deloncle and his MSR want the national revolution to be carried out by more than decrees. They want all the 'bastards' in the place swept away, so that there will be no more Jews, nor Freemasons, able to do any further harm."

Did Schueller sincerely adhere to this nauseating profession of faith? Did he prosaically hope that these functions would offer him a foothold toward becoming Economics Minister under Pétain? It was a waste of time and effort, in any case. He "settled" for writing in reviews like *La France au travail* (*France at Work*) and *L'Atelier* (*The Workshop*), in which he suggested, among other things, calculating wages in proportion to the benefit to the company, which would disgust any workman who had heard of Marx.

At the end of the war, the Purification Committee for the chemical industries, insensitive to the innovative ideas of the owner of L'Oréal, affirmed that he "organized in the factories conferences favorable to collaboration, encouraged the departure to Germany of French workers and financed the collaborationist movements of the MSR and the RNP."[2]

The perfumier, who feared above all an incriminating sentence, strove to find support in the Resistance circles. He did not have to look far: a micro-network of four friends who could always compensate for their numerical weakness by their effectiveness, all had reason to help him out.

There were only four of them, but so precocious! These young people, all provincial, had jointly flirted in their youth with French Action. During their higher education, they were all placed with the Marist fathers of 104, rue de Vaugirard. And, not to miss a thing, at least two of them could display honorable patents of the Resistance.

The youngest of the team, André Bettencourt, was closest to Eugène Schueller. Holed up in Normandy, with his family, at the beginning of the war, this lawyer's son (himself studying law) would send articles to *La Terre française* (*The French Land*), a weekly Pétainist magazine published in Paris. Between 1940 and 1942, he ran a column entitled "Ahoy, Young People!" Rather prolix, he would write 64 articles in two years; some of them were frankly anti-Semitic. That's an embarrassing biographical item for a man who would become a Minister under General de Gaulle.

There were signs that this journalistic collaboration would put him in touch with Schueller. On December 6, 1941, the apprentice journalist published a dithyrambic report on a book by the perfumer, *La Révolution de l'économie* (*The Revolution of the Economy*). Schueller was captivated by this young man so sure in his taste, and all the family felt the same. Eight years later, in 1950, Liliane Schueller, his only daughter, married André Bettencourt.

Another friend from "104," François Mitterrand, owed a debt to Schueller. At the end of the war, without a political appointment, he had to provide for his family. A miracle of friendship: François Paves, another protagonist of the "gang of four," introduced him to Schueller. Thanks to Bettencourt, Dalle himself had begun working at Monsavon in 1942. At the end of 1945, the young activist thus brought his friend

François into the cosmetic group. The transitory Minister for General de Gaulle became director of the Modern and Parisian Publications Company, a property of Eugène Schueller, the jewel of which was *Votre Beauté* (*Your Beauty*) — an esthetics magazine that throughout the war sang the merits of hair coloring and the virtues of the national revolution! Cosmetic journalism was not the future President of the Republic's cup of tea, but this job enabled him to hold on while waiting for the State to pay him for his official functions.

When Schueller got his first warning from the purification committee, Mitterrand was in the midst of a legislature election campaign. The "104" network thus delegated another member of the Resistance, Pierre de Bénouville, formerly of the college at Saint-Paul of Angoulême and the "104."

A long-timer in this informal lobby, Bénouville was part of the patriotic Right wing, anti-German, and proud to have chosen the Resistance from the start while certain Socialists had gone for Vichy. He was proud, and rightly so, of having been a "real" member of the Resistance. His undeniable credits (he was a "Compagnon of the Liberation," a resistance fighter) made him an invaluable instrument for certain ones who pursued the "double game" and found themselves in difficulty with the courts of purification.

At the end of June, 1946, he arose spontaneously before the committee of purification that was planning to give the owner of L'Oréal a hard time. He briefly explained, reveals Michel Bar-Zohar (an Israeli writer and deputy of the Knesset, who investigated the dark years of L'Oréal at length),[3] having met Schueller once in 1943 and that Schueller had promised him money for the Resistance. The testimony was apparently not sufficiently convincing, since the file went up another level. This time, a new commission recommended forbidding Schueller to exert any leadership function and passing on his file to Justice.

Bénouville intervened twice more, to the General Secretary of the commission, then to the prefect of the Seine. Better, the certificate signed by his hand on December 27, 1946, in favor of Schueller made a difference. General Bénouville certified that he had used information from the industrialist from 1942 until March 1944, passed on by the intermediary of a future "very well-known" deputy whose name he modestly forbore to mention. The prefect of the Seine stopped the trial in progress. A final release was dated April 20, 1948. The "104" network had done its job well. It had just contributed, without realizing it, to the creation of a means of reclassification (for the better) for those being purged.

For once Eugène Schueller got out of the mess, his cosmetics empire came to the assistance of those friends from before the war who had been compromised during the occupation. The chemist thus gave Jacques Corrèze a chance, Corrèze having been the faithful right arm of the head of La Cagoule, Eugène Deloncle.

La Bûche ["the Log"], as his Cagoulard friends called him (they remembered that he used to work as a decorator at the shop "Au Bûcheron" [the Woodcutter]), had rather a checkered past. Accomplice to several assassinations perpetrated by La Cagoule before the war, during the Occupation he and his henchmen seized about sixty shops belonging to Israelites, then collaborated in the Institute of Jewish Questions before fighting on the eastern front under the German uniform until April 1942. An exemplary course for a collaborationist! Late scruples or political opportunism? He would claim he had returned some services rendered some minor services to the Resistance at the end of the war. Rescued by Schueller, Corrèze in his turn would protect other old mates or their families, thus creating, at the very heart of L'Oréal, a kind of multi-stage network.

Although he was sentenced in 1948 to ten years in prison during the La Cagoule trial, a penalty combined with the ten years handed down by the Court of the Seine for his activities during the Occupation, Corrèze came out of prison in 1950 due to the favorable climate of national reconciliation that prevailed at that time.

Upon his exit from prison, Schueller sent him to his new right-hand man, François Dalle, who had moved up several levels since his entry into the legal department of Monsavon in 1942. Dalle swears that, at that time, he was unaware of all Corrèze's dark past. "He had a clean criminal record," he said to Le Nouvel economiste, "he had been amnestied."[4] "I gave him a shit job, as representative," he said on television in November 1991. In fact, Corrèze would be amnestied only in 1959. His criminal record was thus still loaded when he began as representative at L'Oréal in 1950.

Corrèze may not have boasted to his recruiter about his war-time exploits. But how could Dalle, a well-informed man, have been unaware of the lawsuit against La Cagoule that was in all the newspapers two years before? "La Bûche" was a "superstar" in the case, with his photograph constantly on the front page.

"The shit job" led its holder to Spain as soon as he signed up. That is a country that he already knew, having taken refuge there at the end of 1937 when the Interior Minister Marx Dormoy started hunting Cagoulards. Once he arrived, Corrèze joined forces with a man who was already selling the house products, Frederic Bonnet. Together, they created a company, "Productos Capillares" (Procasa), of which L'Oréal has still owns 18.4% of the shares today.

L'Oréal was not the only cosmetics company to have use Corrèze's services in Spain. Most surprising was the firm Helena Rubinstein, whose owner is a convinced militant Zionist. She asked the person who had shamelessly requisitioned, during the war, the Lica headquarters and the art merchant Wildenstein's and the former minister Georges Mandel's apartments, as well as several Jewish stores, to be the sales representative of her Spanish company "Albesa"! Corrèze, one suspects, was carefully dissimulating his past as a professional anti-Semite. Similarly, this employer was unaware that Corrèze continued to maintain ties with former "collaborationists" like himself, who were under the benevolent protection of Serano Sunner, Franco's brother-in-law.

Everyone was trying to survive thanks to channels of mutual aid that were more or less under surveillance by the allied services. The most surrealist, certainly, is the astonishing network "88," which was still in full swing in the 1960's. Composed of former Gestapo agents and other collaborationists of every type, affiliated with a German central unit, it was baptized "88" in reference to the eighth letter of the alphabet: "HH" for "Heil Hitler"!

Corrèze knew this fraternity. And for good reason — one of his best friends, Henri Deloncle, was part of it. Involved by his brother Eugène in the disastrous ventures of La Cagoule, Deloncle, like the other members of the secret organization, always justified this membership by a visceral anti-Communism. But he was lucky: imprisoned in October 1945 at La Santé, awaiting the trial that would judge the Cagoulards in 1948, he was released in December by error. He quickly left France. The whole Deloncle family followed him to Madrid. However, this was a family bereft of its "chief." Eugène Deloncle was indeed cut down on January 7, 1944 in the early morning at his residence by the German Gestapo who suspected him (with reason) of having been in the service of Admiral Canaris, who was hostile to Hitler.

Jacques Corrèze, an intimate friend of Eugène and Mercedes

Deloncle, was present in the apartment; he had taken refuge in the bathroom. Louis, Eugène's son, then 18 years old, had less luck; seeking to protect his father, he was seriously wounded by a burst of machine-gun fire.

Upon his fortuitous exit from prison, Henri Deloncle had taken on board his nephew Louis in Madrid. Louis' sister, Claude, also formed part of the caravan with her husband, Guy Servant, a former militiaman enrolled in the LVF, and their son Thierry. Mercedes Deloncle was not far behind, in the wake of Corrèze, whose wife she became.

Little by little, the "family" filled out with the arrival of "cousin" Jean Filliol, La Cagoule's designated gunman. He escaped during the headlong flight of the Militia through Germany and Italy, and he returned to France without any incident in 1946. Faithful to his sinister reputation, he put together some money by hitting up certain Cagoulard industrialists, all of whom were rather glad to see him winging his way toward other lands, where he would remain unpunished. (He still enjoyed a few months of peaceful retirement in the Balearic Islands.)

Corrèze certainly wanted to help his old friend Filliol, but to recruit him into Procasa would be a little too conspicuous all the same. He was given three death sentences *in absentia* in 1948 for his brilliant exploits as a Cagoulard and a militiaman. Conscious of his burdened past, he borrowed his wife's name, Lamy. The Resistance fighters from the underground around Vienna would, indeed, never forget this figure, head of the service that helped the Germans "choose" L'Oradour-sur-Glane for exerting their reprisals.

It was impossible for Corrèze to help him directly. He hired his son, André, at Procasa. That was a subsidiary where one really had a sense of family. Just imagine —the son of Eugène Deloncle, Louis, was engaged there at the same time as his nephew, Thierry Servant, the son of his sister Claude.

The Parisian headquarters of L'Oréal was not spared in this recycling. The son of Michel Harispe, Corrèze's faithful second at MSR in his maneuvers during the black years, found a place there. "In the early 1950's," writes Pierre Assouline in *La Fleuve Combelle*,[5] "L'Oréal-Monsavon was the province of the unpatriotic . . . Berlingot Dop was the paragon. Eugène Schueller watched over his domain. He preferred young people from advertising. . . Since the amnesty, he was constantly recovering those who had fallen." Lucien Combelle, the former director of National Revolution was one of these, and he in specific was engaged for a time in the advertising department.

But it was Jacques Corrèze, extremely knowledgeable in business, who made the most spectacular career within the cosmetic group. After a few years of training in Spain, Schueller had him pack his bags for Latin America, where some former acquaintances whose legal positions were delicate were already hatching intrigues.

So much for the "shit job"! While crossing the Atlantic, Corrèze was promoted. The mission which L'Oréal entrusted to him was highly strategic: to establish the French cosmetic range on the American market. Better to start with Latin America, that was little concerned with the *curriculum vitae* of its adopted citizens.

And then, there were the friends, already established for a few years. Among them was Jean Azéma, formerly with French Action and La Cagoule in Filliol's 17th team. A talented journalist, he wrote for *Cri du people* (*The People's Cry*), the newspaper of the French People's Party (PPF), before being overtaken with enthusiasm for the Belgian collaborator Leon Degrelle. His passion was so strong that he even adopted the uniform of the Wallonia division of the SS! Condemned in absentia to life imprisonment, he began a new career as an advertising executive at the Yuste agency. A happy coincidence: L'Oréal chose this agency to conduct its advertising campaigns in Latin America. In Mexico City, another trustworthy member of the MSR, Jacques Piquet, worked in data processing for L'Oréal. Azéma's and Piquet's history shocked Jean Lévy, one of the company's executives doing a tour of duty in America. Upon his return, he spoke to François Dalle about it. "Don't dig up the muck," he was heard to answer.[6]

An infamous past does not prevent one from being selective about the company one keeps, far from it. Corrèze, conscious of this consideration, openly snubbed a Frenchman whom he knew well and who had taken refuge in Brazil. Jean Bouvyer, an old Cagoulard, was police station chief for Jewish questions from May 1941 to April 1944. A friend of the Mitterrand family, during the Occupation he was engaged to one of the future President's sisters. He feels that Corrèze dropped him. It is true. Too boastful, to much a braggart, Bouvyer would tarnish a man on his way up.

"La Bûche," indeed, kept climbing in the L'Oréal hierarchy. Although his guardian, Schueller, died in 1957, the new chairman, François Dalle, had full confidence in him. Better still, when Corrèze founded the company "Cosmair" in Delaware in 1961, he did not forget his friends, and kept in close contact with André Bettencourt and Henri Deloncle.

Cosmair, of which Corrèze was named "Chairman, in charge of strategy for the western hemisphere," was a real cash pump. Neither an agent nor a subsidiary, Cosmair was an extremely privileged importer of the L'Oréal product range, and transferred only modest royalties to the home base: 1% on consumer goods and 1.5% on professional products — unheard of. Thanks to these advantageous conditions and to Corrèze's know-how, the American firm thrived. The profit realized upon the sale of Cosmair to Nestlé, already a shareholder in L'Oréal, was quite cute: approximately $800 million.

That was a winning formula that Corrèze sought to replicate with Helena Rubinstein, by then a property of Colgate. When this multinational, which bought the business for $142 million in 1973 from the famous cosmetic expert's heirs, decided to sell, L'Oréal said it was not interested. Pure propaganda, show the Frydman brothers, intended to persuade the Arab countries who were boycotting any firms in league with Israel; Helena Rubinstein did, indeed, have factories in that country.

Officially, Helena Rubinstein was bought out (far below the price paid by Colgate) by an American company, Albi, that was acting, it was rumored in economic circles, in the name of "mysterious investors." Shortly thereafter, Albi was bought by Palac, which then resold it to. . . L'Oréal. In the course of events, the "mysterious investors" made a few more million dollars in profit.

More generally, the luxury trades (haute couture, perfumes and cognac) which had shown themselves overall to be, at the very least, obliging to the Germans during the Occupation, turned out after the war to be quite as accommodating to the heavily compromised Vichyists. Jean Leguay, deputy general of the police force under Vichy, one of the organizers of the raid of Vel d'Hiv, was hire in 1946 by Nina Ricci in the United States. Nina Ricci, who in 1941was a member, along with 200 other managers of French enterprises, of the "European Club," a "European Committee for Economic Collaboration" in which French and German were equal partners.

His past caught up with Leguay just before his death (just like Corrèze, who died in 1991). Leguay the former prefect, accessory to the deportation of thousands of foreign and French Jews, was accused in 1979 of "crimes against humanity." Bad luck. At 69 years, he had just completed a second career without any concern. In 1955, he had even succeeded in being rehabilitated: the Council of State had kindly cancelled the only sanction it had given him in 1945, the revocation of the prefectoral corps. The whole affair had been tied up quickly: the aforementioned Council took a decision in consideration only of the file that it had put together.

His reputation cleared after ten years of service at Nina Ricci, Leguay returned to Europe with head held high, to work for his new employer, Warner Lambert, an American cosmetic firm. There he finished out his career, between Paris and New York, without ever breaking off with his old friends.

On Sinecure Street

On his return to France in 1955, Leguay visited his former boss, René Bousquet, General Secretary with the police force under Pierre Laval. A brilliant technocrat, he was so sure of himself that he imagined he could negotiate as equals with the Germans. But, from compromising to being compromised, he had ended up handling the bureaucratic management of the deportations of Jews and others who were being cited with increasing pressure as "anti-nationals" by the occupying entity.

After a stay at Fresnes, Bousquet found an influential position at the Bank of Indochine in 1950. There, he hired Pierre Leguay, the young brother of the one who, in the black years, had been his delegate in the occupied zone. Later, other sons of those who had been purged came to the bank or its subsidiary companies thanks to Bousquet. The staff, who understood these special favors, ironically called such recruits the "Bousqueteers." One example was Jean-Claude Cathala, son of Maurice Cathala, the former Vichy Finance Minister, one of Bousquet's first bosses in 1930; he was propelled upward in a rum company in Bordeaux, owned by the Bank.

These informal micro-networks recycled the former companions of the technocratic Collaboration far more effectively than did the "Association of the Purged" founded by the sub-prefect Pierre-Henry or the "Association of those who have been distanced from the Government" (sic) founded by Jean Dides, a former specialist in Jewish questions for the Police Prefecture from 1942 to 1944. An irrevocable solidarity as created in the first months of the Liberation between men who, at the time of their glory, mingled urbanely in the gilded salons of the Ritz Hotel and suddenly found themselves sharing monk-like cells in the prison of Fresnes! Several regulars from the "Round Table" lunches that, during 1942, used to bring together politicians, high-ranking officials, and heads of the French and German enterprises every three weeks at the Ritz, now went to eat together for a few months, or a few years, in a less select location.

The bankers Henri Ardant (Société Générale), Hypolite Worms, Gabriel Le Roy Ladurie, Jacques Barnaud (all three of Worms Bank), André Laurent-Atthalin (Paribas), Paul Baudouin (Bank of Indodine), the industrialist Louis Renault, his nephew the former minister François Lehideux, would meet behind bars René Bousquet, Pierre Laval, the ambassador Fernand de Brinon, the former minister Jean Bichelonne, and also Sacha Guitry and Tino Rossi! All these prisoners were busily preparing their defenses and . . . their reconversion.

For the most adroit, Fresnes became a kind of labor exchange. The "employment interviews" were all the easier since the regimen was not very strict for these "political" prisoners. The "upper crust" of the Collaboration thus visited from one cell to another. Georges Albertini, the former number two of the RNP with Marcel Déat, did not have to go far to meet his future employer. He shared cell No. 257 with Perruggia, the famous bootmaker from rue de la Paix, and with Hypolite Worms, the prestigious bank manager of the same name that provided so many cadres to the Vichy regime.

It was not the bootmaker who offered him a job, but the banker. The former humanities professor so impressed the big bourgeois with his conversation and his discretion, that he promised to help him when he got out. A promise kept: Albertini, upon his release, gave him an office and a salary, and let him set up his new undertakings as he saw fit.

Hypolite Worms, who so likes to lend a hand (his close contact Xavier Vallat, police chief for Jewish questions, was recruited to a subsidiary of his bank) was also a guardian angel to René Bousquet. Temporarily released in July 1948, the burdensome prefect was hired, while waiting for his trial, at a public works company affiliated with Worms. But Bousquet's real "protector," who would enable him to start a new career, was Paul Baudouin, the transitory Vichy Minister for Foreign

Affairs and chairman of the Bank of Indochine until 1944.

In Fresnes, the former banker Baudoin also worked to help young administration officials when he got out of prison. In one fell swoop, the bureaucracy that headed up the anti-Jewish raids (a subject that was avoided completely during his trial) was engaged in 1950 at the Bank of Indochine where Baudouin discreetly served as "technical adviser."

This "Vichyist" bank redeemed itself with the Liberation by elevating to its to its top position Jean Laurent, a finance inspector and member of several resistance networks. Laurent was moderately Gaullist, which one suspects must have pleased Bousquet, who was trying to fix up some other "victims" of purification. In the muffled corridors of the bank, he would cross paths with, among others, the former chairman of the Bank of Paris and the Netherlands, Paul de Thomasson, and Jean de Sailly, ex-director of the Vichy Economic Board. Did Bousquet ever discuss the past with them? "He didn't blush about it, nor speak about it any more that was necessary," says Pascale Froment, author of a biography of this character.[7]

Quickly promoted to Deputy Chairman, his talents as a born leader apparently being something of a marvel, he was also named president of a series of subsidies, and a director of many companies. He thus graced with his presence the Société financière pour la France et les pays d'outre mers (Financial company for France and the countries overseas) chaired by the Pétainist Edmond Giscard d'Estaing, father of the future President of the Republic, and the board of directors of Baccarat Crystal, whose chairman was René de Chambrun, the faithful son-in-law of Pierre Laval.

Maurice Renand, another unrepentant Lavallist, also sat on this council. A finance inspector, this former director of the administrative and financial services of the Presidency of the Council, removed during the Liberation (and reinstated thereafter), was rescued in 1949 by his father, boss of Samaritaine, who gave up his seat to him. Simple coincidence or fidelity once again? To head up the great store's press service, Maurice Renand recruited the elder daughter of Marcel Bucard, the founder of the francist Party, who was shot in March, 1946. "He wasn't paying attention to my name when he hired me," she claims. "But I do not think that he would have been opposed to my being recruited!"[8] That is euphemistic, for little is left to chance in the recruitment and hiring in which Bousquet excelled.

He was taught how to use the networks before the war, especially by the powerful radical leader of South-west, Maurice Sarraut. After the Liberation, this innate sense of mutual aid did not leave him. Once he was re-situated himself, he was quick to use all his connections (he had kept on the "good side" of the high public office) to recommend friends who were in delicate positions with the purification commissions. Due to his friendly pressure, his lawyer, Pierre Doublet, Esq., thus hired into his office a few prefects who had been kicked out.

But there was one man in particular who would help him to recycle his closer friends. A man who shared his anti-Gaullisme. A man through whom he seemed to live, by proxy, so much he recognized himself in his ambitious rise.

Did he already know François Mitterrand when, shortly after acquittal in June, 1949, he sought to help "a friend who has a problem"? He did not ask him directly but he addressed himself to a close contact of the one who was already one of the brilliant hopes of the 4th Republic. Yves Cazaux, delegated to the rebuilding of Amiens, was one of those civil servants who preferred to give up their career advance during the black years rather than compromising themselves. But he felt an inexplicable fascination for Bousquet.

From Amiens, Cazaux alerted Mitterrand via a common friend, Jean-Paul Martin. During the Occupation, Martin had worked under Bousquet's orders in the Interior. But he was also in regular contact with the leaders of the Movement of the Prisoners of War, and among them a certain captain Morland, alias François Mitterrand.

Martin was demoted in January 1945, he was even exiled for a while in Sweden, but when he came back in 1947 he found a shelter as a "press attaché" for the Minister for Ex-Servicemen, Mitterrand.

The "friend" that Bousquet wanted to help, with the assistance of Cazaux and Martin, was named Jehan de Carayon. This civil servant, worried at the Liberation, would also join the cabinet of Mitterrand, who had gone from being Minister for Ex-Serviceman to that of France Overseas. Four years later Mitterrand, as Minister for the Interior, gave Carayon another boost by reinstating his legal rights.

In 1954, the "Bousquet network" was discreetly re-established in this same Ministry for the Interior. Mitterrand, still assisted by the faithful Martin, made room in his cabinet another friend of René Bousquet, Jacques Saunier, Deputy Manager of General Information during the Occupation, who was thrown out without pension during the Liberation. Not content to make him his representative, the lenient minister named Saunier a prefect. After this ministerial passage which definitively "cleansed" them, all these men would continue their administrative careers, from now on forged into a tight network of mutual recognition with regard to the future President of the Republic. Once at the Elysée, he still did not forget them. On October 11, 1983, Jean-Paul Martin received the rosette of an Officer of the Legion of Honor and Jacques Saunier received a plaque as a high officer.

My friends' friends. The proverb seems to apply magnificently to Mitterrand and Bousquet. Among the latter's right-hand men in Vichy was Pierre Saury. Known in the Resistance under the name of "Paule," he nevertheless had to make himself forgotten with the Liberation. Like other civil servants whose situations were a little bit ambiguous, he was dispatched to administer the French forces in Germany. Returned in Paris in the early 1950's, the former radical teacher who had strayed into the police force got re-settled in certain ministerial cabinets before becoming, in 1956 — can you believe it? — Representative to the Minister of Justice, François Mitterrand. In 1961, he was even promoted to substitute for Deputy Mitterrand, who accepted him as a confidant. His burial in 1973 brought together his two guardians, Bousquet and Mitterrand, who were linked by a reciprocal fascination and some mutual services rendered.

The Bousquet network is an example of recycling that was particularly successful in the prefectoral body. With the Liberation, most of its members needed some serious "whitewashing." The prefect René Bargeton collected (a labor of Titan) the biographies of the 1,985 prefects who had been in office from September 1870 to May 1982.[9] An analysis of the biographical highlights of the prefects during the Occupation (some 220 passed through, from August 1940 to November 1944, in the 87 French departments, in eight successive waves) is revealing as to their routes and their networks of protection.

On one side, the heroes: 36 prefects and sub-prefects died after deportation and 35 others were removed, but returned to France in 1945. On the other side were the "passive resisters, the zealots of the National Revolution, partisans of the Vichy regime who (in the image of René Bousquet) collaborated correctly, courteously, but coldly, in the name of maintaining law and order, while trying to safeguard French interests, there were the resolute collaborators with the Germans, often animated by a savage hatred anti-Communist, and finally, the prudent ones who represent the majority of the epoch, managing the immediate demands while trying to prepare for the day after."[10] The most "collaborationist" were condemned to death (six, including three who were shot without trial) or to severe prison sentences (fourteen of them, while the majority were dismissed, crossed off the list of executive candidates, and placed in mandatory retirement.

Some of the younger people among this "pestiferous lot" of the administration were recycled in the big company structures. Anyway, the majority of the heads of enterprises and their trade-union organizations hardly shone by their spirit of resistance, so that the calling card of a former prefect, once purified, and a solid address book, were of considerable interest. Thus, Marcel Ribière, former State Councillor, prefect of the Alpes-Maritimes from September 1940 to April 1943, was ejected from the cadres in 1944 (but reinstated as honorary prefect in 1954); in 1948 he was named president of Nation-Capitalization and of Nation-Life before becoming in 1968 vice-president of Foncière-Life. Similarly, Frantz Lambert, prefect of the Ardennes in January 1944, suspended without discussion, was retired on July 1, 1946 but was rehabilitated by the Trade Union of Furnishing and became its General Secretary. As for Marc Freund-Valade, prefect of the area of Limoges in 1944, whose dismissal the Council of State would cancel in 1947 — he became vice-president of the Employers' Federation of the Somme, then worked for the Picardy Chamber of Commerce. For his part, Victor Leydet, who managed to have his case dismissed in the court of Douai in August 1945 in spite of the extreme reservations of the local resistance representatives, presided over the fate of the Société Générale de Surveillance before becoming chairman of the Crepin Laboratories in Rouen. Charles Roger-Machart, a former tax inspector who made the jump, before the war, to the Crédit foncier égyptien, simply regained his former position. And the lists go on.

But the company leadership started earlier with the hiring of a small group of purged, for whom it had a different kind of delicate treatment in mind. The leader of the troop, André Boutemy, distinguished himself during the Occupation as director of General Information (RG), prefect of the Loire, then of the area of Lyon. Suspended in November 1944, dismissed in 1945, jailed in Saint-Etienne and then at Fresnes, before seeing his file classified, he was more like a businessman than a high-ranking official. As Bousquet would testify in his favor, this ambitious man could not bear having the war interrupt a promising career. He too convinced himself that he got through this period as a technician and not as a political actor. Affable by nature, Boutemy diversified his contact list during the last months of the war. In Lyon, he saved the mayor, Georges Villiers, from the firing squad that the Gestapo intended for him.

And that was a stroke of luck for Boutemy. Villiers became president of the National Center of French Employers (CNPF) in 1946. He would discreetly bring in the former prefect as a political advisor. The former head of the RG was propelled to the top of the enigmatic "Cabinet of Administrative and Political Research," and installed in well-appointed offices in the 8th arrondissement. Officially intended "to collect and to distribute documentation," the research office was used to distribute the manna of patronage to the political class, with the exception of the Communists.

Being wary, Boutemy involved two friends "in his ideas." The first, Henri Cado, general manager of the national police force under Vichy, had troubles when the Liberation came: he was dismissed in July 45, and then retired from office. The second, André-Paul Sadon, an itinerant prefect throughout the years of the Occupation, had approximately the same experience: dismissal, and retirement from office, before the measure was revoked in 1950.

Another member of the Bousquet clan, Jean Weber, a former civil servant in the Interior, joined these pals of the company leadership. André Boutemy had other ambitions: having spent so much time among the politicians who were beholden to him, he wound up dreaming of a career as a notable. Elected senator in 1952 by none too vigilant Great Electors, he already thought of becoming a minister! That was too exposed a position, but he insisted, and accepted with delighted, in January 1953, the Ministry for Public health which the President of the Council (his friend René Mayer) offered to him. But his past caught up with him. The Communist deputies forced his resignation. Suddenly, he had to reach out to his friend Cado. Having failed to see that only the shadows enabled these discreet marionnettists to work their connections like so many threads, André Boutemy ruined his career all by himself.

A Funny Sort of Appendix

Georges Albertini, another *éminence grise*, would never make that mistake. Since he got out of Poissy's central prison, after having spent four years in the jails of Fresnes and Épinal, you could say that Albertini cultivated extreme discretion. In the year 1950, the great majority of the bank clerks at Worms would have had difficulty to identify this small, well-groomed man with the round glasses, who took care not to use the imposing entrance to 45 Haussmann Boulevard to get to his office. And they were quite unaware that on Friday evenings, he would get together, a few hundreds of meters from there, at No. 86, with an astonishing group of anti-Communists most of whom knew each other in the RNP.

"In 1948," admits Guy Lemonnier, alias Claude Harmel, Albertini's assistant at the RNP, "we were wondering how to get ourselves accepted by the political personnel in office." Albertini and Lemonnier were radically different in temperament, one extraverted, the other not, but they were very complementary and knew each other since 1938 when both were active on the pacifist fringes of the Socialist party. A good dozen former militants of the Left who had been caught up by the fascistic trend would thus find in the protective shelter of 86 Haussmann boulevard the ideal outlet for their lost illusions and their bad choices. None of them was seeking a professional sinecure there. Albertini, who did not begrudge a certain middle-class standing for himself, paid his collaborators skimpily. Apparently he was persuaded that it was an honor to work for "the cause." In 1981, Guy Lemonnier, editor of *East and West*, had to settle for $600 per month!

Some got tired of this semi-voluntary militancy. Such was the case of Jean Madiran, a nostalgic Pétainist, who left to found the fundamentalist review *Itinéraires*, then the extremist daily newspaper *Présent*. And also Roland Goguillot, alias Roland-the-Lefty, former leader of the RNP youth, and future general adviser for the National Front in Franche-Comté; he left the review in 1959, to render his services to publications of the far Right.

But most of the early recruits had no choice. Not everyone found a protector, like Albertini, so gracious as Hypolite Worms. When Guy Lemonnier left Fresnes in November 1947, after more than two years of detention,[11] he had no resources. A humanities professor at the College of Brest before the war, he no longer had the right to practice. "I certainly found some openings in the private sector, but every time, the boss would say to me: 'What will my enterprise committee say?'"

A friend sub-contracted to him a historical book on anarchism, until Georges Albertini, who had just gotten out of prison, recommended him in May 1948 to the Secretary of the trade union FO-Métallurgie, Leon Chevolme. He had just founded the discreet "Bureau of Economic and Social Studies and Documentation," the BEDES, which was savagely anti-Communist. Guy Lemonnier then became, under the signature of Claude Harmel (and more episodically that of René Milon) the salaried editor of the modest review whose offices were also the base of Albertini's first network. While planning their future activities, the two friends concocted a monthly bulleting (15 published issues), entitled *"Dictionnaire des girouettes"* (Dictionary of Weather Vanes), where they railed, anonymously, at the "false resisters" who turned coat as the occasion demanded!

They also ranted against those who retrieved their virginal purity thanks to the Communist Party, a channel that was not well-known but was effective for those who had been purged. "People from the RNP were very coveted for they made reliable activists," Guy Lemonnier says with irony. He himself was approached by Maurice Bouvier-Ajam, the ex-head of the Institute of Corporate and Social Studies. Moving without undue distress from the *francisque* (the Vichy battle-axe symbol) to the sickle, this curious "headhunter" promised, in exchange for the CP card, to discharge the collaborationist blemishes. A renowned professor of economics, author of a work on corporate development in the collection "Que sais-je" recuperated himself in this manner. Albertini too was contacted, by Georges Cogniot, one of the leaders of the CP (a real resistant, that one).

At the other end of these trajectories, Albertini was recruiting former Communists who were compromised in the Collaboration, Henri Barbé and Pierre Celor, two fonts of erudition on the internal history of the CP. Even while these two ex-cadres of the Comintern both suffered from the relentless Stalinist crusher, and ended up being removed (Pierre Celor) or removing themselves (Henri Barbé), they were enemy brothers whom Albertini had to manage. Celor did not forgive Barbé for having taken part in 1932 in a kind of "Moscow trial" against him. It didn't bother Albertini, who was very attached to these recruits who had another point in common besides their virulent anti-Communism: they had both converted to Catholicism! Barbé even became a regular freelance journalist for the fundamentalist review *Itinéraires* under the prolific Madiran. The other convert in the Albertini clan, Leon Emery, was a former professor at the teacher training school in Lyon. Scorning the justice of the men, would these former collaborators prefer to rely on a less demanding divine sentence?

One of the pillars of this network of former "socialo-collabos" used the pseudonym Lucien Laurat; his true name was Otto Maschi. This former member of the Austrian CP was a professor at the oriental school of Moscow and had as a student a certain Ho-Chi-Minh. Arriving in France, he joined the SFIO (the French Socialist party from 1905 to 1971) and launched a magazine called *Marxist Combat*, renamed *Idea and Action* in 1936. Imprisoned upon the Liberation, he was expelled from the SFIO for having collaborated in various economic and social organizations during the Occupation.

Laurat was not the only one who owed friend Albertini for offering him a second ideological chance. Thanks to his relations with a judge on the commission for pardons, Déat's former assistant got some of the sanctions reduced. Young people, some of whom were disconsolate at having ruined their lives by making "a bad choice," felt an almost filial admiration for him. Such was the case of Michel Courage, a former member of the Socialist Students, propaganda chief of the JNP (the youth movement of the RNP); he would help fund anti-Communists publications with Jacques Guionet and Roland Silly, two other ex-JNP's, who also appreciated this "family" on which they could always depend.

The "Pen-Pushers'" Bunker

All the historians agree: purification was more severe for the "pen-pushers" than for business leaders and politicians. There was too much information, they were too exposed. The situation was hardly bright for this "community reduced to cackling," to use the term of one of those who fled to Sigmaringen, where many collaborationists ended up at the end of the war, before being exiled in Latin America. Their dream? To return to France.

The amnesty laws of 1951 and 1953, then the judicial regulations in the 1970's gave them that opportunity. Where could they get fixed up again, if not in the "friendly" press that specialized in protecting the purged? *Rivarol*, launched immediately following the war, became the home port of the collaborationist press. Its founder, René Malliavin (who led it until 1970) was legal adviser to the Agence Inter-France during the Occupation. At his side were the militiaman Emmanuel Allot (alias François Brigneau), the former Youth Commissar under Vichy, Maurice Gaït, the ex-SS Bernard Laignoux, Pierre Lucchini (alias Pierre Dominique), a Leftist pacifist, director of the French Office of Information under Vichy, the writer Lucien Rebatet (alias François Vinneuil), the director of the *Cri de Peuple* Henri Lèbre, etc.

Pierre-Antoine Cousteau, CAP to his friends, the editor of *Je Suis partout* (*I Am Everywhere*), converted during the PPF exodus to Germany to Radio-Fatherland, the French version of "The Voice of the Reich," exited prison in 1953 and was rehabilitated at *Rivarol*. His brother, the commander Jacques-Yves Cousteau, who was achieving considerable notoriety with his film *The World of Silence,* wished to inculcate precisely those virtues to him. He begged his brother to keep quiet, in vain; he didn't care, he told his family ☐ it was a matter of honor, he had to speak out, to debate, to protest. . . He got together with two notorious anti-Semites, Henry Coston and Jacques Ploncard d'Assac, and together they produced a monthly magazine, *French Lectures*, which gave a forum to Paul Rassinier, a former Communist who was deported for deeds of resistance, but who hurt himself with nauseating revisionist theses.

René Malliavin, who similarly founded the *Writings of Paris*, was happy to help fix up his peers. His facilities at 354 rue Saint-Honoré, served as temporary offices for Georges Albertini and his friends from *East and West* until 1952. But, to save appearances, the review displayed an imaginary address, No. 600 rue Saint-Honoré, which never existed.

Happy, at first, to find refuge there, the purified journalists ended up feeling a little confined in these congenial newspapers. Some were eyeing the press that came from the Resistance, an ideal venue for being absolved for the past. There, the idea of the network shows its real strength: one could get a reference to good addresses, those of the lenient, or voluntarily amnesiac, owners or department heads. Many scribes from the collaborationist youth press were thus helped after the war to get fixed up again, some in *Valiant Hearts* (Catholic), others at

Vaillant (Communist).

No newspaper can could feel certain that it was spared this underhand infiltration. Witness the former "street pedlar of the king," an activist of the PPF and prolific journalist, Robert-Jullien Courtine. During the Occupation, he wrote for *L'Atelier* (*The Workshop*), *Le Réveil du Peuple* (*People's Wake Up Call*), *La France au Travail* (*France at Work*), *Au Pilori* (*At the Pillory*), *Le Bulletin d'Information anti-maçonnique* (*The Anti-Masonic News Bulletin*), and he contributed to Radio Paris. After the war, he took refuge within the very selective newspaper *Le Monde*; the readers there were already being treated to delicious columns signed by La Reynière, in homage to a famous cook. But they are unaware of that the culinary expert used to relish the delights of Jew-baiting in his column in the 1940's! And that he continued in the same vein, across the Rhine, with Radio-Fatherland, the PPF's transmitter.

As a refugee initially in Baden-Baden, where he found himself in the company of Celine and his cat Bébert, he ended up joining the fine team of *I Am Everywhere* in Bad-Mergentheim. Jean Hérold-Pasture told of this piteous exodus in his memoirs, written in the Fresnes prison in 1945 while he was awaiting execution. He drew a wild portrait of the journalist, who apparently had only one concern during this time of troubles: his dog "Bobby." The Americans at the gates, Courtine fled to Austria and crossed the Swiss border by night, through waist-deep snow, in the company of Cousteau, Pâquis and a few others. The head of *Le Monde*, Hubert Beuve-Méry, accepted him a few years later over the protests of some journalists who had fought in the Resistance and who did not forget his writings. His professional anti-Semitism had, indeed, led him in the 1940's to track "the Jewish influence," making personal denunciations in every sector. Particularly obsessed, one of his articles even asked, in all seriousness, "Was Christopher Columbus, admiral of trinkets, Jewish?"

In this small band where everyone helps each other while, at the same time, spying on each other, everything is known, but everyone respects the law of silence. Those who had listened to Europe No. 1 were of course unaware that the very erudite "Mr. Larousse" was actually Lucien Combelle, and that during the Occupation he was one of the youngest newspaper editors. Veteran of French Action, close friend of Drieu La Rochelle, one-time secretary to Gide, editor-in-chief of the weekly magazine *Révolution nationale*, he barely escaped the death penalty demanded by the government commissioner.

In the 1970's, the listeners of Radio-Sud were likewise unaware that many of the "voices" on the airwaves were perfectly happy that the station was based in Andorra, out of reach of the French courts. Former journalists who had been part of *I Am Everywhere* and other anti-Semite sheets, they took shelter behind their microphones, far from Paris. Alas, the Gaullist Pierre Lefranc, appointed chairman of Sofirad in 1965 and preoccupied with cutting costs, intended to repatriate everyone to Toulouse. It took him quite some time to comprehend the stubborn refusal of certain of the journalists.

Television, in the 1960's, accommodated a young journalist from Strasbourg who had wasted his talent under the Occupation in *I Am Everywhere*, and *Combat*, the weekly magazine of the Militia. "An ambitious young journalist could not pass up such an opportunity to launch his career," wrote Pierre Assouline. Nothing astonishing in that. What is more shocking is to find, immediately after the Liberation, so blemished a journalist working under a pseudonym in places such as *Carrefour* and *Parisien Libéré*. The case of Charles-François Bauer makes people wonder — his fellow-members of both the Resistance and the Collaboration as well.[12] They would be even more surprised when they saw him nonchalantly interviewing all the movie stars under his new patronym, François Chalais. But watch out, anyone who dared to recall Bauer's diabolical past: the journalist, deceased in May 1996, explained without raising an eyebrow that he had been a Resistance agent who had infiltrated the others!

His buddy Roland Goguillot, alias Roland Gaucher, who did his training at the *National-Populaire* of the RNP, didn't bother with any such justifications. Upon his exit from prison, he scraped by with *East and West, Journal des Indépendants*, and *Ecrits de Paris*. Redeemed in 1961 at *Auto-Journal*, he ended up specializing in the press of the far Right (*Minute, National Hebdo*). At *Auto-Journal*, he was not out of his element; in fact, the paper had brought in several former collaborators of whom the most "famous" is Marc Augier, who had been a correspondent at the Russian front for LVF newspaper; he was condemned to death, and then amnestied in 1953.

In August, 1940, Augier (then editor-in-chief of the weekly magazine *La Gerbe*, or *Fireworks*) received a visit from a 20-year-old man. "My name is Robert Hersant. I've come to work for the Marshal."[13] Augier politely turned him away. As head of "Youth Front," a subsidiary of Pierre Clémenti's small National Collectivist Party, Hersant distinguished himself nonetheless at the beginning of the Occupation by breaking the windows of some Jewish shops on the Champs-Elysées. But the "Youth Front" experiment was short-lived. Clémenti and his cronies were wary of this ambitious young person who was liable to steal the show. Discouraged, he signed up with les Chantiers de Jeunesse (another youth organization) and took over the management of the Marshal-Pétain Center at Brévannes, the largest in the Paris area. This was a milieu that Marc Augier frequented, and he was working with the "Young People of the New Europe." On January 31, 1942, Hersant and Augier find themselves having a cup of tea, on rue de Lille, at the German embassy, in the company of Abel Bonnard, Minister for State Education, the journalists Jean Luchaire and Robert Brasillach, the writer Pierre Drieu La Rochelle, and a few others.

These common memories created a bond between the press baron and the reject. Hersant not only gave him work with *Auto-Journal*, he provided a house in which Augier, who was writing under the pseudonym of Saint-Loup, died in 1990 after having written an enormous literary opus that was revered by those who longed for the New Europe.

In Hersant's career, the "friends from Brévannes," in fact all the "Marshal's youngsters," made a difference. They formed a core that followed him in his rise after the Liberation: Bernard Gougenot lent his name in 1950 to the creation of the *Auto-Journal*; Jacques Lemoy became future director of the same newspaper; André Boussemart, his right-hand man, would become the director of Sirlo, *Le Figaro*'s printer. And let's not forget his associate, Jean-Marie Balestre, the most compromised of the group. In 1942, he supervised the recruitment of young people into the French Waffen SS to go to the Eastern Front.

Just like Marc Augier, the writer Raymond Abellio had dozens of admirers after the war. Converted to esotericism, this "X," who was a pacifist on the Left in 1939, attracted a large audience with books where mysticism disputed the syncretic explanations of the universe.

The Liberation had, however, been difficult for the one who had been known in the political sphere under the name of Georges Soulès. Little by little, he regained his footing thanks to a network of friendships the pillar of which was Laval's gracious chief assistant, Jean Jardin. Jardin met the young Soulès when the latter was making such a good impression on Eugène Deloncle at the MSR. At Vichy, it was Jardin who controlled the funds for the political parties. And every month, from the summer of 1942 to the end of 1944, Soulès would go to the Hotel du Parc to receive his payola from the MSR. That created a durable bond that persisted even after the Liberation, when Jardin relocated to Vevey, Switzerland.

This latter provided him with both lodging and cover in exchange for working as a tutor to his son Pascal, the future successful screenwriter, and he had him sign a contract for three books with a publisher that he was sponsoring — Le Cheval Ailé (the Winged Horse), a hotbed of Vichyists that was short of writers. And Abellio was not the only writer to profit from Jardin's "editorial network;" Jardin was also a friendly advisor to the Éditions du Table Rond from 1943 onward.

After the amnesty law of 1951, Abellio returned to France. He spent thirty hours in La Santé prison before being acquitted on October 17, 1952 by the Paris military tribunal. Jardin, who never was tried and who remained on good terms with both camps, had given favorable testimony. Abellio then started a new career as a consultant, which was hardly flamboyant; but he was helped along by his literary admirers. Among them was Jean-Pierre François, a discreet financier and a friend of François Mitterrand, whose presidential campaigns he helped fund. Of Austrian origin, he was a flourishing banker living in Switzerland but with antennas in France. And that enabled him to support Abellio discreetly in the 1970's. But above all, the network of the old École Polytechnique alums came to Abellio's aid; he and two engineers founded a consulting company, of which he was the general manager. Although he revisited his past in his Mémoires, Abellio had nothing more to do with politics and until his death he took refuge in mysticism.

Le Pen, Here We Are

While some former collaborators like Georges Albertini still regard themselves as "authentic Socialists" and hang onto their convictions from before war, the better to obscure a cumbersome past, others persist in drifting toward the far Right. Witness Roland Goguillot, alias Roland Gaucher, alias Roland Varaigne, the former national inspector from Jeunnesses nationals populaires, who has not disavowed any of his old commitments and who openly scorns "distance" that

Déat's assistant put between himself and his past.

Was he any more at ease with Jean-Marie Le Pen? Whether he did or did not, Roland Gaucher in any case found a new family in the National Front that Le Pen tried to promote in the 1970's.

Le Pen never boasted about that. And, as long as his electoral percentages bordered on zero, nobody, fundamentally, was really concerned by these doubtful relations. However, he was assisted from the first by some enthusiasts of the "National Revolution."

The most "prestigious," if one dares say so, was Victor Barthélémy. He was right-hand man to Jacques Doriot, the head of the French Popular Party (PPF). After having been an invaluable auxiliary of Moscow in the 1930's, "the ex-Bolshevik" allied himself with Berlin in the 1940's. And so the intimate companion of Doriot turns up a few years later under the protection of the transitory Poujadist deputy, a young extremist who made a lot of noise but had little to offer in the way of ideas and strategy.

Condemned at the end of the war for high treason and intelligence for the enemy *in camera* before a military tribunal, Barthélémy, executor of Doriot who died on a road in Germany, came out of it rather well: with just a few months of prison. But, like Albertini who developed a taste for power during the Occupation, he was unwilling to remain inactive. He longed for "real" responsibilities. The role of semi-official advisor to the Italian Giorgio Almirante, the leader of the Fascist MSI, was not enough for him. Thanks to Le Pen, he came out of obscurity, more or less. In May 1975, at the FN congress at Grand Motte, he became General Secretary. This nomination went pretty much unnoticed. Le Pen was hardly making waves, and then, who still remembered Victor Barthélémy? Roland Gaucher did; he'd traveled just about the same perilous route in 1945 via Italy and Switzerland. Thanks to his advice, he published *A Secret History of the CP*, in 1974, before joining the National Front in 1981.

Barthélémy would shape the new Right-wing party, which was still just a clique, according to methods that he learned under Stalin, then under Hitler. "At the Communist Internationale, at Doriot's PPF and at the National Front," notes Guy Konopnicki in his meticulous study on Le Pen's *Filières noires* (*Black Connections*),[14] "he applied the same technique. You need old men to ensure legitimacy. You need specific organizations to recruit, milieu by milieu, women, young people, ex-servicemen, businessmen, fundamentalists, Catholics, repatriates, the press. . ." In short, the old collaborationist taught his young pupil the art of assembling networks to reach power.

This old guard had at least three merits: it was discreet, it was experienced, and it was grateful. In exchange for Le Pen's protection, it offered an unfailing loyalty to him. Thus a few German soldiers were found, as if by miracle, in the vicinity of this powerful figure who did not mind singing German military songs. He knew them by heart. He would — after all, for a long time he had been publishing them in association with former a Waffen SS, Leon Gaultier, at the Société de l'Édition et de relations publiques (SERP). Other nostalgics who found refuge in the obliging bosom of the FN include Pierre Bousquet, from the Charlemagne division of the Waffen SS, a one-time treasurer of this party on the "extreme Right." Then there was Paul Malagutti, member of the PPF at the age of 17, who was accused after the war of having stood guard during a massacre of eight resisters near Cannes. Condemned to death, *in absentia*, he was exonerated in 1953. This very old acquaintance of Le Pen had participated in the birth of the National Front and was a regional advisor since 1986.

Until his death in October 1996, Malagutti was constantly militating for the FN — just like the old Waffenstüber, André Dufraisse, a real estate agent who died in 1994 but whose political heritage is maintained by his widow, Martine Lehideux. Even after Dufraisse disappeared, an annual banquet still brings together survivors of the 638th Wehrmacht regiment in a restaurant at Rueil-Malmaison.

Meanwhile, the Le Pen family was extended, but the past still binds some members secretly. Some "children of the purges" are active "for memory's sake." Such is the case of the journalist Jean-François Chiappe, son of the prefect Angelo Chiappe, one of the rare high-ranking civil servants who was shot during the Liberation by the Resistance workers. Similarly, Alain Jamet, one of the sons of Claude Jamet, a pacifist journalist condemned after the Liberation for having criticized the British and American military actions during the war; he became an FN regional adviser for Languedoc-Roussillon. Simon Sabiani, a Marseillais big shot of the PPF who was condemned to death *in absentia* and remained exiled in Spain until he died; his daughter Agathe took up the family torch. This former social adjunct was number three on the FN short list put together by Bruno Mégret in February 1997 for the mayoral election in Vitrolles. A pillar of "French Fraternity," the charitable affiliate of Le Pen, she was active in the Rhone delta in the name of "Popular Frontism." Also implicated was François-Xavier Sidos, nephew of the militiaman Pierre Sidos (the founder of Young Nation) and grandson of François (who was shot after the Liberation); he is both a city councilman for Epinay-sur-Seine and member of the movement's network "Armées."

Le Pen doesn't like it much when anyone brings up the dubious past of his friends or their parents. He blew up when François Léotard recalled, at a conference organized on "nationalist populism" on June 16, 1996 at Châteauvallon, that some of the FN bigwigs were former volunteers in the German army. Aggressively evoking "that sort of civil war that the Second World War had been for some Frenchmen," he defended his group while asserting that "the FN accepts in its ranks Frenchmen from wherever they come, provided that they love France." It only remains to be seen what kind of France. . .

Chapter 9

Militants

The old vs. the modern: a cleavage as old as Christendom. But in modern France it takes on very particular contours. From 1905, the date of the separation of the Church and the State, until the historical private school battles in 1984, the Catholics never presented a united front to the passing whims of the century. The Church always rocked between the temptation to live in the current era and the will to remain faithful to a certain tradition. It's a question of time and of . . . the Pope. However, the reign of Jean-Paul II put the fundamentalists and their networks in the saddle.

The fundamentalists? They come from afar. In 1909, Mgr Umberto Benigni, under-secretary of the Congregation of Extraordinary Ecclesiastical Matters, created in Italy quite a curious institution, intended to remain in the half-light of the Vatican antechambers. He called it the *Sodalitium pianum* (or St. Pius League of Black and White), code name: the Fir Plantation. In spirit, it was an "anti-modernistic international secret network." The first fundamentalist conspiracy was born. Its goal was to fight, by every means — denunciation, calumny, putting together false files, intimidation — in short, nothing but the most charitable actions, against the "moderns" within the Church.

In France, this was the "Belle époque," but not for everyone. In 1905, during the third year of the Combes ministry, the Parliament approved the "law of separation of the Church and the State," presented to the Chamber by the Socialist Aristide Briand. This text put an end to all the secular privileges that Catholicism had enjoyed in France. It also balanced out a long estrangement between the republican government and the Vatican. The president of the Council, Emile Combes, a former sub-deacon who set out to destroy that which he had once adored, applied the new law with rigor. He even had just prohibited any activity of teaching to the members of the congregations, and he entered into open conflict with Rome about the appointment of bishops. However, Pius X had just succeeded the very conciliatory Leon XIII. This meant the rupture of diplomatic relations. France, a lay State, was an exceptional situation in the heart of Europe.

Those who love tradition could not get over it. The horizon seemed to be blocked by the long-lasting establishment of a parliamentary regime charged with a delirious degree of laicity.

It was too much for Mgr Benigni (future supporter of Mussolini's Fascism) and his friends, that even inside of the Church modernistic currents were thriving, people who were not even shocked by the law of 1905; in their eyes, this required an energetic and severe response. Thus arose the famous Sapinière, made up of ecclesiastics who were established in every country of Europe. An internal police force of the Church, it received the discreet support of a very rigid Pius X, signatory of an encyclical opposed to modernism. *Sodalitium Pianum* resorted to methods inspired by the Inquisition, "to cleanse" the Church but also, in France, to destabilize the parliamentary democracy.

As in any self-respecting secret society, the initiates of the Fir Plantation (who called each other "cousins") adopted a language with code words. It wasn't really a whole ciphered system such as the foreign ministries use, but rather a curious vocabulary (417 words) that they would substitute for ordinary words. These James Bonds of the holy font thus wrote in the language they called "roich" — the word "roich" is composed of the French initials of Pius X's motto, "Restaure Omnia in Christo," (To restore all things in Christ"). In "roich," bishops were called "aunts," priests were "nephews," were "sisters-in-law," the Jews were "pork butchers," the ambassadors were "dentists," the propagandists were "electricians," the modernizers were the "patients," Christian-Democrats were "oranges," republicans were "hardware merchants," and the Freemasons were "greenery." Pope Pius X was also addressed by a frankly surrealistic nickname: Baroness Micheline!

The plotters of the Fir Plantation found their best support among certain members of French Action who were, however, repudiated by Rome following several writings by Maurras, following the example of *Chemin de paradis* (*The Way of Paradise*), which was blacklisted in 1914. But French Action emphasized order and authority, two values dear to the Benigni clan. Certain priests even become militants in the Maurrassian movement. One such was the reverend father Floch, director of the French Seminary in Rome, who was relieved of his functions in 1927 because of his activism. Meanwhile, this friend of the Fir Plantation counted among his young seminarians a certain Marcel Lefebvre, who a few decades later would cause a schism within the Church.

Was the Fir Plantation an effective conspiracy or, more simply, a handful of old greybeard reactionaries, who enjoyed secret codes and file cards? The sociologist Emile Poulat, a prominent specialist on "fundamental Catholicism," studied this ecclesiastical network at length.[1] He says, "They kept track of everything that was produced by the modernistic Catholics, made a big deal about it and dispatched the products of their investigations to Rome. But they did not display a great virtuosity in this work."

In any case, the activities coordinated by Mgr Benigni stopped abruptly on December 8, 1921. Very much against his hopes, the prelate was constrained by the hierarchy to dissolve his micro-network, tiny in numerical strength but sufficient to inspire, after the war, a fundamentalist revival. The Fir Plantation had plenty to smile about. Spies in mitres? This marked the beginning of a war of networks with fluctuating allegiances.

The progressivists went along their way. Curiously, it was the war of 1914 that instilled the first modernistic inclinations among the young priests. "The very laic Third Republic," explains Jacques Duquesne, a journalist specializing in religious questions, "had decreed that in the name of equal treatment, the priests should perform their military service like everyone else. Upon their mobilization they discovered, rucksacks on their backs, the misery of the popular classes."

Catholic Action, created at the end of the 19th century, was the fulcrum of this movement. And it recruited very successfully, thanks to this trend. Christian Working Youth (JOC), one of its affiliates founded in 1927, attracted many activists and acquired notoriety and influence in a sphere where, so recently, extremely condescending patronesses had held the monopoly over the soul and the revealed truth.

Quite a new phenomenon: Catholics openly asserting themselves as members of the working class!

In the intellectual sphere, 1932 marked the creation of the *Esprit* (*Spirit*) review by Emmanuel Mounier. The philosopher who developed ideas that were "disturbing" for the adherents of the "Church of the Order" so dear to the very reactionary Charles Maurras, proposed a synthesis between Christianity and Socialism. Mounier sought to convince people that it was not only possible but desirable that Catholics should involve themselves in society. How to make the plotters of the defunct Fir Plantation grit their teeth!

Five years later, the creation of the SGEN (General Trade Union of National Education) went almost unnoticed. However, that organization brought together teachers and professors who were certainly Christian, but who were eager to promote a social culture "where the emphasis would be on lay disciplines and studies, abstracted from any denominational reference." One may as well declare a revolution! Its promoter, Paul Vignaux, was an enlightened practitioner of what the "Leftist Cathos" would carry out even more remarkably. A former pupil of the École normale supérieure on rue d'Ulm, a historian specializing in medieval philosophy, he was a pure product of Catholic Action. His creed: "Republican Catholicism." His destiny: to head up, after the war, the deconfessionalization of the CFTC to which his union had been affiliated since 1919.

The Left, For Christ

The post-war period marked the apogee of those who made up "the Left for Christ." The clerical hierarchy did not conduct itself, to put it mildly, with a noteworthy degree of heroism during the German Occupation. If examples are set at the top, the one set by Rome did not really contribute to awakening anyone's conscience. Quite a few "traditionalists" were in the lead roles in pontificating Vichyism. A refugee in the United States after having called the Gestapo's attention to himself at the beginning of the Occupation, Paul Vignaux wrote in 1943, "In Vichy France, the Catholic world was divided and at a loss: many traditionalists (who called themselves nationalists) turned out to be filled with resentment — resentment against the Third Republic, the democratic and workers' tradition, the French revolution. Brooding over the defeat that was, they thought, a good lesson for these people that fundamentally they did not much like, many of these hard core defenders of Catholicism failed to see the danger of Hitler." At the opposite pole, the JOC organized resistance networks against the occupying forces, and was actively working to get young people out of the STO (*service du travail obligatoire*, the mandatory labor requisitioned during the war). Upon the Liberation, they were crowned with victory, while certain "traditionalists" had to drop out of sight. The relation of forces shifted irremediably. The "Cathos of the Left" gained the upper hand; and they would keep it for three decades.

During the war, another denominational movement took its first clandestine steps. In 1942, some old scouts created "Vie Nouvelle" (New Life). They sought to change society through the virtues of education and a certain Christian humanism. Organized in "district fraternities," as networks that were not acknowledged as such, the activists would discuss subversive subjects like colonialism, the right to criticize, the couple, and sexuality. They wanted to consider social evolution independently of the Church doctrines. The underlying idea at New Life was, in truth, very modern: that Christians might, aside from their faith, relate to the facts of society — starting with those of their own daily life — via judgments that are not automatically dictated by the doctrines of the Church.

The great innovation that cemented the Catholic networks in this promising post-war period was activism. The JOC had popularized it in the 1930's, and some priests began to repeat it from the pulpit: a good Catholic must engage. Certainly — but where? "Initially, within the Catholic organizations," Jacques Duquesne comments. "That is what explains the rise of Christian trade unionism. The important thing was that a catalyst was given. In France, at the beginning of the century, the ACJF tried out the slogan: 'Social, because Catholic.' Shortly after the war, it supplemented with a new formula: 'Civic, because Social.' They chose 'civic' because the political word alarmed people, but showed that its members had reached the limits of a simple social action and had to engage in political action."

Engagement, consequently, started cropping up everywhere. Ella Sauvageot, wife of the director of *Le Monde* and head of Catholic Life, brought together in her salon Dominicans, Jesuits, Christian militants progressivists as well as intellectuals and journalists, around a "personality." Another woman, somewhat older, Germaine Malaterre-

Saddler, deputy of France for the family businesses with the SDN before the war, and an ardent adherent of the Catholic Left, would host her Christian-Democrat friends in her apartment on avenue Kléber. Under the Popular Front, she served as an intermediary between Leon Blum and Pius XI: she had, indeed, undertaken to reconcile the Church with the first socialist government. A "go-between" for the bishops of the resistance during the black years, after the war she reactivated her "Roman" network.

The younger people, activists in various youth movements, workers as well as students, also set out to influence French society. Edmond Michelet and André Colin, whose daughter Anne-Marie Idrac would become Secretary of State for Transportation in May 1995, were part of this wave. In the same way, the JOC member Paul Vignaux succeeded the JOC Eugène Descamps as leader of the CFTC. Christian Working Youth was the training ground for another emblematic figure of this committed Catholicism: Georges Montaron, future head of *Témoignage chrétien* (*Christian Testimony*), and "godfather" of some big names in the press and audiovisual industries like Hervé Bourges and Jean Boissonnat. This last is a pure "product" of Coed Christian Youth (JEC) from the 1950's. He assumed national responsibilities, and had the occasion to hook up with the future political scientist René Rémond and a few Leftist politicians-to-be: André Labarrère, Henri Nallet, Jean-Pierre Sueur, etc.

Christian Agricultural Youth (JAC), also provided its batch of future leaders who would be shoulder-to-shoulder throughout their careers. The young Michel Debatisse devoted all his activist energies to JAC before he founded the CNJA (National Center of Young Farmers) that would propel him to the head of a ministry in the government under Raymond Barre. At the JAC, he met another pillar of the "peasant" network, Lucien Douroux, the future president of Crédit Agricole. They became friends and brother-in-laws, since he married his sister.

At the center of this myriad of associations an interesting institution thrived: the "Social Weeks." Created at the end of the 19th century in the wake of the encyclical *Rerum novarum* (1891), every year after the war this traveling university would join together nearly 3,000 people around topical subjects. In the 1990's, René Rémond sat on their management committee under the presidency of Jean Boissonnat. And together with Jacques Delors, formerly of New Life, the same ones also were the driving forces for the November 1996 Social Weeks on the topic: "Between Modernization and Nations, What Kind of Europe?"

But all these coteries, if we can call them that, were deeply worried in the 1950's by another pertinent topic, decolonization. In 1948, a "Social Week" bluntly underlined the point that "all training normally completes itself in emancipation and must lead toward that." With the intensification of the war in Indochina, and the Algerian conflict that was heating up, the message was clear. These battlefields would consecrate the divorce between the Christian-Democrats of the MRP (Mouvement républicain populaire, a right-of-center party) and the Cathos of the Left. While the latter, revolted by torture, set themselves "in the direction of progress," not all joined the FLN support networks. A core of priests and lay workers did, however, shelter Algerian nationalists, and served as liaison officers or helped print leaflets.

Once the colonial wars were over, the attention of the "Cathos of Left" turned again toward domestic politics. The first election of the President of the Republic by universal vote, planned for 1965, was announced. The great question: how to put an end to the electoral tête-à-tête between de Gaulle and the Communists?

The operations began in 1963. The young agricultural unionists of the CNJA, under the wing of Michel Debatisse, talked for a long time with the workers of the JOC and the militants of the CFTC. Of these debates was born the GROP (Workers' and Peasants' Research Group) which would maintain, from the beginning, close ties with the club Jean-Moulin.

Initially, this gathering of high-ranking civil servants had no religious overtones. In May 1958, Jean Moulin's former secretary Daniel Cordier thought to create it in the company of some friends, from the Resistance, like him — the diplomat Stéphane Hessel, and the fellow traveler of the Communist Party Marcel Degliame-Fouché. These paradigms of clandestinity, ulcerated by the de Gaullian authoritarianism, were looking to serve again. But their savoir-faire was not sufficient for the second round.

Contrary to all expectation, de Gaulle did not take power after a putsch. He was designated in all legality by the Chamber, with the blessing of the political parties. What to do? — Fight against the increasing personal power, for democracy and the respect of personal freedoms. But this network hardly impressed the General. "We have young functionaries," he grumbled, "who in the evening will criticize to their buddies in the opposition the very ministerial acts to which they have, in the course of the day, devoted their intelligence."

In 1959, the network came out of anonymity under Georges Suffert, former editor of *Christian Testimony*. Promoted to General Secretary, he opened the doors of the Club to the CFTC and the GROP. Marcel Gonin, head of education and research at the CFTC and Lucien Douroux, who had gone from JAC to CNJA, came to the meetings. This small band gravitated toward the economic journalists Jean Boissonnat and Gilbert Mathieu, and the sociologist Michel Crozier. The finance inspector François Bloch-Lainé, then president of the Caisse des dépôts (public works fund), a leader in the Jean-Moulin club, contributed to the political efforts of the GROP in the company of two academics who also wore several associative caps: the lawyers Maurice Duverger and Georges Lavau.

All these networks more or less actively cooperated in the operation "M. X.," that aimed at putting Gaston Defferre in the saddle to face General de Gaulle. On December 16, 1963, a "Proclamation on the Presidential Election" took up a full page of *Le Monde* signed by the GROP, the Jean Moulin Club, Citoyens 60, the 2,000 Lyonais members of the Tocqueville Club, and the Marseillais members of New Democracy. In addition to pleading for a single candidate on the Left, all called for a restoration of the political debate.

On June 6 and 7, 1964, Vichy hosted "Bases of Democracy," an event organized largely by the signatories of the "presidential" proclamation; this meeting illustrates the flourishing health of clubs. But the "M. X." idea did not carry the day. They wanted Gaston Defferre, a makeshift in an SFIO that was at the end of its rope, but it was François Mitterrand, supported by Christian Testimony.

But the Cathos of the Left still had ideas. In the autumn of 1965 about fifteen of them, including Jean Boissonnat, Michel Debatisse, Eugène Descamps, Jean-Marie Domenach, Henri Nallet, René Rémond, and Jacques Duquesne, organized a weekend at Dourdan, in the Essonne. They invited a hundred of their counterparts to speculate about the way to "support the dialogue between the world and the people of God."

This was a vast question on a topic that was quintessentially post-conciliar, in that Vatican II had defined the precisely Church as "the people of God." Quite a symbol, the consequences of which gave despair to the "archéos" and was honey to the "moderns."

But the "moderns" would pay dearly for the Church's exaggerated will to prevail beyond its walls and to militate at all costs in political parties and trade unions. "After Vatican II, it was only a question of engaging in every sphere of society. The "Church boutique" was deserted by the progressivists on order of the clerks," explains Christian Terras, editor of the iconoclastic Christian magazine *Golias*. "Then, in 1978, it was all the easier for the new Pope, Jean-Paul II, to further bar the door preserving those conservative bases, since he encountered practically no resistance within the institution." Jean-Paul II indeed came to power with the support of some savagely conservative networks, among them Opus Dei, some of whose active members were his close collaborators.

The Cardinal's Shock Troops

How far away it seems, the time of dialogue, the "people of God" and the weekends at Dourdan! Aligned on the positions of Jean-Paul II — he saw his spiritual advance as a reflection of his own — the cardinal of Paris, Jean-Marie Lustiger, one of the most influential personalities of the Church of France, had only to dialogue, to ask questions about the way of living with faith in modernity. He believed and he advanced. It is as simple as that.

Those who knew him as a student, a member of the UNEF union, claiming a status of "young intellectual worker" in 1946, those who thought that his old friendship with Jean Gélamur (the former president of the group Bayard Presse, whom he met in 1969 at the parish of Sainte-Jeanne de Chantal) and who thought he would establish good relations with the Catho-Social networks, were promptly disabused. The cardinal-archbishop scorned Catholic Action. At least, that is the impression he left on all those who had the occasion to address that question with him. Jean-Paul II went to Saint-Siège in 1978, Jean-Marie Lustiger to Paris in 1981, and the tandem worked together wonderfully. Endowed, according to public opinion, with a difficult nature, the cardinal lacked a consensual spirit. That was a defect that kept him from (among other things) ever being elected to the head of the Episcopal Conference by his fellow-member bishops. But this nasty temper did not isolate him. Set on crossing swords with these progressive "tramps," he was able to sew up a system devoted to him, to feed the chains of complicities, and to find solid bases of support outside the

Church that enabled him to shore up his position.

He surrounded himself, as so many others have done, with old friends. He had fans at the Richelieu Center, where he was chaplain to the Parisian students, among the vicars of Sainte-Jeanne de Chantal where he was curate for in the days of Cardinal Marty. As for the youngest recruits, they swore him allegiance without reservation. "Some were very proud of it," notes Christian Terras. "'We are the Cardinal's shock troops,' they would say proudly. All those who inherited positions of trust passed through these channels."

For example, Mgr André Vingt-Trois, his faithful right arm. Gifted enough, they say, to achieve unanimity against him, this former vicar of Sainte-Jeanne de Chantal became a virtuoso of office plurality. Named auxiliary bishop (not without effort), he was responsible for the strategic sectors of development and information in the bishopric.

Did Cardinal Lustiger consider the Issy-les-Moulineaux seminary to be unsatisfactory? No problem — he created another in Paris, directed by Mgr. Vingt-Trois. And with considerable results, moreover, since half of the French priests are ordained in the capital. Did the same cardinal consider that the lay people were short of places to reflect on their faith? He founded "The Cathedral School," which offered courses on the Scriptures, the Fathers of the Church, religious literature, and had *Cahiers* (Books) published by the bishopric to treat with the Christian mystery. The jewel of this institution, called the "Leadership School," welcomed the élite among the parishioners. Regarded as a kind of Catholic ENA, it gave in two years a thorough training on the study of the scriptures.

There still, Mgr Vingt-Trois held the reins. Just as he jealously watched over the two diocesan media channels: Radio Notre-Dame and the weekly magazine *Paris Notre-Dame*, which seldom opened its columns to forums for debate. Radio Notre-Dame constituted a radio network with several dozen decentralized stations in "friendly" dioceses that could select at will from its programs. These were programs that did not give much voice to any opposing viewpoints, contrary to the Lyons Radio Fourvière, a pluralist and ecumenical radio station supervised by his rival Mgr Decourtray. The two men hardly got along with each other, and it was quite an effort, they say, for Mgr Lustiger to accompany him on a return visit to Mitterrand before the great 1984 demonstration at Versailles in favor of private teaching.

Radio Notre-Dame was on this occasion an effective link in the religious schooling network. Lustiger was instinctively wary of the newspapers classified as "Catholic," like *La Croix* (*the Cross*) and *Life*, which made a point of retaining their independence and their critical direction. Suddenly, the cardinal decided to maintain his own network of "lay" journalists like Georges Suffert at *Le Figaro*, Jean Daniel of *Le Nouvel observateur*, Henri Tincq of *Le Monde*, and Jean-Pierre Elkabbach.

Failing to achieve unanimity with his fellows in the other bishoprics, the Cardinal-Archbishop of Paris wove multiple alliances with the politico-economic and intellectual world — thanks to a talented recruiter: the chaplain of the École normale supérieure, Jean-Robert Armogathe. It was he who brought in, in particular, Jean Duchesne, formerly from the ENS and a distinguished teacher of English. He promoted him to both personal advisor and "ghost-writer" of the Cardinal. The scholar thus wrote the speech establishing Cardinal Lustiger in the French Academy. But he also looked after the preparation of foreign press releases, negotiated the publication of his writings with book publishers and organized luncheons with selected intellectuals.

That Club was based around the *Communio* review, the French version of which was chaired by Jean Duchesne and inspired by the philosopher Jean-Luc Marion. Founded in 1972 by theologians and prelates from the Vatican (including the very rigorous Cardinal Ratzinger), *Communio* conveys to the élites the thought of Jean-Paul II, who is himself an assiduous reader of the review. Very critical on the philosophers of the Enlightenment, it offers its columns to a small network of ENS alumni, which serves as the cardinal's laboratory of ideas.

The political and economic networks of the archbishop's palace were tightly structured. Still, some high-ranking civil servants were part of it, including Michel de Virville. This former assistant to Jean-Pierre Soisson, at the Labor Ministry, became known to the general public as General Secretary of Renault. It was he who oversaw the closing of the Belgian factory of Vilvorde and its calamitous media coverage. The Cardinal charged his wife Martine with all the catechesis — a task traditionally reserved for a monk, but Mrs. de Virville was a trusted friend. The former director of the ENA René Lenoir, finance inspectors François Bloch-Lainé and Philippe Rouvillois, Jacques Chirac's promotion chief at the ENA, the Giscardian former Culture Minister Jean-Philippe Lecat, RPR president of Ile-de-France area Michel Giraud, a great dispenser of subsidies, and the pro-Fabius Philippe Essig, former director of the SNCF — they made up a sufficiently eclectic politico-administrative tableau to be useful at any time.

Consider Roger Fauroux, former Minister of Industry in the Michel Rocard government, ex-director of the ENA. A one-time financial adviser to the Cardinal, he opened to him the doors of the Catholic business world whose leading lights are men like Michel Albert, Jacques Calvet, Olivier Lecerf, and Jean-Noël Bongrain. These business friends were also part of the board of directors of the association "Art, Culture and Faith," created in 1989, to subsidize exhibitions and artists who reconcile aesthetics with a celebration of faith.

Relying on lay support among dogmatically reliable people equipped with excellent social positions — that is one of the secret bases of the Lustiger edifice. Conscious of the risk that there might be some questionable aspects to these institutions, he nevertheless was also interested in other, more "basic" social groups. These included the charismatics, the "Fools of the Holy Spirit" inspired by American Pentacostalism, who were fond of miraculous healings and other wonders. He did not necessarily share their ideas, but these communities can sometimes provide good fishing grounds for future priests. Suspected of cult tendencies, the charismatic sects appreciated being legitimated. . . And this cardinalesque emolument offered another advantage: the possibility of alleviating an insatiable thirst for prayers in friendly parishes. That was the case in particular with the Church of the Trinity where one of their own was named by the agreeable archbishop.

Similarly, the community of Emmanuel, one of the most important charismatic gatherings, includes several faithful members among the journalists of Radio Notre-Dame. Many of these were former students or teachers from the Catholic School journalism in Brussels, "European Media Studies" (EMS). That is a denominational school liberally subsidized by Piet Dierksen, the Dutch owner of the amusement park "Center Parcs," who is himself a faithful fan.

The charismatic tribe wove ties with the group Médias Participation, a Belgian holding company that re-issued the old Ampère editions of Rémy Montagne, a fundamentalist editor who passed away at the end of the 1980's. The Cardinal looks on this citadel (enriched since 1986 by Dargaud, Fleurus, Mame, etc), with all the more benevolence since it counterbalances the influence of groups like Bayard and Malesherbes Publications. Their publications are, indeed, hardly in tune with the sanctity of the archbishop's palace.

Some members of the network "Communio" contribute to Médias Participations, which also publishes the newspaper *Famille Chrétien*. With an edition of nearly 100,000 copies, this weekly magazine discusses the topics of "the reconquest," with articles presented camera-ready by the Vatican. One of the leaders of Media Participation, Jacques Jonet, belongs to the Chevaliers du Rouvre, a Belgian "order" comparable to the very fundamentalist Chevaliers of Notre-Dame. One of the former directors of *Famille Chrétien*, André Josan, was also one of these French knights who used to participate in some of the episcopal events.

Onto this Lustiger nebula is grafted a galaxy of approximately 600 young people, priests and priest candidate, all members of the Congregation of the Brothers of Saint-Jean. Baptized the "little gray guys" by their detractors, these "soldiers of the Church" of unyielding faith live under the supervision of a former Dominican brother, Marie-Dominique Philippe. Once an adviser to the Pope, he is allied to the Bonduelle family, which is one of most flourishing in the agro-food industry and which liberally subsidizes these good works.

Having parachuted into the dioceses where the ultra-conservative bishops prevail (ten in all, including Ars, Gap and Le Puy), they are dreaded by the Catholics progressives who see in them the base of logistical supports for the anti-abortion networks, among others.

"Christo-Marxist" Methods

"Our approach is a little bit Leftist. It resembles the Trotskyite methods. And it's even rather Christo-Marxist. We have three objectives: conscientization, dynamization, mobilization. Conscientization refers to one central idea: the embryo is a human being and not a substance. We incite our sympathizers to act on this idea. That is the phase of dynamization. They in turn are charged with mobilizing (through intermediaries) the opinion of the members of Parliament and other influential groups." These remarks made in *L'Express*[2] by sociologist Dominique Ansery, a theorist of the anti-birth control fight, have a familiar ring. Didn't the Cagoulards of the 1930's dream of founding a "moral society," distant from the "Bolsheviks" but inspired nevertheless by their methods?

The public is used to seeing the far Left putting on "agitprop" shows, whether in support of immigrants without papers or the homeless. Surprise rallies at a subway station or sit-ins at a church for the former, closing down a building for the latter — calls to the media, calls to the politicians, the Leftists are on the move.

By astonishing imitation, fundamentalists of all types, Moslems as well as Christians, have internalized this method. In the same way that the Islamists knowingly decide to hold an "Operation 'Headscarf'" at such and such college, the "pro-life" contingent dreams up commando actions in the wards that practice new forms of birth control. These "resistance fighters," who do not hesitate to compare the legal practice of abortion to genocide against the Jews, act according to perfectly developed techniques. "The idea is simple," says Fiametta Venner, who has dissected their strategy,[3] "a group of people recruited by word of mouth finds itself in a church, and after listening to a mass for the memory of unborn children, moves on toward a hospital designated by Xavier Dor, the founder of 'S.O.S.', they kneel in the corridors and pray, singing canticles."

The capacity to mobilize these networks — more than a score of them — is astonishing. It is not that their troops are so infinite, since one often finds the same faces from one fundamentalist clique to another, but their determination, even their fanaticism, are impressive. When, in fall 1988, the Health Ministry accepted the broader use of RU 486, "the day-after pill" discovered by Professor Etienne-Emile Beaulieu and manufactured by the Roussel-Uclaf laboratories, the "Christo-Marxist" steamroller started its engine. Insulting letters and threats of boycott arrived *en masse* at the plant and headquarters of the company (whose chairman is a devout Catholic) to denounce this "abortion pill." The Association for Conscientious Objection to Any Participation In Abortion (APCOA), which had already encouraged its members to deduct from their taxes the sum corresponding to the research grants underwriting the pill, recommended this time to buy a share in Roussel-Uclaf so that they could attend the general meetings and denounce the industrialist's "humiliating activities."

Alarmed by the turn of events that started to take on its market, the chairman retreated one month later. Which brought the greatest satisfaction to Catholic family associations and the bishops who were meeting in plenary assembly in Lourdes. But, by the same token, the protests against "religious conservatism" had multiplied so much that the Minister of Health, Claude Evin, gave Roussel-Uclaf notice to start distributing its product. Message received.

But it took more than that to make these "moral crusaders" give up. So, TV Antenna 2 devoted a "Special" to criticizing the movement? Traditionalist family associations mobilized their forces to protest against its broadcast. It is true that "Families of France," whose national leaders of the sector "Life-Family-Education" were spear-pointing the anti-birth control combat, and the review *Christian Family*, were not shown to advantage. The show was indeed broadcast, but Families of France managed all the same to get itself designated as a "legal" organization.

These conservatives also know how to put modernity to the service of tradition. The president of the APCOA, Michel Raoult, still has a computer file listing all the elected officials' positions on birth control. For their part, the Coordination of the Rosaries for the Respect for Life, a prayer organization that goes into action prior to any "rescue operations" (the modest name for anti-abortion commandos), have also set up a server on which the four hundred organizers of rosaries can work. Lastly, two sympathetic media outlets, Radio-Courtesy and Radio Notre-Dame, relay the information transmitted by the "rescuers" on their various activities.

There are, indeed, myriad networks organized by professional corporations. Catholic doctors affiliated with these cliques, obedient to the Pope, obviously offer no help to women seeking abortion. They encourage childbirth for adoption via a specialized service. Similarly, many pharmacists refuse to sell condoms, and lawyers devise amendments to oppose the application of the Veil law (de-criminalizing abortion) and prepare the defense for anti-abortion commandos. But one of the most surprising links is that with certain "fundamentalist" insurance companies.

Actually, when you think about it, it's not that odd. When abortion is covered by insurance plans or State aid, that costs the companies dearly. What cleverer way to discourage candidates for interrupted pregnancy than to refuse this "wicked" coverage to them? Jacques Rousset, a former executive at a Lyons insurer that used to reimburse abortion expenses without any problems, thought he could convince most of his colleagues to delete this service. In fact, his "Association for the Protection of Life and Health," associated with the April group, was one of the rare insurance companies to notify its members that it would no longer pay for abortions. But he taught the others, as well: according to him, six other mutual insurance companies (one of which targets students in Paris) have now given in to the pressures of militants "for the respect for life."

The moral support lent by many ecclesiastics to these "rescue operations" is hardly astonishing. What is it more surprising is to find some of them actively participating in them. Don Gerard Calvet, prior of very the fundamentalist Sainte-Madeleine monastery of Barroux, in Vaucluse, is one of most combative. Chained together with seven lay persons, he led a prolonged sit-in in October 1994 in the abortion clinic in a hospital in Grenoble, until the gendarmes dislodged him by force. Publicly blessed by Cardinal Lustiger at the time of his lawsuit ("This is a morally well-founded protest of conscience") he pulled in other monks who would, in their turn, be arrested.

Torn between their natural fidelity to the Pope and their will to live in modern times, Catholics progressives are constantly losing ground. On contraception and abortion, the episcopate's hostility weighs heavily. This has become, for the most conservative, a guarantee of importance. Thus, the progressives are marginalized, whereas the fundamentalists are flourishing, supported not only by the Catholic hierarchy but also by solid "denominational" political relations.

The Son-in-Law and His Friends

The most admirable godmother of the "pro-life" movement, in public opinion, is the very Catholic deputy of Yvelines, Christine Boutin. Changing from the PR to the UDF, then to the Center of Social Democrats (which became "Democratic Force"), this barrister, a mother of five children, tows along a hard core of some twenty implacable supporters who all refused to vote for the "wicked" laws — the Veil law de-criminalizing abortion, of course, as well as its renewal, and then the coverage for abortion costs and, more recently, the law on bioethics. Even though this is only an informal and modest parliamentary group, it is feared for its activism. After all, its members belong to a string of associations, the purpose of all of them being, under different names, "to support life." One of them, which Boutin has labeled "The Cartel for Life," encompasses some dozen micro-associations, some of which flirt with the far Right, a favorite fish pond for anti-abortion activists. Wasn't Doctor Xavier Dor, who invented "rescue operations," active in the Party of New Forces before moving to the National Front? Didn't the tenors of the Catholic faction of the FN, like Bernard Antony, Marie-France Stirbois and Bruno Gollnish (who are constantly squabbling with the "pagans" of the movement), pride themselves on being members of the Honor Committee of "Let Them Live"? As for Thierry Bauzard, General Secretary of the "League for Life," he straight-forwardly domiciled his organization at the headquarters of the National Front, in Saint-Cloud. At least, there is nothing ambiguous there.

But the happiest victory of the followers of the "pro-life" movement was to find an ally in the government. Secretary of State for the Budget in the first Juppé government, then for Health in the second, Hervé Gaymard had the honor of being the real-life husband of a daughter of professor Jerome Lejeune. Deceased on Easter Day, 1994, Lejeune's funeral was celebrated with ostentation at Notre-Dame by Cardinal Lustiger (this professor of fundamental genetics at the Necker hospital had devoted all his life to the fight against abortion). Moreover, Jean-Paul II, who had named him a member of the Pontifical Academy of Sciences, largely relied on him to promote papal morals in France. The Institute of France, of which he was member, rejected him nonetheless when Professor Lejeune sought to involve it in this combat. Therefore, the Pope decided at the beginning of 1991 to create his own "Pontifical Academy of Social Sciences," with an auxiliary, the "Pontifical Academy for Life," of which Professor Lejeune was quite naturally the president. According to Catholics on the Left ("Marxists," their adversaries call them), this Academy is designed as a network of political oversight rather than as an erudite society. Its seventy members, dispersed throughout the world, are connected by a computer network that enables them to hold teleconferences and to intervene immediately in the local public life, upon instruction from the Holy See.[4] That Academy would take a prominent role in the drafting of the eleventh papal encyclical *Evangelium Vitae*, which largely deals with "respect for life."

Shortly after his death the professor's widow, Birthe Lejeune, her five children, her daughter-in-law and her two sons-in-law decided to create an association, "Friends of Professor Lejeune." The whole family, a network in and of itself, asserted its heritage. Mrs. Lejeune became an honorary member honor of the Pontifical Academy for Life; the eldest daughter, Anouk and her husband, the philosopher Jean-Marie Mayer, are members of the Pontifical Council for the Family; one of the sons, Damien, is a priest with Opus Dei, a movement that is well-established in the Pontifical Academy; another daughter, Karine, is an anti-abortion activist with her husband Jean-Marie Le Méné, public auditor at the Court of Auditors. As for their sister Clara's husband, Hervé Gaymard, elected deputy in 1993, if he knows what he is doing, his involvement is beyond doubt.

Some major figures joined forces with this family network to associate some prestigious sizes: President Jacques Chirac, whose wife Bernadette never made a secret of her hostility to the Veil law, the chairman of the pharmaceutical laboratories Pierre Fabre, professors Lucien Israel and Alain Carpentier, Christine Boutin and Philippe de Villiers, and of course, Jean-Marie Lustiger.

They all helped the Lejeune family with a delicate mission: to obtain recognition as a public service organization for the "Jerome Lejeune Foundation." Usually, the procedure requires several years and in most cases does not, in the end, lead to the desired status. A miracle: just one year was enough for the Lejeune family, initially to collect the million necessary for the initial endowment of any Foundation, then to be granted the prestigious (and profitable, since donors to a Foundation enjoy tax deductions) label. Registered on March 25, 1995, the request led to the publication of a decree on March 21, 1996 in the *Journal Officiel*.

Warped minds saw this unusual celerity as the result of friendly pressure from "Mr. Son-in-Law," the Secretary of State for Health. This was challenged at once by the family, always so loyal. The brother-in-law, Jean-Marie Le Méné, hastened to point out that Hervé Gaymard was not even a member of the famous Foundation. Clara Lejeune-Gaymard was indignant, for her part, that anyone could suspect for a single moment that this Foundation would finance the activities of anti-abortion commandos with money that had been collected for the fight against trisomy 21! The Lejeune Foundation, she insisted, had only a "scientific purpose" and no other objectives but "to support research on diseases affecting the intelligence."

Maybe it is giving too much honor to Hervé Gaymard to credit him with having such influence. After all, the friends of the famous professor also benefit from the best possible relation with the President of the Republic and his wife. On the other hand, it is perfectly clear that in the position that he occupies, the son-in-law of Jerome Lejeune is a sure ally for all those who are trying, by any means possible (including the most violent), to oppose the Veil law. Yesterday the deputy keen to demand that the Constitutional Council repeal the law on bioethics, he will surely not be the minister who grants abortion centers the best working conditions and pay levels suited to a correct application of the law.

Catholically Incorrect

Is anyone resisting the rise to power of these "archeos" within the Church? Not Catholic Action and its allies, which exist now only in a vegetative state. Voices of protest are nevertheless raised, whether media-friendly like Mgr Gaillot, or more reserved like Mgr Rouet in Poitiers. These two bishops, and some others, more anonymous, discreetly support the rebels who for ten years have been collecting around a Lyons review, *Golias*, which often takes a grumbling, even satirical, tone that would not disgrace the *Canard enchaîné*.

The magazine took the name of Golias quite simply in reference (and homage!) to a bishop of the Middle Ages, renowned for his rebellious spirit. The head and founder, Christian Terras, is a forty-something special educator in the Lyons suburbs. He comes from (no surprise here!) Coed Christian Youth! To put it mildly, this former chorus boy and his cohorts, tired like him of "the Catholically correct," irritate the highest authorities of the Church, especially Cardinal Lustiger, who hates Golias. "The archbishopric of Paris put pressure on the Catholic bookshops so that they would not represent us," says Christian Terras. "And since these bookshops' largest accounts are often the catechism teachers, they do not always have the means of resisting pressure from the Catholic hierarchy."

Golias, of course, does not give in to pressure. An iconoclast, in 1990 it published a "rogues' gallery" of the bishops, where each biographical note is preceded by one to five meters in imitation of the exhortation to faith and fidelity in the penitentials. Suffice it to say that this "consumer's guide" is not prominently displayed in the sacristies! In 1991, *Golias* followed up with an "anniversary" issue devoted to the ten years of Jean-Marie Lustiger at the bishopric of Paris. Still more insolent, this "special edition" classified the capital's priests according to the flexibility of their episcopal spine. The same year, the magazine presented an exhaustive investigation into "God's Right-wing" and deciphered the connections between various fundamentalist movements. Next, they came out with an article entitled "Opium Dei," (a distortion of "Opus Dei"), a lampoon of the order, discussing and spelling out its ramifications in the French establishment. In 1995, *Golias* created a real scandal by attacking, by name, the Rwandan priests who facilitated the genocide (including Father Wenceslas, who had taken refuge in France). It also showed that the European clergy had obligingly granted them asylum.

All these investigations could not be carried out without a network of accessories at the very heart of the institution. That was a sign that rebellion was mounting. Already, on September 22, 1996, the day of Jean-Paul II's celebration of the 1500th anniversary of the baptism of Clovis, in Rheims, a handful of young Catholics, about thirty fighters, publicly demonstrated against the excessive media coverage of the papal voyage. Their banners? Two statements still quite timid. The first, for Christian Testimony, proclaimed "We Too Are the Church," the second, Jesuit in inspiration, took a name that was more telegenic: "Rights and Freedom in the Churches!"

That day, they were mixed together with a procession organized by lay people and even (a real scandal in the eyes of the Church hierarchy), with Freemasons! They all joined together under the same heading, "Clovis is not France." This was not the first time that Catholics had gotten together with the laymen. Any time they wanted to take on the extreme Right or defend personal freedom in the field of conduct, the friends of *Golias* were ready to make a pact with the "devil," be they Trotskyites, intractable militant pro-birth-control activists from Family Planning or the lay members of the "Voltaire Network," which were particularly active against all the "counter-revolutionary" lobbies eager to restore a new moral order.

It would be difficult to find any better proselyte than the initiator of that network. Thierry Meyssan had the faith of converted and the expertise of those who know their adversaries from the inside. Educated by the Jesuits — like Voltaire! — this faithful reader of *Osservatore Romano*, the official journal of the Vatican, indeed had quite a number of confrontations with the traditional Catholics. Breaking off with a family from the good bourgeoisie of Bordeaux, who repudiated him due to homosexuality, he wound up in a religious court that annulled his marriage. Destroyer of "Holy-Mafia," that is, Opus Dei, lobbyist in the anti-abortion battle, Freemason at his most desperate moments, he smelled strongly of fire and brimstone.

Occasional ally of the progressive Catholics, he became the *bête noire* of the most conservative. He offended them most at the time of the vote in Parliament on an article in the new Penal Code criminalizing the "manufacture, transport, and the distribution . . . of any message of violent or pornographic character or likely to seriously denigrate human dignity." Attacked by pro-family associations who were fighting against "loose morals," Meyssan and his friends fought back by declaring (in good faith?) that freedom of expression was threatened. Really.

Was it a failure? Not completely. For the network extended, with the support of personalities as varied as Senator Henri Caillavet, the screenwriter Jean-Claude Carrière, sociologist Pierre Bourdieu, and former Minister Jack Lang. Of course, there was a small militant and anonymous core that furtively hunted down the intrigues of the "fundamentalists." They always used the same technique, "to mobilize different people so that, in the aggregate, they all say pretty much one thing." That was how it happened in the "Garaudy-Abbé Pierre" case. Public figures on all sides noisily expressed their horror. They were alerted by the Voltaire network, that discreetly broadcast (before it is was made public) the astonishing letter of support addressed by the former abbot to the anti-Semite philosopher. In this battle, the friends of *Golias* were not the least virulent; they published a major investigation into this affair.

In the fight against fundamentalism, it was fated that part of this movement would find itself united on another front — that of the "head scarf." Only one part only, for many Catholics, even the progressives, are very reserved on this subject. It is indeed a question that touches on the freedom to express one's beliefs. However, where does this freedom stop, and where do proselytism and provocation start?

The lay people themselves could not avoid the debate. A whole "communitarian" network developed, preferring the right to be different; they had the support of sociologists like Alain Touraine and political scientists like Olivier Duhamel. To counter them, a certain resistance was organized around the pure and hardfast lay approach, conscious that the Moslem fundamentalists were refining their own networks to better protect those who were wearing the scarves. The association "Initiative Republicaine" was thus created on December 7, 1992 — the year of the bicentenary of the Republic — by a Freemason, Bernard Teper, then spokesman of the Grand Orient. But this activity did not involve the Obedience, which was rather reticent to participate in any ostentatiously pro-layman action. "Anybody who contacted us," he says, "we asked them to give us between ten and thirty names. That is how one creates a network."

Guards of secularity to the point of caricature, some of them got together in Paris on April 8, 1995 to celebrate the "So-Called Holy Friday" for an anticlerical banquet with, at the center, a bloody piece of beef! Still, one year later in their anti-papal demonstration they welcomed the support of Catholics who were turned off by a Vaticanesque hierarchy that they judged to be reactionary.

This curious alliance of the compass and the baptismal font is justified, in their eyes, by the threat from fundamentalists of all types, who are better organized and more dangerous than the almost folkloric plots of the "anti-modernists" of the Fir Plantation.

Chapter 10

BECOMING PRESIDENT

Every Wednesday, they meet in the old dining room of an apartment in a Haussmann building at 266, Saint-Germain boulevard. This is a practice that they have kept up since the time when they had a chief, a program, quarrels — in short, everything that makes up the ordinary life of a member of the Socialist Party. They are still there, ten to thirty of them depending on the week, but their heart is not really in it any more. Since Michel Rocard, shortly after the May 1995 presidential election, announced that he intended to go his own way, the Rocardian network is not what it once was.

One year later, the receptionist at "266" still hasn't gotten used to the change. He still finds himself reaching for the telephone with a snappy: "Hello! Michel Rocard's office!" The network, since then, survives after a fashion. The friends of "Rocky," as his closest buddies call him, even invented an acronym for him, ARES, which resounds like the name of the son of Zeus and Hera, mythical god of wars and battles! ARES, as in "Action for the Revival of Socialism," whose central core was nevertheless extended to nearly two thousand sympathizers. "At the heart of the network, there are several kinds of orphans," comments one of them. "The emotional ones, who like to feel like they have found a family, followers of political cocooning; the careerists, in the search of a platform from which new leaders might emerge, in whose entourage they could position themselves; and all those who are having a bit of an identity crisis given that the Socialist party seems to be dying out." Is this a way of taking revenge for having been abandoned? Clearly, no one appeals to the "chief" in these weekly meetings. "On the contrary," laughs one of the participants. "It's considered good form to 'slay the father' and to recall in bitter, caustic tones what a longwinded exposé we have escaped, due to our mentor's absence!"

Ah, how good self-management sounded in yesterday's conversations! But how difficult it is to survive on one's own, when the man to whom one has given allegiance leaves without warning. Painful as it was for his followers, Rocard's move was logical, given that he was only a virtual candidate in the presidential election of 1995. What good is it to maintain networks, when the prospect of becoming President of the Republic has disappeared?

If it's a question of character and convictions, the man in any event never went for that system of emoluments and services rendered. However, that approach is pretty much a requisite for any candidate who decides to aspire to the supreme burden.

Some make it to the highest levels of politics, if not by accident, at least without having been methodically trained for it. Simone Veil, Raymond Barre, and even Edouard Balladur are of this species. Propelled by chance or need, they arrive with neither networks, team, nor close guard. It's a miracle of power: the "faithful" are often revealed as if by magic. Balladur had an amusing experience with it: he found himself, thanks to ministerial glory and miraculous surveys, at the head of influential coteries of businessmen, administrative officers and elected officials who were attracted by this rising star. But those complicities are fragile and they are not enough, as we have seen, to attract masses of votes from one's fellow-citizens.

A politician's first network is the party where he first tests his capacity as a born leader. Even the scantly careerist Georges Pompidou understood, in 1966, the need to make a UNR of his own, made up of a new generation of Gaullists, more modern than his companions from the RPF. Valéry Giscard d'Estaing himself, a young technocrat more at ease in the corridors of the ministries than on the militants' ramparts, sacrificed to the rules of political life by creating the Independent Republicans. Only it is not given to everyone to create a real party that is entirely devoted to you. "It is not enough for him (the President) to have talent, character, an honest Prime Minister, the devotion of the ministers and the more or less factitious vote of the deputies," notes Arthur Conte, "he needs thousands of faithful supporters to keep his flame burning in the depths of the country. However," he says, analyzing VGE's failure in May 1981, "the President did not have, or could not constitute, such phalanxes. He really only had a weak club. It is ridiculous."[1]

If psychology has any integral part to play in politics, it is in the art of building these famous "phalanxes." It requires a temperament both brutal and two-sided, impatient and cherishing, dominating and alluring. Two men, under the Fifth Republic, made a success of this type of rough dealing, each one taking over a party without a drop of blood. François Mitterrand, the first, took the leadership of the SP at Epinay in 1971. Three years later Jacques Chirac, Prime Minister to VGE, who was afraid of being destroyed by both the Elysée and the Gaullists, took over the UDR without any concern and in 1976 created the RPR, an apparatus militantly devoted to him. "Both set out to attack an old guard that still had some strength — whether we are talking about the barons of Gaullism (Chaban, Guichard, etc.) or the apparatchiks of Socialism (Mollet, Savary, etc.) — and the old guard was firmly committed to not to let itself be dislodged," compares Franz-Olivier Giesbert in his biography of Jacques Chirac. "They did not take them as traitors since they gave them notice, a little beforehand, of their intentions. Then, they won them over, one by one, like a bunch of grapes."[2] In fact, each one in his own way had already understood that "great careers are hammered out through small services."

Well before setting out to the attack a town hall, or a district or a party, it is necessary to ensure one's relationships, the most various and the most layered possible. To cultivate these requires many qualities. It demands that one be sufficiently charismatic to be able to attract talented people, the ability to cultivate an eclectic following of good quality, to make several clans work together without any becoming excessively jealous, and the ability to make use of all and sundry without them neutralizing each other.

As much as natural prestige is a gift — "a kind of sympathy inspired in others," "a fluid of authority such that one cannot distinguish just what it consists of," as de Gaulle wrote in *Le Fil de l'épée* (*The Path of the Sword*) — so the achievement and then the maintenance of these successive loyalties require "a true vocation," including vitality and patience, method and ambition, audacity and meticulousness.

After the war, the young Gaullist general Chaban-Delmas had these qualities. His eye on Bordeaux, where he did not know a soul, he conquered the city, charming a dowager of Chartrons here, winning over an old Pétainist there, persuading a radical socialist elsewhere, all influential in their respective milieux. As reinforcement, he could count on his buddies from the Resistance, his "founding" network. The latter supported him in 1946 to eliminate his principal competitor, Mr. Odun, a radical lawyer.

Helped by a commando of old mates from the Normandy-Niemen fleet on the evening when the candidates had to deposit their lists with the prefecture, Chaban did not hesitate to burst all the tires of the cars of his fellow candidates who were still reflecting in the Café de la Renaissance. "It's 11:00pm, Mr. Odun will have not time to register his candidature."[3]. . . Little by little, the one called "Charming-Delmas" or "Mister Trade Union" accumulated friendships. He multiplied the "stables" from which to draw workers who would slave away on his plans for a "New Society," and flattered the "external personalities" who would help him round up support outside the Paris seraglio.

On the other hand, he lacked an activist base to launch out in a national adventure: he was one "Companion" among others. He tried indeed in 1956 to create the "Republican-Socialists," a name supposed to attract the survivors of the RPF who were undone by the 4th Republic. But he failed when Mitterrand showed up, to reinvigorate René Pleven and the UDSR, a small fringe party, the ideal springboard for gaining the fidelity of the deputies with few votes. And then, no one is perfect: Chaban stumbled in February 1972 on a tax technicality, a legal loophole that enabled him to avoid the tax but which had a bad effect on public opinion. A disastrous televised campaign completely discredited him in the 1974 race for the Elysée. All the same, he succeeded in being elected a deputy from 1947 to 1986 and mayor of Bordeaux until 1995!

The Stalags as a Hunting Ground

The war, crucible of many political careers, also allowed François Mitterrand to launch out in the adventure of politicking. Without the networks from stalag 9A in Prussia and 9C in Thuringia, could he have taken off also quickly? He was already determined in 1943 to be the one and only official representative of the prisoners of war, and he began by whispering in the ear of Michel Caillau, de Gaulle's nephew, to give him the leadership of a movement that the Gaullists and Communists were disputing. He moved into the breach without any qualms, and just as easily turned his back on one of his friends who would have been just as legitimate a candidate as he, to fly away to London, then Algiers to meet the General. Already, he could count on a first circle of faithful supporters: during the first days of the liberation of Paris, his companions in captivity Patrice Pelat and Jean Munier, guns in hand, took over the places that Morland (Mitterand's name in the Resistance) wanted to occupy. Among them was the Parisian site of the old Vichyist commissariat for prisoners of war.

This spot was especially strategic since Mitterrand intended to make the two million prisoners his first base of "political goodwill." A very staunch trio supported him from the moment he was nominated to the Ministry for Ex-Serviceman in January 1947: his brother Robert (whom he named to be his chief assistant), aided by Georges Beauchamp, and another old friend from the stalags, Jean Védrine. The three men would support him unremittingly in his conquest of power; and he would reward their constancy well.

Right after the war, he remembered his friend Pol Pilven, who was arrested in his place by the Gestapo in Vichy and was deported. Upon his return, Mitterrand helped him get into L'Oréal as the head of a subsidiary. Pilven's nephew Pierre Bordry (the right-hand man of Alain Poher, the *éminence grise* of the centrist president of the Senate) would also, during a time of thorny political negotiations, have occasion to experience Mitterrand's ability to show his recognition.

This first network had a major impact on the future President. Once at the Elysée, his former companions in captivity were cherished: presidential decorations, travel, receptions. . . And their children were not forgotten. Védrine's son Hubert was named advisor for diplomatic affairs in 1981, before becoming the Elysée spokesman in 1988. He would run into Paulette Decraene there (the daughter of Léopold Moreau, another comrade from the stalag, recruited as personal secretary already before, and promoted again in 1993 as general inspector at the Ministry of Culture. Brigitte Finifter, daughter of Bernard, from stalag 9, was responsible for overseeing the free radios. Veronique Né-iertz, his faithful archivist at the SP who was named minister in 1984, had an uncle who was a Jesuit, deported to Dachau; Mitterrand knew him in Vichy and regularly inquired about his welfare.

Throughout his career, Mitterrand was influenced by personal feeling, without that being the only criteria. His friends from youth, from the institution of Saint-Paul d'Angoulême like Pierre Guillain de Bénouville, or from his home as a student at 104 rue de Vaugirard (like André Bettencourt and François Paves), buddies from the regiment at Lourcine (Georges Dayan) and those from the stalags, the tribe of Ni-vernais, the family extended to include groupies and mistresses — all these took precedence over his comrades from the Party. It happened that the two categories merged, in some cases, but the majority were more attached to the man than to his ideas. He did not ask them to be Socialist, but to be faithful. Like him.

He was particularly attached to André Rousselet, the former owner of Havas, who was his first chief assistant at the Elysée. They had a long family history: André's father, Marcel Rousselet, was presi-dent of the County Court of the Seine in 1959 at the time of "the attack on the Observatory." Justice had required of some explanations of Senator Mitterrand regarding that attack. The matter was finally clas-sified. At the time André Rousselet and François Mitterrand were al-ready acquainted: Rousselet had been Mitterand's assistant at the Inte-rior Ministry in 1957. But this affair, which permanently tarnished a promising career, linked them far better than any political motion they may have both supported.

The list of all these links explaining the promotions, the missions entrusted, the decorations conferred, would be endless. Betting on fi-delities born of an astonishing emotional geopolitics, Mitterrand pushed to the extreme what he himself called "clannishness," the "tribal spirit." "It is very powerful," he explained in an issue of the review *Autrement,* on the topic of friendship. "Today's world, including the na-tions that are the most modern in the field of technological develop-ments and science, continues to be a conglomerate of tribes."

In politics, the tribal sense, however, redounds only to the benefit of the chief. Contrary to other networks that really expand only hori-zontally — the mutual support among the Corsicans or Savoyards, for example — in politics, the gang is structured vertically, from the base toward the top. But effectiveness presupposes discipline.

The failure of the famous "Léo's Gang" testifies to that. During the first cohabitation, from 1986 to 1988, these young ministers with high ambitions were renowned for their indestructible friendship. These admirable feelings did not stand up to the loss of three ministerial portfolios, the revelation of financial irregularities, and legal problems on the part of one of the musketeers, Gerard Longuet. In the same manner, the "renewers" of the RPR, Alain Carignon, Michel Black, Charles Millon, Michele Barzach and their consorts, who presented themselves arm in arm as the best friends in the world in order to break up the "archeos" in the RPR, failed. This small troop, inhibited in its action by the rivalry among its members, lasted only one summer. In the world of politics, far more than in any other field, the network really only helps one person.

Protectors with Heart, and Protectors with Cash

If Jacques Chirac allowed himself to be recruited in the 1960's into what Claude Imbert called in *L'Express* the "young wolves," a small group of bright young stars from the national Assembly who were dispatched to the Southwest of France to conquer hostile strongholds, he did not go hunting with the pack for long. Of the same breed as his predecessor, the new tenant of the Elysée always had a taste for graceful mediation, friendly subsidies and services rendered. This convivial practice that Philippe Séguin amusingly summarizes as "Chirac's approach: How's your Dad, how's your Mom?" — obviously does not forge a new political platform, but it does make it possible to promote one.

Following the emotions, like Mitterrand, under a "Bulldozer" exterior (one of his nicknames at Science-Po university), Chirac prefers the most faithful over the most intelligent. Of course, like all his peers he surrounds himself with technocrats who have applied their talents to making the machine of State run smoothly. When Alain Juppé was installed at Matignon, 38% of his ministers' cabinets were ENA alumni. That's a good score for a candidate who was constantly vilifying the élites throughout his presidential campaign! Himself a former student in Vauban's class (1959), where he forged a longlasting friendship with Jacques Friedmann and the centrist Bernard Stasi, he was good at remembering his schoolmates from the ENA when the occasion merited.

However, by nature he was inclined to prefer henchmen who would devote themselves to restoring his fluctuating popularity, no matter what. Jean-Louis Debré, Jacques Toubon, Bernard Pons are such men. This last never forgot that Chirac had exerted himself to convince Pompidou to invest him with the district of Figeac, in the Lot. At the time, he was only a young doctor, a neophyte activist. That was in 1966: Chirac was already positioned as the chief of the Gaullist future deputies who had just taken over the Socialist-Communist territory. Among them, in addition to Pons, there were Jean Charbonnel and Pierre Mazeaud. They all swore mutual assistance during an alcoholized evening not far from the abbey of Solignac. Chirac scrupulously respected this oath, helping his comrades, particularly Pons, to profit from the largesse of the airframe manufacturer Marcel Dassault, a friend and customer of his banking father. It is services like these that seal perpetual devotion.

"So many friends betrayed him during Balladur's hour of glory that the solidity of his supposed networks became more than dubious," one of his close relations notes bitterly. From cowardice to half-treason, the 'Chirac Gang' shrank in the course of the 1995 presidential campaign. "Maurice (Ulrich), Dominique (Villepin), Jean-Pierre (Denis), Claude (Chirac), Christine (Albanel): doesn't it sound like the title of a film by Sautet?," jokes the Corrézien Denis Tillinac, himself a pillar of this restricted clique. "He called them up separately; then he brought them together, and held conclaves around a rectangular table where commands were aligned as in a military order."[4] A few months later, the "Chirac Gang" was at the helm, with "faithful" soldiers at the outposts: Dominique de Villepin, General Secretary of the Elysée with Jean-Pierre Denis as assistant, Maurice Ulrich, the oldest of the gang (70 years old) as a "sage," his daughter Claude as omnipresent public relations adviser, Christine Albanel, eternal presidential ghost-writer, in charge of Culture, and Tillinac himself at Francophonie.

Doctor Pons, who belonged to another layer of Chirac's entourage, was not comfortable with the assumption that this new "band" could now, on its own, take over all the presidential networks. He was convinced that there always exists a "guard of the heart," that is even more devoted to its idol; and he set to work frantically to reactivate it. To support this idolatry he chose the somnolent "Association of the

Friends of Jacques Chirac," founded in 1988 by the late Raymond Thuillier. As President of this empty shell since June 1996, he organized the first sizeable event on the 15th of October. That evening, 240 guests gathered in a room in the 17th arrondissement, his old Parisian stronghold, for a Chiraqi banquet, where loin of lamb and honey pastries were accompanied by toasts to the beloved Jacques. The seating plan was like a career plan revisited: every stage in Chirac's rise, and the supporters who which accompanied them, were represented there.

There were his friends from the Carnot Academy in Paris, the members of the informal little club that young Chirac, a major from Saumur, had created upon his return from Algeria (and whose principal activity consisted of sipping whisky with Michel François-Poncet, future head of Paribas and Dominique de Martinière, future tax director.) Also round the tables of the loyal were his battle companions from the electoral struggles, some of them survivors of the "oath of Solignac," and supportive businessmen like François Pinault, Bernard Esambert, vice-president of Lagardère and an old Pompidou supporter, and Jerome Monod (the influential chairman of Lyonnaise des Eaux, affiliated with the Corrézien network through his wife Françoise, grand-daughter of Henri Queuille, the former president of the Council who anointed Chirac at Ussel. The Corréziens from Meymac, from Egletons and the plateau of Millevaches also came to the events. "They came, they were all there. . ." One table, even more fetishistic than the others, was adorned with a mysterious sign: 19 FLX 75. This was no secret code for members of the special services, but more prosaically it was the license plate of the car that zipped over from Town Hall to the HQ on avenue Iéna, May 7, 1995, carrying the new President of the Republic. . . And 19 is also the number of the départemente of Corrèze.

The good Doctor Pons was right to circle up the wagon train. But while the "guard of the heart" could do a good job of maintaining the Chiraqi flame, it was insignificant compared to the "Money guard," those financial networks that helped the mayor of Paris rise to the Elysée throne. One finds all kinds among these generous givers: disinterested militants, crooks, interlopers of equivocal intention, cadres from the RPR to with ambiguous morals, elected officials who owed a favor, business leaders needing to barter and bribe their way into the municipal markets.

In short, all sorts of lowlifes; an explosive mixture that explains why, for three years, Chirakia has been poisoned by "incidents." These ongoing legal worries have revealed a flaw in the Chiraqi networks of solidarity. As soon as any "sensitive" personalities are put under investigation and thus exposed to the curiosity of the media, the first reflex is to drop them in order to protect the chief.

The former minister for Cooperation under Balladur, Michel Roussin, indicted in November 1994 for conspiring to misappropriate public funds (since then, the case was dropped), was asked to resign and to keep a low profile. Being thrown out was extremely painful for the former chief assistant to the mayor of Paris; he was used to dealing with "special" cases and to maintaining close relations with Louise-Yvonne Casetta, the behind-the-scenes treasurer of the RPR. Barred from the national office of the Chiraquian Party immediately after the presidential elections, he also had to leave his apartment on Saint-Germain-des-Prés, as it was property of the City of Paris. When it became clear that he was planning to return to his post as a deputy after his case was dismissed, he was given to understand that it would be inadvisable to reappear on the political scene. In short, he was under quarantine. Then they changed their minds. The new mayor Jean Tiberi rehabilitated him as assistant of the "Cooperation," while Eiffage, a "friendly" construction company, gave him a comfortable salary as an export consultant; and, as the cherry on the cake, the CNPF offered him the presidency of the Africa-Caribbean-Pacific commission!

People who have been dumped are always liable to the temptation to go and tell their little secrets to a judge, either to relieve their consciences or to be avenged. So, it's better discreetly to take them in hand. A dubious promoter whose deals collapse, on the heels of his legal troubles, may find that new markets are proposed where he can get by, and a Parisian civil servant who is a little too smart is promoted to a prefecture in the provinces, while still another is fixed up again in a safe sinecure.

This attention includes of course the guidance of a specialized lawyer, ready to pamper his customers as much as possible. Louise-Yvonne Casetta, a former perfume saleswoman who traveled for a time in the wake of the ex-treasurer of the Party, former minister Robert Galley, and then of the General Secretary Jean-François Mancel, was hardly prepared to face legal thunderbolts with her head held high and mouth sealed shut. She thus enjoyed the affectionate attention of her former employers. Admittedly, "rue de Lille," i.e. the head office of the RPR, loudly announced at the beginning of 1996 that she was no longer part of the staff. In fact, she was not dropped. From the very start of her troubles, this plump forty-something, slow of pace but energetic in character, let it be known that she "could not bear to go to prison." Message received. Everyone circled 'round and advised her to take as lawyer Jacques Vergès, Esq., whose associate Alex Ursulet was the husband of Fréderique Pons, daughter of Bernard Pons. The family discussions must be very lively: Fréderique Pons is herself the lawyer of Jean-Claude Méry, who was indicted for abusing social funds and for fraud.

This intermediary specialized in "contributions for the Church of Chirac," who had as many friends among the people's deputies as among the business leaders, endured her prison stay with difficulty. But many good hearts toiled to rehabilitate her. The obliging Générale des Eaux would use her talents as intercessor in selling buildings in Paris, and the administration was invited to look kindly on her real estate projects.

Jacques Chirac pretends to scorn networks — "Networks? Do I have a head for keeping track of networks?" he shot back in November 1994 to two journalists from *Le Figaro*, who had inquired about the candidate's companions from the good old days (and bad old days). He repeats to anyone who will listen that his best allies are the activists and the Corréziens. But the President, who has a horror of society life, who prefers Line Renaud over Alain Minc, makes sure nonetheless that his financial connections are not allowed to erode. If just one of the nine judges responsible in one way or another for the financing of the RPR, the Party he has led for twenty years, expose any misconduct that may have occurred during his conquest of power, that would be a real earthquake that even his guard of the heart would have trouble to contain.

Le Pen's Closest Friends

If Chirakia were imperiled by this means, it would only delight his constant enemy, Le Pen. Too cliquish to have built real funding circuits in its own support, the National Front has not yet had time to be besmirched by "business." That does not mean that "President Le Pen," as his friends call him, has not garnered any profitable money connections. The chief of the National Front found his way into the club of the rich, thanks to the affluence provided by an inheritance from Hubert Lambert, wealthy heir of a line of industrialists, in 1976. Before, he was always short of money and he lived on the generosity of a friend in the hotel business for a long time. Those lean years seem quite remote today. Le Pen has friends in the loftiest circles.

But does his party derive much benefit from that? When his public relations director Lorrain de Sainte-Affrique resigned abruptly, he was constrained to take legal action against the National Front to get his due. Activists have to pay for their own travel, and the deputies have to finance their own campaigns. Apparently, Le Pen does not mix his personal financial networks and those of his party.

His friendships with billionaires are not enough to fill the National Front's till. Le Pen, an impulsive and unmethodical big-mouth, had never been able to structure a party. Too epicurean, too lazy, he always left it to others, yesterday Jean-Pierre Stirbois, today Bruno Mégret, Bruno Gollnisch and Jean-Michel Dubois, his special envoy to the business world, to round up donors. He himself has had great difficulty in drumming up reliable support. His fellow traveler from the early days, Doctor Jean-Maurice Demarquet, gave up, denouncing both his anti-Semitism and the conditions according to which Le Pen had inherited Hubert Lambert — in his opinion contestable. The young activists of Ordre Nouveau (the New Order) and Occident, like Alain Robert and Gerard Longuet who were understudies with him, preferred "more worthy" godfathers. Only the old collaborationists whom he rehabilitated and the more extremist among the young people were still with him when he announced for the 1974 presidential election. But the result was poor: 0.74% of the votes!

Ten years later, the "divine surprise" of the 1984 European elections — 10.95% of the votes — changed the scene. For the first time, Le Pen could aspire to creating "a real" party. For the ten years that followed the first electoral successes, the organization slid. But, since the strikes of December 1995, the "extending rays" of the Front seem to have spread and refracted as if by miracle within certain professional circles. What changed is that the FN decided to use social causes to supplement its preferred topics, immigration and insecurity. But this new strategy resembles infiltration. Until then, its followers had come from certain closed intellectual circles, the Horizon Club, Renaissance, clubs of the New Right, etc., from the fundamentalists committees of

Christian-Solidarity, or from anti-birth control associations like the League for Life led by Martine Lehideux, André Dufraisse's widow. The first professional field that the FN penetrated was the police force. Jean-Pierre Stirbois supervised its infiltration into the police stations via certain individuals who longed for the days of the OAS. At the time, he tried (in vain) to take over the Independent Professional Federation of the Police (FPIP). Today, the president of the National Front-Police is none other than Jean-Paul Laurendeau, former Secretary General of the FPIP. The success of the FNP is snowballing: it is the fourth largest police union, out of eighteen, with 7.45% of the votes. But its prohibition, decreed on March 10, 1997 by the court of Evry, is likely to stop this irresistible rise.

That police officers of the far Right FPIP would succumb to the charms of the National Front is hardly surprising. That prison wardens who were part of CGT for more than twenty years would move over, bag and baggage, to the FN-Penitentiary trade union is more unexpected. But that is what happened with its founder, Damien Francès, after 26 years of honest service in the Leftist trade union. Hardly had he created his extremist organization — in September 1996 — and memberships poured in. Thirty prisons out of 181 expressed interest and five sections were formed.

Getting into the schools and colleges was more difficult. The few attempts to penetrate the National Trade Union of Lycées and Colleges (SNALC) ran up against the resistance of the teachers' trade unions. Similarly, attempts to penetrate the federations of pupils' parents were rejected.

The same phenomenon is at work with the RATP, where 100 out of 40,000 agents belong to Force Nationale-Transport, considered to be a non-representative professional organization. On the other hand, the National Front had a tremendous breakthrough in the HLM, reaching second position in 1996 behind the powerful National Confederation of Housing in 7 organizations out of 11. This score especially shows the FN's ability to take over forums deserted by others.

These diffuse "groups" are more the emanation of a party that of a man. Admittedly, one can always assert that the first is in the service of the second. But Le Pen is not an ordinary politician. A gang leader, he has always been wary of "lobbies," of "factions," of anything that might obstruct his freedom and his autocratic power. This propensity for defying everyone and everything limits the maneuverability of a potential "Le Pen network."

Juniors at the Elysée

For the first time since the Liberation, the next presidential election, in 2002, will be played out without the networks derived from the Resistance playing a significant part. From the first French election by universal vote, in 1965, to that of 1995, these networks have exerted their influence (increasingly weak, one suspects, over the course of time). These groups did not have a natural vocation for playing politics. But the Club of 22 (which invariably gathers 22 Companions of the Liberation, of all different persuasions), the Jedburgh brotherhood and the Marco network, where not a few old members of the "services" are found, Le Clerc's men, those of the Communist "Fabien," plus many homologous associations, are mobilized every time, discreetly or not, for whichever candidate seems to them to defend best the spirit of the Resistance.

In 1981, these old networks were still active. In fact, they gave the Left-wing candidate the edge. They did not accept Giscard d'Estaing's suspension, during his seven years in office, of the commemoration of the Nazi defeat on May 8, 1945. And what is worse, VGE also put flowers on the grave of Marshal Pétain on November 11, 1978. The *francisque* was forgotten, the Pétainist civil servant had disappeared. Mitterrand was the only "resistance" candidate; he knew it, and he took full advantage.

In 1988, in the lead-up to the presidential election, the resistance armies were mobilized again. For another Left-wing candidate: Michel Rocard. The artisan who crafted this offensive was Stéphane Hessel ("Greco," in the Resistance), a former ambassador and close adviser of Rocard. The latter was too young to have begun his career in clandestinity, but he belonged to a family that proved its mettle in those days. His father, the physicist Yves Rocard, worked to protect London from the Nazi V1 and V2 rockets. His uncle, an eminent German specialist, helped intercept German telephone calls. Hessel was not the only resister to propagandize on behalf of "young" Rocard. He was assisted by a rheumatologist, Doctor André Solomon, a former FTP that Rocard engaged in Matignon in 1988.

For the 1995 presidential election, the Resistance acted more discreetly — for lack of combatants, unfortunately. Between Chirac and Jospin, neither of whom could plead a family tradition in the underground, Chirac's de Gaullism won out. In recognition, the new President started his term by a symbolic visit. On May 17, 1995, at the break of day, in a drizzling rain, at the deserted cemetery of Colombey-les-Deux-Églises, Chirac deposited a tricolor sheaf in the shape of a Cross of Lorraine on the tomb of General de Gaulle. In a few hours, he would take possession of the Elysée. The old Gaullist barons appreciated the gesture.

Chirac also marked the end of an epoch — that in which the historical choices made by politicians colored their entire careers. In process of extinction, the resistance networks will be able neither to impede, nor to support a candidate for the 2002 presidential election. Deprived of their tutelage, will the juniors in the Elysée forsake the networks of activists, the clans and the tribes, and settle for merely being "telegenic"?

Some of them have networks already waiting to go to work, just the same. On the Right, via "Idea-Action," Alain Madelin has collected nearly 4000 members among business leaders, elected officials and students. On the Left, Martine Aubry, within her Foundation Action, is reaping the goodwill of grass-roots militants and the support of the moneyed classes. These two potential candidates in power are the only ones who are trying to transform their personal relations into a more or less structured apparatus, just in case.

Laurent Fabius, who spins straw into gold in such cases, saw his hopes dashed by the contaminated blood business. Constrained to make a strategic retreat, he has returned to his home terrain among the elected officials, first cultivated in 1988 at the time when he was using the generous facilities of the Hotel de Lassay to receive great hordes of deputies and general advisers likely to increase his following. The matrix set up by his wife Françoise during the first cohabitation around the clubs "Spaces 89" and "Here and Now" has been more or less eroded, but if need be, he knows he can count on his hyperactive wife to reactivate them. She is the one who organizes, every autumn in Clichy, the big shindig for the "Fabiusie": elected officials, collaborators, friends from youth, nobody would be out of place.

His rival, Lionel Jospin, who has the good fortune of being able to rely on the Socialist party, is however a man alone or nearly so, anti-Mitterrand and without his own close supporters. Admittedly, he does have some friends — at least two: the faithful Claude Allègre, a geophysicist whom he knew as an amateur basketball player at in the early 1960's, and the not-to-be-overlooked Daniel Vaillant, a consummate connoisseur of the Party and its intrigues. His sister Noëlle Chatelet, who had tried during the presidential campaign to form a support committee of superstars, artists and intellectuals, suggested to her brother to stay in touch with them. "There are commissions in the Party, one can simply go there," is the answer she hears. Two men, two tactics: Fabius is courting favors, Jospin is courting experts.

Still more masochistic than Jospin is Philippe Séguin, the president of the National Assembly. He takes pleasure in his voluntary loneliness. "I am alone, I will always be alone," he repeats every chance he gets. Indirect coquetry or genuine misanthropy? The truth is somewhere between the two. Openly refusing to follow the example of Laurent Fabius by building a "hotel Seguinism" at the Hotel de Lassay, he lets his friends organize networks in his stead.

The faithful Jean de Boishue, whom he met in Olivier Guichard's office, briefly Secretary of State for Higher Education under Juppé, does his part. "We are building Séguinism without Séguin," he says with some irony. Together with Étienne Pinte, the deputy-mayor of Versailles, and the latter's son, representative to the National Assembly, and Robert Karutchi, the chief assistant of "President Séguin," he performs the "triage between the careerists and the committed." That's not easy, given that the anti-Juppé reflex works so automatically in favor of Séguin, who will eventually have to recognize his followers, in a whole nebula of fans-clubs: "Tomorrow France," open to the professional echelons, "Human Condition," reserved for elected officials, "Assembly for Another Policy" (RAP), an association of young people built around networks in every départemente. Lastly, the "Association for a Citizens' Republic," created in the wake of his campaign against Maastricht, boasts a few thousands members. Not bad, for a man who is "alone" and who, moreover, cultivates the friendship of large owners like Marc Ladreit de Lacharrière, and of intellectuals like Alexandre Adler, Jean-Paul Fitoussi, and Maurice Allais. And who, if he made it to Matignon, could also count on some "elephants" of the majority, hostile like he is to the "politically correct" and "the only way."

Necessary but not enough in themselves, the networks are not the single magic wand that will give access to the highest burden of the State. But the man who beat the record of presidential longevity under the Fifth Republic testifies to their determining role. Mitterrand raised the manipulation of his clans into an art of management. Polishing throughout his career a persona as a charismatic leader, methodically incorporating all the actors from his multiple lives, maintaining them carefully and methodically, Mitterrand leaves to posterity, no matter what one thinks of his character, a "model" of the Head of State and political behavior where networks played the greatest role.

* * *

At the end of this voyage through the landscape of networks, should we conclude that France is an exception? Indeed, no other democratic country seems to be shaped to such a degree by parallel hierarchies and obscure complicities. In the Anglo-Saxon countries, the network is almost institutionalized. In Great Britain, the career channels are very openly structured around association with former college or university pals, and sports associations, while the famous "clubs" also form part of the landscape, as well as the political parties and the trade unions. In the United States, the immoderate taste for transparency inhibits the effective operation and the enduring establishment of clans, which operate most successfully outside of the spotlight. Only Japan would appear to rival France, to some extent. But networks, over there, thrive only at the tops of the large companies in the capital and only in relation to narrowly overlapping interests. Nothing in common, therefore, with the bonds which, in the Hexagon of France, link the Freemasons as well as the aristocrats, the homosexuals, the business leaders, the hunters, the former Trotskyites, the Jews, the fundamentalist Catholics and the Corsicans...

An old French tropism? Under the *ancien régime*, enlightened intellectuals and the bourgeoisie, progressive aristocrats and critical prelates formed confidential coteries to prepare a better world. In the 19th century, political instability led to the burgeoning of clubs and other societies of thought, often inspired by conspirators dressed in silk. See Balzac's Thirteen. See Flaubert and Maupassant, too, who sometimes use it as the backdrop of their romances.

Networks have lived on through all the Republics; because they are the product of a certain French state of mind, they resist every institutional evolution.

Never, however, have they seemed to be so much in evidence as they are today — as if our times particularly supported the emergence of a furtive social geography. The degradation of democratic values, real or imagined, surely has something to do with it. It nourishes a distrust of elites, and results in each one seeking success, assistance or comfort by non-official channels. The meritocratic social elevator, which yesterday meant having a degree from a good school, admission to a great university, is starting to get hung up. Furthermore, people now prefer upward channels that may be less academic, but are likely to recreate a feeling of belonging. The same values, shared pastimes, common origins, related interests, similar errors of youth, convergent beliefs. . . They all seem to be helping to create the social fabric — for better or worse — for legitimate mutual assistance, but also for unjustified enrichment.

These networks fill the vacuum left by the intermediary bodies that are semi-bankrupt. The political parties are desperately looking for activists, the unions no longer represent anyone but themselves, associations (yesterday so esteemed) are besmirched by scandals like that of the ARC. Since the organizations that were stamped and approved seem to have broken down, the troubled citizen finds it easy to turn to clandestine and vague ones.

This is an attraction easy to satisfy in a country of shadows and light, where transparency hardly exists. This fog allows people at both ends of the spectrum to go on, sheltered from view and from public judgment. In this direction, the strength of the networks is an excellent barometer of democratic life.

Should we deplore it or rejoice? Well-established in the French landscape, they adapt and shift, whatever regime is in place. Reforms come and go, the networks remain.

Footnotes

Chapter 1

1. Honoré de Balzac, *Histoire des Treize*, Presses Pocket, 1992.
2. *Le Monde*, 14 mai 1996.
3. Régis Debray, *Loués soient nos seigneurs*, Gallimard, 1996.
4. Roger Faligot, Rémi Kauffer, *Les Résistants*, Fayard, 1989.
5. See the chapter, "Protecting Each Other."
6. See the chapter, "Helping Each Other."
7. See the chapter, "Bulding a Career."
8. Philippe Labro, *Des feux mal éteints*, Gallimard, 1967.
9. See the chapter, "Bulding a Career."
10. *L'Evénement du Jeudi*, July 25, 1996.
11. Which was definitely was not done.
12. See the chapter, "Monopolies."
13. Chouchen: a liqueur based on hydromel.

Chapter 2

1. Yannick Le Bourdonnec, *Le Miracle breton*, Calmann-Lévy, 1996.
2. *Jeune Afrique*, March 2, 1995.
3. Pierre Dauzier et Denis Tillinac, *Les Corréziens*, Robert Laffont.
4. Alain Guédé et Hervé Liffran, *La Razzia*, Stock, 1995.
5. "La Menace, Histoire d'une interdiction avortée," *Gai-Pied Hebdo*, no 263.
6. Frédéric Martel, *Le Rose et le Noir*, Seuil, 1996.
7. Hodder et Stoughton éditeurs.
8. *Politis*, mai 1993.
9. *L'Evénement du Jeudi*, June 20, 1996.

10. *Le Point*, November 14, 1992.
11. Robert Laffont et Bibliophane, 1990.

Chapter 3

1. Claude Askolovitch, Sylvain Attal, *La France du piston*, Robert Laffont, 1992.
2. *Nous serons tous des protestants*, Plon, 1976.
3. Alain Guédé, Hervé Liffran, *La Razzia*, Stock, 1995.
4. Robert Laffont.
5. See the chapter, "Protecting Each Other."
6. See the chapter, "Getting Rich." The English translation of *Grand Fortunes* is available from Algora Publishing, in New York.
7. *L'Expansion*, September 12, 1994.
8. *Actes de la recherche en sciences sociales*, no 31, January 1980.
9. Plon, 1994.
10. Payot, 1996.
11. *Le Courrier du Jockey Club*, no 10, December 1990, by François-Xavier de Vivier.
12. *Métailié*, 1993.
13. *Rapport Equinoxe : dérives bancaires, le système bancaire français à l'épreuve du Crédit Lyonnais*, éditions Les Djinns, 1995.

Chapter 4

1. See Eric Leser, *Crazy Lyonnais*, Calmann-Lévy, 1995.
2. *L'Expansion*, March 3, 1994.
3. Seuil, 1973.
4. See the chapter, "Militants."
5. *L'Histoire,* September 1985.
6. Cited by Hervé Hamon and Patrick Rotman in *Génération*, Seuil, 1987.
7. See the chapter, "Protecting Each Other."
8. December 15, 1992.
9. March 18, 1993.
10. September 17, 1992.
11. April 1990.
12. Jean-Emile *Vié, Mémoires d'un directeur des Renseignements généraux*, Albin Michel, 1988.

Chapter 5

1. *L'Express,* March 4, 1988.
2. See the chapter, "Building a Career."
3. *L'Evénement du Jeudi*, January 18, 1996.
4. *Carnets d'un Grand Maître*, Editions du Rocher, 1990.
5. Seuil, 1995.
6. *L'Evénement du Jeudi*, 18 to 24 January, 1996.
7. Alain Guédé, Hervé Liffran, *op. cit.*
8. See the chapter, "Making It."

9. Stock, 1996.
10. Albin Michel, 1996.
11. Anne Sabouret, MM.
12. *Lazard Frères et Cie*, Olivier Orban, 1987.
13. *Libération*, October 29, 1994.
14. Cited by Anne de Caumont, *Un prince des affaires*, Grasset, 1996.
15. Which became Alcatel-Alsthom.

Chapter 6

1. Seuil, 1983.
2. Albin Michel, 1988.
3. Evaluation made by *Enjeux-Les Echos*, November 1993.
4. Hervé Hamon and Patrick Rotman, *Les Intellocrates*, Seuil, 1981.
5. Sylvain Attal and Claude Askolovitch, *La France du piston*, Seuil, 1993.
6. Seuil, 1993.
7. Flammarion, 1996.
8. Ghislaine Ottenheimer, *L'Impossible Victoire*, Robert Laffont, 1995.
9. Seuil.
10. January 27,1996.
11. Ramsay.
12. *Le Voleur dans la maison vide*, Plon, 1997.
13. Cited by Jacques Delperrié de Bayac, *L'Histoire de la milice*, Plon, 1994.
14. Henri Charbonneau, *Les Mémoires de Porthos*, Clan, 1967.

Chapter 7

1. See the chapter, "Militants."
2. "Le monde secret de l'Opus Dei," no 30, Summer 1992.
3. *Esprit*, no 224, August-September 1996.
4. Seuil, 1974.
5. Philippe Bourdrel, *La " Cagoule,"* Albin Michel, 1992.
6. *Une histoire sans fard*, Fayard, 1996.
7. No 956.
8. Calmann-Lévy, 1997.
9. Michel Bar-Zohar, *Une Histoire sans fard*, Fayard, 1996.
10. René Bousquet, Stock, 1994.
11. Pierre Rigoulot, *Les Enfants de l'épuration*, Plon, 1993.
12. Author of *l'Annuaire biographique des préfets 1870-1982,* French National Archives.

Chapter 8

1. Under the direction of Jean-Pierre Azéma and François Bedarida, *Vichy et les Français,* Fayard, 1992.
2. Guy Lemonnier and Georges Albertini were amnestied as a result of the law of Janyar 5, 1951.
3. *L'Epuration des intellectuels*, Editions Complexe, 1990.
4. Dominique Pons, *H comme Hersant*, Editions Alain Moreau, 1977.
5. Denoël, 1996.

6. Emile Poulat, *Intégrisme et catholicisme intégral : un réseau secret international anti-moderniste, la Sapinière*, Casterman, 1969.
7. July 8, 1993.

Chapter 9

1. *L'Opposition à l'avortement*, Berg International, 1995.
2. *Golias*, May-June 1995.
3. Arthur Conte, *Les Présidents de la Ve République*, Le Pré aux clercs, 1985.
4. Franz-Olivier Giesbert, *Jacques Chirac*, Seuil, 1987.
5. Arthur Conte, *Les Premiers ministres de la Ve République*, Le Pré aux clercs.
6. Denis Tillinac, *Dernier verre au Danton*, Robert Laffont, 1996.

Also from Algora Publishing:

CLAUDIU A. SECARA
THE NEW COMMONWEALTH
From Bureaucratic Corporatism to Socialist Capitalism

The notion of an elite-driven worldwide perestroika has gained some credibility lately. The book examines in a historical perspective the most intriguing dialectic in the Soviet Union's "collapse" — from socialism to capitalism and back to socialist capitalism — and speculates on the global implications.

IGNACIO RAMONET
THE GEOPOLITICS OF CHAOS

The author, Director of *Le Monde Diplomatique,* presents an original, discriminating and lucid political matrix for understanding what he calls the "current disorder of the world" in terms of Internationalization, Cyberculture and Political Chaos.

TZVETAN TODOROV
A PASSION FOR DEMOCRACY –
Benjamin Constant

The French Revolution rang the death knell not only for a form of society, but also for a way of feeling and of living; and it is still not clear as yet what did we gain from the changes.

MICHEL PINÇON & MONIQUE PINÇON-CHARLOT
GRAND FORTUNES –
Dynasties of Wealth in France

Going back for generations, the fortunes of great families consist of far more than money—they are also symbols of culture and social interaction. In a nation known for democracy and meritocracy, piercing the secrets of the grand fortunes verges on a crime of lèse-majesté . . . *Grand Fortunes* succeeds at that.

CLAUDIU A. SECARA
TIME & EGO –
Judeo-Christian Egotheism and the Anglo-Saxon Industrial Revolution

The first question of abstract reflection that arouses controversy is the problem of Becoming. Being persists, beings constantly change; they are born and they pass away. How can Being change and yet be eternal? The quest for the logical and experimental answer has just taken off.

JEAN-MARIE ABGRALL
SOUL SNATCHERS: THE MECHANICS OF CULTS

Jean-Marie Abgrall, psychiatrist, criminologist, expert witness to the French Court of Appeals, and member of the Inter-Ministry Committee on Cults, is one of the experts most frequently consulted by the European judicial and legislative processes. The fruit of fifteen years of research, his book delivers the first methodical analysis of the sectarian phenomenon, decoding the mental manipulation on behalf of mystified observers as well as victims.

JEAN-CLAUDE GUILLEBAUD
THE TYRANNY OF PLEASURE

The ambition of the book is to pose clearly and without subterfuge the question of sexual morals -- that is, the place of the forbidden -- in a modern society. For almost a whole generation, we have lived in the illusion that this question had ceased to exist. Today the illusion is faded, but a strange and tumultuous distress replaces it. No longer knowing very clearly where we stand, our societies painfully seek answers between unacceptable alternatives: bold-faced permissiveness or nostalgic moralism.

SOPHIE COIGNARD AND MARIE-THÉRÈSE GUICHARD
FRENCH CONNECTIONS –
The Secret History of Networks of Influence

They were born in the same region, went to the same schools, fought the same fights and made the same mistakes in youth. They share the same morals, the same fantasies of success and the same taste for money. They act behind the scenes to help each other, boosting careers, monopolizing business and information, making money, conspiring and, why not, becoming Presidents!

VLADIMIR PLOUGIN
INTELLIGENCE HAS ALWAYS EXISTED

This collection contains the latest works by historians, investigating the most mysterious episodes from Russia's past. All essays are based on thorough studies of preserved documents. The book discusses the establishment of secret services in Kievan Rus, and describes heroes and systems of intelligence and counterintelligence in the 16th-17th centuries. Semen Maltsev, a diplomat of Ivan the Terrible's times is presented as well as the much publicised story of the abduction of "Princess Tarakanova".

JEAN-JACQUES ROSA
EURO ERROR

The European Superstate makes Jean-Jacques Rosa mad, for two reasons. First, actions taken to relieve unemployment have created inflation, but have not reduced unemployment. His second argument is even more intriguing: the 21st century will see the fragmentation of the U. S., not the unification of Europe.

ANDRÉ GAURON
EUROPEAN MISUNDERSTANDING

Few of the books decrying the European Monetary Union raise the level of the discussion to a higher plane. European Misunderstanding is one of these. Gauron gets it right, observing that the real problem facing Europe is its political future, not its economic future.